JAVA™
PROGRAMMING
BY EXAMPLE

ADVANCES IN OBJECT TECHNOLOGY SERIES

Dr. Richard S. Wiener
Series Editor

Editor
Journal of Object-Oriented Programming
SIGS Publications, Inc.
New York, New York

and

Department of Computer Science
University of Colorado
Colorado Springs, Colorado

Additional volumes in preparation

JAVA™
PROGRAMMING
BY EXAMPLE

RAJIV SHARMA
VIVEK SHARMA

CAMBRIDGE
UNIVERSITY PRESS

SIGS
BOOKS

PUBLISHED BY THE PRESS SYNDICATE OF THE UNIVERSITY OF CAMBRIDGE
The Pitt Building, Trumpington Street, Cambridge CB2 1RP, United Kingdom

CAMBRIDGE UNIVERSITY PRESS
The Edinburgh Building, Cambridge CB2 2RU, UK
http: //www.cup.cam.ac.uk
40 West 20th Street, New York, NY 10011-4211, USA
http: //www.cup.org
10 Stamford Road, Oakleigh, Melbourne 3166, Australia

Published in association with SIGS Books

© 1998 Cambridge University Press

Any product mentioned in this book may be a trademark of its company.

First published in 1998

Design and composition by Kevin Callahan/BNGO Books
Cover design by Yin Moy and Tom Jezek

Printed in the United States of America

4|12|00

A catalog record for this book is available from the British Library.

CIP data is on record with the publisher.

ISBN 0-521-644429

We would like to thank our parents, Shri Swayam Prakash and Mrs. Saroj Sharma, for being the guiding lights of our lives. Also, thanks to our wives, Nikki and Anu, for being so understanding.

CONTENTS

## CHAPTER 1

INTRODUCTION TO JAVA

If, like us, you're a software developer who learns through examples and wants theory only as and when required, then this book is for you. It introduces you to Java exclusively through examples. And with our limited sense of humor we've tried to make this book as lively as possible.

So what is Java? It's an object-oriented programming language which is gaining a lot of popularity these days, especially because it fits hand-in-glove with the Internet. And you thought it was some kind of coffee?

We could go into history and tell you how events in the time of Alexander the Great helped shape Java like it looks today, but you can find a lot of that in other books. So, without wasting any more time, let's get to a position where we can start learning the language.

There are a few things you'll need in order to learn Java on your computer. We're assuming that you have Internet access. If not, sell this book and get it! Among other reasons, you'll need it to get all the code in this book off the web site: **http://www.cup.org/Titles/64/0521644429.html**

1.1 Getting Started

You may want to use a browser to view applets. For the uninitiated, applets are not small apples—a section in this chapter explains what they are.

You can use any Java-enabled browser. For instance, you can buy Netscape 3.0 or you can download the HotJava browser provided by Javasoft at their "Download" site.

You may need to do certain things before the browser allows you to run applets (no, you don't have to do a jig on the table in full public view). For instance, in the case of Netscape 3.0 on Solaris, you need to copy a file called `java_30` to one of the following directories:

> The current directory
> /usr/local/netscape/java/classes
> /usr/local/lib/netscape
> HOME/.netscape

You can read the documentation/readme files of your browser to see if any such special thing needs to be done.

Note that applets written with JDK 1.1 specific features will not run on Netscape 3.0 as it doesn't support JDK 1.1. However, we can expect Netscape to support JDK 1.1 in a future release. For the time being if you want to see such an applet, you can use the appletviewer which comes as part of the JDK.

1.1.1 Downloading the Java Development Environment

Open the following site through your browser:

```
http://www.javasoft.com
```

This is the index page of JavaSoft, the business unit of Sun Microsystems, Inc., which develops Java technology.

On the index page JavaSoft has a link called "Download". If you click on this you'll see options for downloading different pieces of software and documentation. You can select Java Development Kit—JDK 1.1. This will lead you to a page from which you can download both the software and the documentation.

There are explicit instructions on how to download the software and unpack it.

For instance, in the case of Solaris, if you're downloading JDK 1.1 , you'll get the file `jdk1.1-solaris2-sparc.sh`. You should execute `sh` with this file name as the command line argument:

```
sh jdk1.1-solaris2-sparc.sh
```

This will unpack the Kit.

In the case of Windows you can either download the software directly by clicking on the JDK 1.1 link or you can download a compressed file and later uncompress it. This file is `jdk1_1-win32-x86.exe`. When you double-click on this, the JDK 1.1 releases will be installed on your system, after which you can delete this .exe to recover some disk space.

You will need to update your path so that the bin directory which contains the Java executables is present in the path. This is required so that you don't have to type the absolute path of the executables when invoking them.

For instance, in case of Solaris using C-shell, you can say:

```
set path=(/home/your_dir/JAVA1.1/jdk1.1/bin path).
```

Here `/home/your_dir/JAVA1.1` is the directory in which you've downloaded the software. Of course, you don't have to use the same directory name!

On Windows you need to set the PATH. You can put this in your `:autoexec.bat`:

```
PATH C:\JDK1.1\BIN; rest of the path
```

There are very good installation instructions on JavaSoft's web page which tell you exactly what is to be done to download the software for your platform.

1.1.2 Theory You Need to Know

Yeah, yeah, we lied. But some theory *is* absolutely necessary. Imagine someone teaching you how to skydive without telling you how the parachute opens! The next few headings may seem boring, but the information will be very helpful for you in understanding some concepts — and then we'll take the 30,000-foot jump.

1.1.2.1 Utilities in the JDK

There are different utilities that come as part of the JDK release. These include the Java compiler, `javac`, an appletviewer used for viewing applets, `javah` which is used for generating headers and stubs for native method integration, the interpreter `java`, and `rmiregistry` and `rmic` which are used for remote method invocation.

If the above paragraph sounds like it's written in an alien language, don't panic. Once you've gone through this book, the terms mentioned above will become part of your coffee-table discussions.

1.1.2.2 Classes in the JDK

For those of you who don't know what classes are, you'll come to know as we progress. But for the time being, you can look upon classes as libraries that contain functionality your code can make use of. For instance, there are classes you can use to make connections with another computer, to write output on your terminal, to draw images, etc.

When you've downloaded the JDK, you should go to the `java` directory. This contains a zip file, `src.zip`. You should unzip this file as it contains the source code of some of the classes that come as part of the JDK.

On Solaris you can type: **unzip src.zip**

On Windows you need to use an unzip utility that maintains long file names. This is because most of the classes have names longer than 8 characters. One such utility is UnZip 5.12 which can be found at the following site:

```
ftp://ftp.uu.net/pub/archiving/zip/WIN32/
```

You can download `unz512xN.exe` and use it for unzipping `src.zip`.

This will create a directory src containing subdirectories such as `java`, `sun` and `sunw`.

Most of the time you will be interested in the `java` directory.

Using Java's notation, if we refer to a directory as `java.src`, you should interpret it with the period replaced by the directory delimiter on your platform. For instance, on Windows, `java.src` would mean `java\src`, while on Unix it would mean `java/src`.

`java.src` contains several subdirectories such as `applet`, `awt`, `io`, `lang`, `net`, `rmi`, etc. Each of these contains Java files which in turn contain classes that provide methods we can make use of in writing our Java applets and applications.

1.1.2.3 Objects, Classes, and Instances

For those of you familiar with C, a class is something like a structure, only it has a much wider scope. A class is a combination of variables and related functions. In object-oriented terminology, functions are known as methods. The variables store the state the class is in, while methods determine what the object can do.

An object can be anything, such as your car or your cup of coffee. A class is an abstract representation of an object.

For example, "a car" can be represented by a class, while "my Honda Civic" will be an object of this type.

Each object has some variables and methods associated with it, and these are exactly what the methods and variables of a class represent.

Let us explain the concept with the help of an example.

```
class lottery
{
    /* Variables */
    name
    winning number
    drawn?

    /* Methods */
    getWinningNumber()
    drawWinningNumber()
}
```

Here we have an object, "lottery". A lottery has a name and a winning number. The name of the lottery is constant, but the winning number changes every day or week. The lottery for a particular date can be in one of two states: drawn or not. For this example, we're using the variable "drawn?". These are the variables associated with the lottery.

For every lottery, the organizers draw the winning number(s). They need a method to do this. Similarly, a lottery ticket buyer needs a method to know what the winning number was. We have put methods in the class for doing this: getWinningNumber() and drawWinningNumber().

We can represent all this information in software using the class "lottery". All the variables and methods that are a part of this class represent the states the lottery can be in and the operations that can be done on it.

So a class is nothing but a software representation of an object.

But the class itself is inert; in order to use it we need to instantiate it. That is, we need to create a copy which represents a specific instance. In the case of the lottery class, instances could be "Super Lotto", "Lucky 5", and so on. All of these instances are distinct copies of the class "lottery". But as we'll learn, all methods and variables need not be copied over to each instance. All instances can share one copy of certain variables/methods and can have local copies of other variables/methods.

1.1.2.4 Instance and Static Variables/Methods

Each instance can have a local copy of variables and methods. This way, Super Lotto's winning number can be different from Lucky 5's winning number. These types of variables and methods are called instance variables, as they're tied to a specific instance.

There can be certain variables and methods that are tied to the class rather than the instance. These are known as class or static variables and methods. In our example, all these lotteries have one thing in common: they're all U.S. lotteries. So we can have a constant whose value is "USA". This constant need not be replicated for each instance as its value is the same for everybody. This is a static variable.

A static variable is like a global variable in C; everybody has access to it, and if one function changes its value, the new value becomes visible to everybody.

There is just one copy of a static variable/method which is used by all instances. Changes made by one get reflected to everybody else.

1.1.2.5 Polymorphism

In languages like C we cannot have two functions with the same name. This restriction has been removed by object-oriented languages. You can have two or more methods with the same name, so long as the number or type of arguments of these methods are different. This is known as polymorphism. The system will decide which of these methods is to be invoked based on the arguments being passed.

Another type of polymorphism involves a class inherited from another, both of them having methods with the same name and arguments. In such cases the method in the inherited class takes precedence over the method in the superclass.

1.1.2.6 Java Data Types

Java offers a good variety of data types and operators that can be used. We have integers, strings, booleans, floats, doubles, and lots more. Assuming that you have a background in C or some other programming language, we don't want to waste precious pages describing these data types. One of the only things that's worth mentioning, however, is the fact that for various data types Java makes use of objects. One very good example is the string type, which is used for storing strings (i.e., an array of characters).

1.1.2.7 Applets and Applications

There are essentially two types of Java programs you will be writing: applets and applications.

Applets are programs that run within a browser or a special tool called appletviewer. The appletviewer tool allows you to view applets as stand-alone Java programs.

Applications, on the other hand, are stand-alone programs which run using the Java interpreter, `java`. They are not executed from within a browser.

Applets can be put in a web page and made accessible to the world. An applet in this case would be a program which is executed when somebody views the web page. This raises concerns of security.

1.1.2.8 Security

What if I read somebody's web page which contains an applet that wipes out my hard disk (or worse, transfers secret notes from my computer and deprives me of my impending Nobel Prize)? To overcome these problems and lots more, there are restrictions on what an applet can do. As an example, applets are not allowed to read/write files. This security has been built into Java so that the Internet is not misused. On the other hand, applications run on the local machine, so restrictions of this type are not imposed.

Using an example, we'll show you how an applet can be converted into an application.

Here's one more definition before we start our free fall.

```
CLASSPATH
```

This is an environment variable which is used for determining directories in which the classes on which your program depends reside. Every program requires at least some of the classes that come as part of the Java kit (whose source code we obtained above by unzipping `src.zip`). So you will need to include a file called `classes.zip` in this environment variable because it contains information about the JDK classes.

You can run your Java classes without being in the same directory in which the classes exist. Alternately, your program could be using multiple classes, not all of which reside in the same directory.

The `CLASSPATH` environment variable is used for specifying the directories in which the classes to be used by your program reside.

For Solaris, you can set it to `<directory_where_JDK_resides>/jdk1.1/lib/classes.zip`. You should also include the current directory, or any other directory where the classes that you wish to use reside. For example, on Solaris (C-shell), you can say:

```
etenv CLASSPATH
.:~/JAVA1.1/jdk1.1/lib/classes.zip:<other_dirs>
```

For Windows you can set it to:

```
<directory_where_JDK_resides>/jdk1.1/lib/classes.zip.
```

You can modify this as:

```
SET CLASSPATH=.;C:\JDK1.1\LIB\CLASSES.ZIP;<other_dirs>
```

`classes.zip` contains information about classes that come as part of the JDK. This should not be unzipped.

In some cases it is not necessary to set this environment variable. This is true if you're invoking your Java program from a directory where all the classes that your program needs to use reside.

When we started writing this book, our objective was to minimize the theory and concentrate on teaching through examples. Obviously, we've failed to keep our promise so far. But now that you have at least a rough idea of classes and instances, we can start cutting to the chase. So, here goes.

1.2 Applications

1.2.1 Example: First Application

Purpose of the Program
This is your first Java application. If you invoke it with a command line argument, it prints out the line "<argument_you_supplied> - Thanks for dropping by!"

Concepts Covered in the Program
This program introduces you to some concepts behind Java applications, such as the `main()` method, strings, constructors, etc.

Source Code

Thanks.java

```
public class Thanks
{
```

```
/* Every application has a main() method in it from where
   execution begins */
public static void main(String[] args)
{
   /* If number of command line arguments is not 1, we
      want to call endMe() */
   if(args.length != 1)
     endMe();
   /* Declaring an instance of the class SayThanks */
   SayThanks sayThanks;
   /* Creating an instance of the class SayThanks, by
      passing the first command line argument to it */
   sayThanks = new SayThanks(args[0]);
   /* Invoke the method sayIt() of the instance created
      above */
   sayThanks.sayIt();
}
static void endMe()
{
   /* This method is called if the application is called
      with a wrong number of  command line arguments */
   /* Print error message on the standard output */
   System.out.println("Usage: java Thanks <argument>");
   /* Exit from the program */
   System.exit(1);
}
}


class SayThanks

{
   /* This is the class whose instance is being created in
      main() above */

   /* Declaring an instance variable, arg, of the type
      String */
   String arg;
   /* Constructor of this class which accepts one String
      argument */
```

```
    SayThanks(String arg0)
    {
      /*Set instance variable arg equal to the argument
        arg0 */
      arg = arg0;
    }

  public void sayIt()
  {
    /* This method is invoked from the main( ) method */

    /* Print the message on the standard output */
    System.out.println(arg + " - Thanks for dropping by");
  }
}
```

To Compile the Program

Set the `java.bin` directory in your path. For example, in C-shell on Solaris:

```
set path=(~/JAVA1.1/jdk1.1/bin path)
```

On Windows you can set the PATH variable to include the JDK1.1\BIN directory. This step is required so that you can access the Java executables (such as the compiler `javac`) from any directory.

Go to the directory in which `Thanks.java` is present and type:

```
javac Thanks.java
```

This will compile the program and create the file `Thanks.class` in the same directory. `Thanks.class` is the byte code which will be read and executed by the interpreter.

To Run the Application Type

```
java Thanks <your_name>
```

Note that we don't say "java Thanks.class", just "java Thanks". `<your_name>` is the command line argument you're passing. If you don't pass this, you will get an error message.

Output of the Program

If invoked as `java Thanks Jim`, the output is:

```
Jim - Thanks for dropping by!
```

If invoked as `java Thanks`, the output is:

```
Usage: java Thanks <argument>
```

Implementation

The program's execution begins in the `main()` method of the class Thanks. We first check whether the number of arguments is 1 or not. If not, we invoke the method `endMe()` which prints an error message and causes the program to exit.

If the number of arguments is correct, we create an instance of the class SayThanks. We pass the command line argument to the constructor of this class, which stores it as a local variable.

Then, using the new instance `sayThanks`, we invoke the method `sayIt()`, which prints out the . . . . Thanks . . . . message.

Now let us look at the individual components that make up this program.

First we create the file `Thanks.java` and declare the class Thanks in it:

```
public class Thanks
```

Here, "public" denotes that the class is accessible to everybody. In other words, another Java program can create an instance of this class and use it.

"Class" is a reserved word, which is used for declaring a class. The word following this, "Thanks", is the name of the class. Note that you *have to* name the Java file `Thanks.java`, i.e., the class name followed by ".java", otherwise the compiler will give an error. Don't believe us? Try it!

Every application has a `main()` method in it. This is the method from which execution begins. This is defined as shown:

```
public static void main(String[] args)
```

This method gets an array of `String` as an argument. The String class is defined in the JDK source directory:

```
<directory_where_you_downloaded_JDK>.java.src.java.lang.String
.java
```

(Remember from the previous section that you should replace the period with your platform's directory delimiter to locate this file on your system.)

The brackets [] indicate that this is an array. So, `String[] args` means that `args` is an array of string objects. The first element of the array is `args[0]`. The rest of the elements are `args[1]`, `args[2]`, and so on.

Each of these strings represents the command line arguments, i.e., the arguments that you supplied while executing the program. So if you invoke this program as `java Thanks some garbage`, `args[0]` will be "some" and `args[1]` will be "garbage".

There is a variable associated with arrays, `length`, which tells us the number of elements in the array. We're making use of this to determine how many arguments have been passed to the program:

```
if(args.length != 1)
```

We're doing this checking because we want the program to be invoked with exactly one argument. We're defining a method in this class for handling the condition when the number of arguments is not equal to one: `endMe()`. If the number of arguments is not equal to one, this method is called:

```
if(args.length != 1)
    endMe();
```

Here's what this method looks like:

```
static void endMe()
```

"Static" indicates that it is a class method, i.e., there is only one copy of this method which is shared by all instances of this class. "Void" indicates that this method doesn't return anything.

This method is supposed to handle the error that occurs when the user has supplied an incorrect number of arguments. What we want to do is: a) print an error message and b) exit out of this program.

The error message is printed out on the standard output. For this we're using the standard output stream that is available to us through the System class, defined in `java.lang.System.java`. The method `println()` prints out the string that is supplied to it as an argument. So:

```
System.out.println("You need to supply exactly one command
line argument");
```

will print on the standard output "You need to supply exactly one command line argument".

To exit the program again we make use of a method in `System.java`, `exit()`. If you take a look at `System.java`, you'll see that `exit()` is defined as a static method. This is the reason we don't need to create an instance of "System" for using this method, i.e., we can directly say `System.exit(1)`.

Going back, if the number of arguments is correct, the method `endMe()` will not be invoked and the interpreter will go to the next line:

```
SayThanks sayThanks;
```

Here we're declaring a variable which will be used within this method. The name of the variable is "sayThanks", and it is of the type "SayThanks". Take a look at the code where "SayThanks" is defined:

```
class SayThanks
```

Obviously, this is a class. And it's not public, so it's not visible to the world (in fact, if we declare it to be public we'll need to create a new file to contain it, `SayThanks.java`). But it *is* visible within this Java file, so the methods which are defined in this file can instantiate this class and invoke its public methods.

So, how do we instantiate the class? For this we have an operator named "new". Using this we can create a new instance of any accessible class. To create the instance we use the notation `new <class_name>()`. This returns a handle to the newly created instance, and we can store it in a variable of the type `:<class_name>`.

We can also supply arguments to a class when its instance is being created, as we're doing in this example:

```
sayThanks = new SayThanks(args[0]);
```

This returns a handle to a new instance of the SayThanks class, which we're storing in the variable `sayThanks` that we declared above.

Now that we have a handle to this class we can invoke its methods. That's exactly what we're doing in the next line:

```
sayThanks.sayIt();
```

Here `sayThanks` is the new instance we created. `sayIt()` is a method defined in the SayThanks class. To access a method or a variable in a class we use the "." notation. So, `sayThanks.sayIt()` means we invoke the method `sayIt()` which is defined in the instance `sayThanks`.

The thing to understand here is that we can't invoke `sayIt()` like we invoked `exit()`, i.e., without instantiating the class. And the reason is that `sayIt()` is not a static method like `exit()`. In other words, we can't simply write `SayThanks.sayIt()` — the compiler will give an error.

Now let's look at the SayThanks class. As we showed above, the class is created with the following line:

```
class SayThanks
```

This class has a variable associated with it, `arg`. This is used to store the first command line argument that was passed to the program. Note that we're not using the word "static" behind this, so it is an instance variable:

```
String arg;
```

Next we come to one of the methods of this class, `SayThanks`. As you may have noticed, the name of this method is the same as that of the class. Such a method is known as a *constructor*.

Just as `main()` is the first method of a Java application that gets invoked, a constructor is the first method of a class that gets invoked when an instance of the class is created.

Java being an object-oriented language allows us to overload methods. This means that there can be more than one method with the same name, as long as their arguments are different. This applies to constructors also.

It is not necessary to specify a constructor. In the Java environment a default constructor is automatically created. This constructor has 0 arguments. So, if you have a class NoConstructor with no constructor, you can still create an instance of it:

```
NoConstructor noCons = new NoConstructor();
```

Alternately, you can have more than one constructor. The constructor which gets invoked is determined by the arguments you're specifying during the creation of the instance. For example if a class Abc has two constructors, Abc(String a) and Abc(int i, int j), if you create an instance using abc = new Abc("Hello"), the first constructor will be called, while if you create it using abc = new Abc(5,10), the second constructor will be called.

In our example, there is just one constructor, which accepts a String argument:

```
SayThanks(String arg0)
```

And the only thing this constructor does is assign the instance variable equal to the argument arg0. This is being done so that other methods can make use of the command line argument. (But it doesn't mean that this is the only thing a constructor can do; you can write whatever code you want in the constructor):

```
arg = arg0;
```

Next, we define a method called sayIt(). This method is going to be invoked by another class, in our case Thanks. So we need to make it public, otherwise other classes won't be able to access it:

```
public void sayIt()
```

We're making use of the println() method to display a string on the standard output. Note the "+" operator. This is the string concatenation operator. By saying arg + " - Thanks for dropping by" we mean that first the string arg will be printed and then on the same line we'll get the string " - Thanks for dropping by":

```
System.out.println(arg + " - Thanks for dropping by");
```

1.3 Applets

Now that you know the basic structure of a Java program, let's explore some more features. In this section we will concentrate on Java applets.

An applet is a Java program that is normally executed when a browser loads a web page. HTML, the language in which web pages are normally written, provides a tag which allows an applet to be included within the page. This tag is a combination of <applet> and </applet>. Within this pair of tags we can specify where the applet resides, its width and height, and a few other things. We can also pass parameters to the applet by specifying them between these tags.

The following example creates your first applet, shown in Figure 1-1.

1.3.1 Example: First Applet

Purpose of the Program

This program introduces you to applets.

Concepts Covered in this Program

Here we show you how applets can be created. We also introduce you to more features of Java and object-oriented programming, such as import and inheritance.

Source Code

```
HTML file: ThankYou.html
```

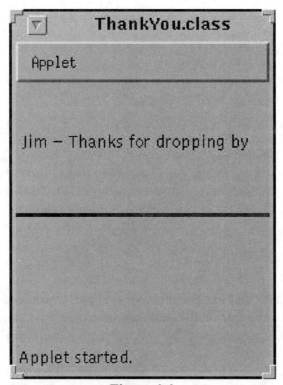

Figure 1-1

```
<HTML>
<HEAD> </HEAD>
<BODY>
<applet codebase="." Code="ThankYou.class" width=200
 height=200>
<param name=nm value="Jim">
</applet>
</BODY>
</HTML>
```

Java file: ThankYou.java

```
/* First "import" all the Java classes that we'll be
   using in this program. Note that classes in the
   java.lang package don't need to be explicitly
   "imported" — they are automatically added when
   compilation is done. */

import java.applet.Applet;
import java.awt.Graphics;
import java.awt.Image;
   /* The class ThankYou should inherit from Applet, so it
      "extends" Applet — this is required for all applets
      */

public class ThankYou extends Applet
{
 Image im;
 public void init()
 {
   /* init() is the initialization method of an applet and
      is called only once in its lifecycle */
   /* Load the image we wish to display */
   im = getImage(getCodeBase(), "rainbowline.gif");
 }
 public void paint(Graphics g)
 {
   // Write the given string at location 5,50 of the
      applet window
```

```
    /* getParameter() gets the value of the parameter "nm"
       as specified in the HTML file from which this applet
       is being loaded */
    g.drawString(getParameter("nm") + " - Thanks for
                                       dropping by",
                                       5, 50);
    // Draw the image we loaded above at location 0,100 of
       the applet window
    g.drawImage(im, 0, 100, this);
  }
}
```

To Compile this Applet

Set the `java.bin` directory in your path as explained in the previous example. Then type `javac ThankYou.java`.

To Run the Applet

```
appletviewer ThankYou.html
```

Alternately you could open the HTML file from a browser such as Netscape or HotJava.

Implementation

As we said earlier, Java provides a set of classes that we can make use of for writing our programs. In the application example you have been unwittingly using some of these classes. For example, you were making use of the System class.

As we will discuss in a later section, in Java, code organization can be done using packages. A package is a collection of classes. The JDK contains a number of packages for use by our programs.

The classes that belong to the `java.lang` package (such as System.class) automatically get linked to our program. But if we want to use some other classes, we need to specifically tell the program which ones we want. In this example, we will be making use of the following classes (besides the `java.lang` classes): `java.applet.Applet.class`, `java.awt.Graphics.class` and `java.awt.Image.class`.

This is made apparent to the program by using the import keyword:

```
import java.applet.Applet;
import java.awt.Graphics;
import java.awt.Image;
```

Here `java.awt` and `java.applet` are packages that contain classes such as Graphics, Image and Applet. The import statement is used to specify that all or some classes of a package are required by our program.

These statements are directives to the compiler that it should include these classes during compilation.

The next statement introduces us to a very important feature of object-oriented programming, inheritance:

```
public class ThankYou extends Applet
```

Since classes represent some objects, we can reuse them to form a new object. For example, if there is a class Fruit, we can reuse it to form something more specific, such as Banana. The advantage of reusing a class is that the original class contains variables and methods associated with all fruits, whereas the Banana or Orange class which is derived from it contains specific variables and methods that apply to this class.

So, the fruit class may contain variables such as weight, color, etc., while the Banana class will contain "length" (which doesn't apply to all fruits) and Orange will contain "diameter".

By defining a class Fruit, we are getting quite a few advantages — we don't need to rewrite the generic code for the implementation of each fruit. And by having the power of extending Fruit to create a new class like Banana which is more specific, our code becomes cleaner and easier.

This concept is known as *inheritance*. By inheriting a class we can create a new class which has all (or some) of the features of the parent class, plus a few more. We can also override methods and variables defined in the parent class. In other words, we can write methods and variables which have the same name in the parent class. When Java encounters this type of a situation it gives precedence to the method or variable defined in the derived class (i.e., the child).

Java allows inheritance through the `extends` keyword. In the above line of code we are saying that the class ThankYou extends Applet. This means that ThankYou has been inherited (or derived) from Applet. In other words, ThankYou can use all the public methods and variables which are defined in the class Applet (or its parents, from which Applet itself has been derived).

It is very important to note that methods or variables that have not been defined with the public keyword may not be available to classes which inherit a particular class. For example, if a method or variable is declared as `private <name_of_method_or_variable>`, then a class which extends this class cannot access this method or variable directly.

Now take a look at `Applet.java` to see what kinds of methods it has. (`Applet.java` is present in the directory `java.applet`.) You'll see several methods such as `init()`,`start()`,`stop()`, etc.

Also, `Applet.java` itself extends Panel, which in turn extends Container. The Container class extends Component. So all public methods or variables declared in all these classes can be used or overridden by our class.

Coming back to our program, we are declaring a variable `im` of the type Image. This will be used for storing an instance of the Image class which is used for storing graphics images:

```
Image im;
```

Next we define the `init()` method. Here we're overriding the `init()` method which is defined in `Applet.java`. So, when the interpreter is executing this applet, it will invoke our `init()` rather than the one defined in `Applet.java`:

```
public void init()
```

The `init()` method is an initialization method and is invoked when the applet is first loaded. We don't call this method directly — the Java interpreter calls it.

Then we make use of another method which is defined in the Applet class, `getImage()`. This is used for loading an image. Note that we're invoking this method just as if it were locally defined. This is because our class has inherited from the Applet class and all the public methods of Applet are available for its use.

The method `getImage()` loads the image and we store it in the variable we declared above, `im`:

```
im = getImage(getCodeBase(), "rainbowline.gif");
```

The parameters of this method are explained in the first example in the chapter on applets. For the time being, just understand that the gif file `rainbowline.gif` will be loaded for use within this applet.

Next, we're overriding the method `paint()`. This method is declared in `java.awt.Component.java`. This method is invoked when some painting needs to be done in the applet. By overriding this method you can specify what you want to draw in your applet window:

```
public void paint(Graphics g)
```

This method takes an instance of the Graphics class as a parameter. An instance of the Graphics class is created for every applet. This is created by the Java interpreter and its handle is passed to the `paint()` method. It can be used for writing to the applet's window.

In our example, we're drawing a string at location 5,50. Here 5 is the position on the X-axis and 50 is the position on the Y-axis. The reference coordinate is the top left corner of the applet's window, which is point 0,0.

```
g.drawString(getParameter("nm") + " - Thanks for dropping
                                  by", 5,50);
```

The string begins with a parameter which is read from the HTML file. In our HTML file, between the <applet   and </applet   tags we have a tag:

```
<param name=nm value="Jim">
```

The `getParameter()` method parses the HTML file and returns the string "Jim" as this is the value associated with the parameter "nm".

Next, we draw the image we loaded above using the `drawImage()` method of Graphics. The image is drawn at location 0,100:

```
g.drawImage(im, 0, 100, this);
```

To review all that we've learned above: we first import various classes we'll need in our applet. Then we define the applet `ThankYou` and inherit it from the Applet class. Next, we override the `init()` method which is called using the initialization of the applet. In doing this we're loading an image which we are later going to display.

Then we override the `paint()` method. This method does the actual writing to the applet window. We first draw a string and then draw the image that was loaded in the `init()` method.

Now let's quickly take a look at the HTML file. Unlike a Java application, an applet resides in an HTML file and to see it in action we need to open the HTML file in a Java-enabled browser (or a special tool like the appletviewer), i.e., we don't directly invoke the compiled class.

For this purpose, HTML supports the tag <applet . With this we specify where the class that needs to be executed resides. We use the reserved words "codebase", which gives the directory in which the class resides, and "code", which gives the name of the class file. The <applet> tag is ended in the normal HTML fashion with </applet . We can specify the width and height of the applet's window using the reserved words "width" and "height". In addition, we can pass parameters to the class by using the reserved words <param name=name_of_the_parameter value="value_of_the_parameter">:

```
<applet codebase="." Code="ThankYou.class" width=200
  height=200>
    <param name=nm value="Jim">
    </applet>
```

The net result is that if you read this HTML file from your browser or say `appletviewer ThankYou.html`, a window of size 200x200 is created and `ThankYou.class` is executed in this window.

(Remember, appletviewer is a special interpreter which comes as part of the JDK. This is used for viewing applets. You can use appletviewer instead of a browser to see your applets in action. In fact it's better to use the appletviewer in the development phase of an applet as it displays any runtime errors it encounters.)

1.4 Converting an Applet into an Application

Now that you know how to create applets and applications, we'll show you how you can convert an applet into an application by putting a wrapper around it, as shown in Figure 1-2.

Example: Converting an Applet into an Application

Purpose of the Program
This program shows how your applets can be converted into applications with a very simple procedure.

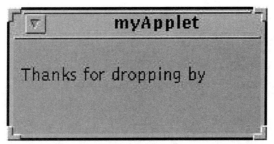

Figure 1-2

Concepts Covered in this Program

By showing how applets can be converted into applications we're showing how you can make use of features offered by applets in your applications.

Source Code

The applet MyApplet.java

```
import java.applet.Applet;
import java.awt.Graphics;
public class MyApplet extends Applet
{
   public void paint(Graphics g)
   {
      g.drawString("Thanks for dropping by", 5, 30);
   }
}
```

The converting application App.java

```
import java.awt.*;
public class App
{
   public static void main(String[] args)
   {
      /* Create a Frame object with "myApplet" as the title
         bar */
      Frame f = new Frame("myApplet");
      /* Create an instance of our applet */
      MyApplet my = new MyApplet();
      /* Initialize and start the applet */
```

```
    my.init();
    my.start();
    /* Add the aplet to the frame */
    f.add("Center", my);
    /* Resize the frame to size 200x100 */
    f.resize(200,100);
    /* Display the frame (and hence, the applet we've
       added to it ) */
    f.show();
  }
}
```

Implementation

`MyApplet` is a simple applet which writes a string in the applet's window. `App.java` contains the class App which uses this applet.

We're doing this by creating a frame and adding the applet to that frame. Frames are GUI components and we discuss them in more detail in the GUI chapter. For this reason we'll not go into the source code of this program, as it will become clear to you only after you've read the GUI chapter.

The basic outline is: a frame, which is a GUI component, is being created. This supplies a window which can be used by applications for writing output. The applet is being added to this window. The `init()` and `start()` methods of the applet are being called. Note that this has to be done because we're not running the applet through a browser or appletviewer which normally calls these methods. We don't need to call the `paint()` method, however, as a frame is also a component and has a `paint()` method associated with it.

1.5 Multi-File Java Programs

What if you have a very large program? You wouldn't want to write everything in one big file. Java allows you to use multiple files for creating your programs. In the next example we show a code that is split into two Java files.

Example: Multi-File Java Program

Purpose of the Program

This program shows how you can write a program that is spread across multiple Java files.

Concepts Covered in this Program

Besides showing how a program can be spread over multiple files, this example also shows how an array can be passed as an argument to a method.

Source Code

ArrayClass1.java

```
class ArrayClass1
{
 public static void main(String arg[])
 {
    int arr[]={1,1,1,1}; /* arr is an integer array
    with all elements equal to 1 */
    ArrayClass1 obj1 = new ArrayClass1();
    ArrayClass2 obj2 = new ArrayClass2();

 /* Print elements of the array before passing it as an
    argument to changeArrVals()*/
    System.out.println("Before array is passed values are
    ");
    obj1.printArrVals(arr);

    obj2.changeArrVal(arr); /* arr is being passed as an
    argument */

    /* Print elements of array after it has been passed
       as an argument */
    System.out.println("After array is passed values are
    ");
    obj1.printArrVals(arr);

    }
 static void printArrVals(int[] arr)
 {
    int i;
    System.out.print("[");
```

```
    /* Traverse all the elements of the array "arr" and
        print them */
    for(i=0; i < arr.length; i++)
    {
        System.out.print(" " + arr[i] + " ");
    }
    System.out.println("]");
  }
 }
```

ArrayClass2.java

```
public class ArrayClass2
{
   /* The method changeArrVal() will change the value of the
      elements of the array "arr" */
   void changeArrVal(int[] arr)
   {
      int i;
      /* Traverse the length of the array and set all
          elements equal to 4 */
      for(i=0; i < arr.length; i++)
      {
   arr[i]=4;
      }
   }
}
```

To Compile

```
javac ArrayClass1.java ArrayClass2.java
```

To Run

```
java ArrayClass1
```

Output of the Program
   Before array is passed, values are:

```
[ 1 1 1 1 ]
```

After array is passed, values are:

```
[ 4 4 4 4 ]
```

Implementation

This program's implementation is spread across two Java files, :Array-Class1.java and ArrayClass2.java. ArrayClass1.java is the top level file as it contains the main() method which, as you may recall, is the first method in an application that is called.

ArrayClass1 creates an integer array with four elements, each initialized to "1":

```
int arr[]={1,1,1,1};
```

Then it creates an instance of itself:

```
ArrayClass1 obj1 = new ArrayClass1();
```

This is being done because we will be calling an instance method, print-ArrVals(), which belongs to it.

We're also creating an instance of ArrayClass2 as we'll be calling an instance method defined in that class, changeArrVal():

```
ArrayClass2 obj2 = new ArrayClass2();
```

Then we print on the screen the message "Before array is passed values are". Now the instance method printArrVals() is called. Since this is an instance method (i.e., it hasn't been declared with the static keyword), we need to use the instance handle obj1 that we created above:

```
obj1.printArrVals(arr);
```

We cannot say printArrayVals() without obj1 as Java will have no way of knowing which instance's printArrayVals() method we wish to invoke.

Note that printArrVals() is defined to take an argument, which is an array of integers:

```
static void printArrVals(int[] arr)
```

It simply prints out all the elements in the array. Then, using the instance of ArrayClass2, we call the method `changeArrVal()` which is defined in that class. The purpose of the method `changeArrVal()` is to change the value of the elements of the integer array:

```
obj2.changeArrVal(arr);
```

And we again print out the new value of this array:

```
obj1.printArrVals(arr);
```

As we can see from the output, when the array is printed the second time, all the elements are "4", as set by `changeArrVal()`. This is because arrays are passed by reference in Java. In other words, if an array is passed as an argument to a method, changes made to the array by that method will be visible to the calling method also; the called method doesn't create and modify a local copy of the array.

Just for the sake of it, let us also look at `ArrayClass2.java`. This is a public class with just one method, `changeArrVal()`. It takes an integer array as an argument:

```
void changeArrVal(int[] arr)
```

It traverses the entire length of the array and sets its elements to "4":

```
for(i=0; i < arr.length; i++)
{
arr[i]=4;
}
```

So, as we've seen, the program has been implemented using two Java files. Similarly, you can use any number of Java files to implement your program.

1.6 Packages

Another way of organizing data is by putting it in packages. You can look upon a package as a library of related classes. All classes and methods in a package must be public for them to be accessible to classes outside the package. A program that wishes to use a package needs to import it.

You've already made use of certain packages such as `java.lang`, `java.awt` and `java.applet`. Out of these, `java.lang` doesn't need to be imported explicitly because the Java compiler adds this by default. However, as we've seen in previous examples, we needed to import some classes from the `java.awt` and `java.applet` packages as we wanted to use them in our program.

Packages help by organizing your data in a clean way. The need for this arises as you start building large applications. You can provide a package to other users. This has an advantage over providing individual classes separately because you can group like classes in one package, thus making it easier for users to locate what they're interested in. For example, the Java packages have all the classes related to network programming in the `java.net` package. So, if we want to look for the Socket class, we know that the first place to search for it would be `java.net`.

Now let's create our own packages and use them.

1.6.1 Example: Creating and Using Packages

Purpose of the Program
In this program we organize our classes by creating packages. These packages are then used by the program `Country.java`.

Concepts Covered in this Program
This program shows how you can organize your classes using the `package` and `import` keywords.

Source Code

First Package

`USA.java`

```
/* The reserved word "package" indicates that the class
   defined in this file, USA, belongs to the package whose
   name is "countries.america" */
package countries.america;
```

```java
public class USA
{
  public USA()
  {
    System.out.println("Constructor of class USA");
  }
}
```

Canada.java

```java
package countries.america;
public class Canada
{
  public Canada()
  {
    System.out.println("Constructor of class Canada");
  }
}
```

Second Package

France.java

```java
/* The reserved word "package" indicates that the class
   defined in this file, France, belongs to the package
   whose name is "countries.europe" */

package countries.europe;

public class France
{
  public France()
  {
    System.out.println("Constructor of class France");
  }
}
```

Italy.java

```
package countries.europe;
public class Italy
{
 public Italy()
 {
    System.out.println("Constructor of class Italy");
 }
}
```

Java File Using These Packages

Country.java

```
/* Since we want to use the classes defined in the packages
   we created above, we need to "import" them (Just like
   we've been importing Java's packages such as java.applet
   */

import countries.america.*;
import countries.europe.*;
public class Country
{
    public static void main(String[] args)
    {
      /*Since we've imported the packages we can use the
        classes just as if they were defined in another
        file accessible to us */
      USA c1 = new USA();
      France c2 = new France();
      Canada c3 = new Canada();
      Italy c4 = new Italy();
    }
}
```

To Compile

Choose a directory where you wish to place your package. Let's say this directory is /home/jim/myPackages.

Change your CLASSPATH to include this, e.g., on Solaris for C-shell:

```
setenv CLASSPATH "/home/jim/myPackages:CLASSPATH"
```

In /home/jim/myPackages create the directory countries, and beneath that create directories europe and america. For example, on Unix:

```
cd /home/jim/myPackages
mkdir countries countries/europe
mkdir countries/america
```

Copy the files USA.java and Canada.java to countries/america. Copy files Italy.java and France.java to countries/europe.
Now compile all these Java files:

```
cd countries/europe; javac *.java;
cd countries/america; javac *.java
```

Your packages are ready now.
Next, go to any directory where you wish to place Country.java. This file uses the packages we created above. Compile it:

```
javac Country.java
```

Output of the Program

```
Constructor of class USA
Constructor of class France
Constructor of class Canada
Constructor of class Italy
```

Implementation

We're creating four Java files, each of which represents a country. In the traditional approach, all of these files as well as Country.java, which uses them, would be lying in one directory. Now, if we implemented a class for each country in the world, there would be more than 150 files lying in one directory, and that would be really cumbersome, to say the least.

What we need here is an organization of our class files so that it's easier to locate the ones we need. Countries can be classified by the continent to which they belong. This is exactly what we're using to organize our data.

We're creating two packages, countries.america and countries.

europe. All class files that represent countries in America will go to the first package and all European countries will go to the second one.

So how does Java recognize this structuring? Well, this is a combination of three things: the "package" statement, the "import" statement, and the CLASSPATH environment variable.

Every package starts with a line that indicates the directory in which all the classes belonging to that package reside. The directory path is not absolute. It is relative to one of the directories in the CLASSPATH environment variable. For example, see `USA.java`:

```
package countries.america;
```

This means that `USA.class` is present in the directory `countries/america` (on Unix) or `countries\america` (on Windows), etc. This path is relative to the CLASSPATH. So if your CLASSPATH is `.:/home/jim/myPackages:/home/jim/someDir`, then `USA.class` could (and should) be present in any of the following directories:

```
./countries/america
/home/jim/myPackages/countries/america
/home/jim/someDir/countries/america
```

There can be any number of classes in this package. Every Java file that defines the class belonging to this package should begin with the line `:package countries.america;`.

Note that if you create the Java file belonging to a package in another directory you will need to move it to the directory mentioned in the "package" line in order for it to be located by programs that use this package.

And here's how a Java file can make use of a package: there is an "import" statement which is written as the first line of a Java program that needs to use a package. For example, see `Country.java`. It uses the packages `countries.america` and `countries.europe`. It first needs to import these packages so that the compiler knows where the classes belonging to the package reside:

```
import countries.america.*;
import countries.europe.*;
```

Here * means all the classes belonging to the package `countries.america`. Note that we can also selectively import class files. For instance, if

`Country.java` didn't need to instantiate France, it could have the following import statements:

```
import countries.america.*;
import countries.europe.Italy;
```

The only other thing you need to notice is that only the classes and methods that are declared public are available for use by programs importing these packages. That applies even to constructors. So we have a constructor declared with the public keyword:

```
public USA()
```

And we have the classes also declared with the public keyword.

1.7 Interfaces

Writing good software involves a design phase in which you lay down your ideas before the actual implementation is done. Interfaces play a very important role here. An interface is a class that defines a set of methods to be implemented by another object.

An interface contains methods like any other class. The difference is that these methods are empty — they don't do anything. It's the responsibility of the class using the interface to write the implementation of the method.

In short, if a class proclaims to implement a given interface, it is telling the world, "I've implemented at least all the methods of this interface and maybe some more methods of my own." You create an interface just so that your design can be done. Later you can use this interface in a class to do the actual work.

Instead of creating an example, let's look at an existing interface: the Runnable interface which is present in `java.lang.Runnable.java`.

An interface is created by using the `interface` keyword. So Runnable is defined as:

```
public interface Runnable
```

It declares only one method, `run()`. Note that there is no implementation provided in the interface. The implementation needs to be provided by the class that uses this interface.

We'll be using this interface in the applets chapter for creating animations, and that's where you'll get a better idea of what interfaces are. We will also be using a number of other interfaces in the GUI chapter, where we also show how to use multiple interfaces.

However just so you're not left groping in the dark, here's how you use an interface. A class that needs to use an interface must use the keyword `implements`. It must also give an implementation to all the methods that are declared in the interface.

So a class that wishes to use the Runnable interface would look like this:

```
class AClass implements Runnable
{
  public void run()
  {
    System.out.println("Do something meaningful");
    .....
  }
}
```

We don't expect you to grasp everything in this chapter in the first go. A lot has been said here which you will come to understand over a period of time. We'll be revisiting a lot of things discussed here in the subsequent chapters, and that's where you'll get a real feel for it.

So, for the time being, treat this chapter like one of those movies you just have to watch more than once to understand how John Travolta ended up munching burgers in a restaurant after being killed.

APPLETS

Have you ever wondered how people manage to put all those pretty pictures in their web pages, much less move them around and make them talk? Well, we are going to discuss all these exciting things in this chapter. It is divided into eight sections. Each of these sections reveals some of the magic behind all the cool stuff on the web.

2.1 An Introduction to Applets

This section introduces you to a very simple applet — one that displays a single image and also writes a string. As we go further in this chapter you will come to know how these images and strings are modified and manipulated. We will discuss how animation can be done using both text and images, and we will show how sound files can be accommodated in your applets.

Java Development Kit 1.1 is not supported by most popular browsers as of this writing, and because of that, applets written with 1.1 won't run in browsers. You may use the appletviewer or Java's own browser, HotJava, to view these applets.

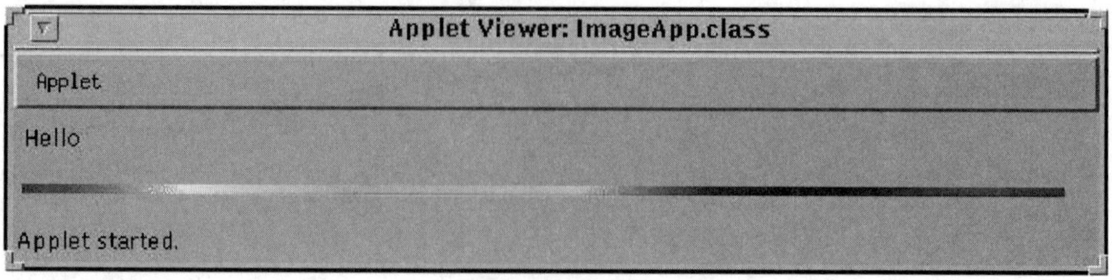

Figure 2-1

2.1.1 Example: Introductory Applet

Purpose of the Program

This is an introductory program in which we show how images and strings are drawn. When you run this applet it will display the text "Hello" and the rainbow image as shown in Figure 2-1. This program will build the base for the next topics of discussion.

Concepts Covered in this Program

This program gives you a basic introduction to applets, and tells you about some of the common methods that are used in writing an applet.

Source Code

For an explanation of the source code, see the Implementation section that follows. Code portions that have been explained in detail are in bold.

HTML FILE: *ImageApp.htm*

```
<HTML>
<HEAD>  </HEAD>
<BODY>
<applet codebase="http://myserver/HTML_DIR"
code=ImageApp.class width=600 height=60>
</applet>
</BODY>
</HTML>
```

JAVA FILE: *ImageApp.java*

```
import java.awt.*;
import java.applet.Applet;
public class ImageApp extends Applet
{
        /* The image to be loaded will be stored in the
           instance variable image1 */
        Image image1;
        public void init()
        {
                / *Load the image med_rainbow.gif which exists
                   in directory "GIF" relative to the "codebase"
                   defined in the HTML file */
                image1 = getImage(getCodeBase(),
                        "GIF/med_rainbow.gif");

        }
        public void paint(Graphics g)
        {
                /* Draw the String "Hello" and paint the image
                   we loaded above */
                g.drawString("Hello ", 5,20);
                g.drawImage(image1, 5, 40, this);

        }
}
```

How to Compile and Run this Applet

To Compile the Applet:
Type javac ImageApp.java

To Run the Applet:
You can use either of the following two approaches:

1. Open the HTML file through a browser such as Netscape. Assuming your HTML file is present in /HTML_DIR on the HTTP server myserver, open the URL http://myserver/HTML_DIR/ImageApp.htm.

2. Assuming that your ImageApp.class is in the same directory as your HTML file ImageApp.htm, replace http://myserver/HTML_DIR/ImageApp.htm with "." (a period). Otherwise, replace the URL with the directory in which the class file exists, relative to the directory in which the HTML file is pre-

sent. Go to the directory in which ImageApp.htm is present. Then run appletviewer: appletviewer ImageApp.htm.

Implementation

```
import java.awt.*;
import java.applet.Applet;
```

The first two lines of this applet are "importing" some other classes which will be used by it. We know that we will require the Applet class and also some classes of the Abstract Window Toolkit (AWT).

Look at the source listing of Java as provided by Sunsoft. This should have been created when you unzipped the file `src.zip`. You will see that in the `jdk1.1` directory there is a `src` directory, which in turn contains a `java` directory. This has a few other directories under it such as `awt`, `applet`, etc. Each of these subdirectories contains the classes that are available for use in our Java programs.

We will be referring to this source listing quite frequently. Here's an example explaining the notation we'll be using: `java.awt.Graphics.java` will mean the directory `<Dir_where_you_downloaded_JDK>/jdk1.1/src/java/awt/Graphics.java` on Unix systems and `<Dir_where_you_downloaded_JDK>\jdk1.1\src\java\awt\Graphics.java` on Windows.

So, by saying import `java.awt.*`, we are saying that we will be requiring all the classes present in the `java.awt` directory.

Next we declare the class. The name of the class is ImageApp. Note that it's important to name the file `ImageApp.java`, i.e., the class name followed by ".java", otherwise the compiler will return with an error.

```
public class ImageApp extends Applet
```

By saying that "ImageApp extends Applet" we mean to say that this class has been derived from the Applet class.

As we explained in Chapter 1, in object-oriented lingo this is known as "inheritance."

Then we go on to declare a variable, `image1`. This is an object of the type Image. We can use the Image class, which is defined in `java.awt.Image.java`, as we have imported `java.awt.*`. It is used for storing and manipulating images.

```
Image image1;
```

In classes extending Applet, we can specify various methods which will be executed at different stages. These methods don't need to be called by our code — the order in which are they are executed is determined by Java itself. But we can always override these methods to get the functionality we want. For this we need to understand a couple of things: a) when these methods are called and b) what sort of code we should write in them.

An applet goes through an initialization phase. For this the method `init()` is invoked.

Normally, images are loaded during this phase, as image loading is a one-time activity. So that's exactly what we're doing here; we're overriding the default `init()` method by writing our own implementation:

```
public void init()
{
    image1 = getImage(getCodeBase(),"GIF/med_rainbow.gif");
}
```

This method uses the `getImage()` method which is provided by the Applet class. The variations of this method are documented in Java's source listing in `java.applet.Applet.java`. `getCodeBase()` is a method that reads the base location of the graphics file from your HTML file.

In your HTML file you will have something like:

```
<applet codebase="http://myserver/HTML_DIR"
code=ImageApp.class width=600 height=60>
</applet>
```

The method `getCodeBase()` tells `getImage()` that the base directory to be used for locating the file is HTML_DIR on the machine `myserver`. This is derived from the `codebase` argument in the HTML file. Note that the second argument to `getImage()` is the path of the actual gif file, relative to the codebase. So, in the current example, your gif file should exist on the machine `myserver` in the location "/HTML_DIR/GIF/med_rainbow.gif. You can change this to whatever machine and directory you want, so long as you have an HTTP server running on it.

The HTML file also specifies that the code of the applet is present in `ImageApp.class`, and that the width and height of the applet are 600 and 60, respectively.

Next, we come to the **paint()** method. This is the method that does the actual graphics output. It gets a handle to the Graphics Context as an argument. The Graphics Context can be viewed as an instance of the Graphics class, whose methods you will use to write output to the applet:

```
public void paint(Graphics g)
```

Here g is the Graphics Context.

The Graphics class is quite rich, and you should study the variations, which are all described in java.awt.Graphics.java. We are using two of them here:

```
g.drawString("Hello ", 5,20);
g.drawImage(image1, 5, 40, this);
```

The first one draws the string Hello on the applet at location 5 on the x axis and 20 on the y axis. Play around with these numbers until you get a proper feeling for what they actually represent. But for now, the upper left corner of your applet is location 0,0.

Similarly, drawImage() draws the image that you loaded earlier at location 5,40. The last parameter, this, is a special keyword — it specifies the current instance of the applet. In most cases we will be specifying this parameter as this.

There are a few more applet methods that are usually overridden, such as start() and stop(), and we will discuss them later on.

Now you have gone through an entire applet. Absorb all the information you've gathered here before moving to the next section, where we actually begin to ride the roller coaster with some of the most interesting topics: animation and sound.

2.2 Animation: Using a Single Image

Gone are the days when a simple image in an HTML file was sufficient to buy you the admiration of your colleagues (or the sometimes-coveted title of nerd). Now your page needs to have at least some sort of animation and maybe some sound, too. In the next few sections we are going to teach you, slowly and steadily, how to achieve this goal. And who knows—you may be able to impress that someone special (or save yourself from being fired, whatever the case may be). And we're going to do it so smoothly that you'll be there before you know it.

In keeping with the overall idea behind this book, we will teach you strictly through examples how you can create animations. In each example, the need for learning a particular concept has been inserted. And we teach you not only the concept, but also how to fish for new methods when the need arises.

For those of you whose bosses use the infamous words, "Take your time, but I want it ready by tomorrow morning," we have lots of material in this chapter that can be cut and pasted. But don't forget to replace some of our images and text with your own (just a piece of advice for the unfortunate ones whose bosses might have a copy of this book on their own desks).

To teach you how to fish, each Implementation section introduces some new concepts and methods. It also tells you where you can find more information about these and a lot of other methods you can use in your programs. As in previous chapters, we will be referring you to Java's source listing, which can be downloaded as part of the Java Development Kit from Sunsoft's site:

`http://www.javasoft.com`

For Solaris, if you `untar` the release you will see a directory called `jdk1.1/src/java` which contains all the source code. References to files like `awt/Graphics.java` should be construed to mean that we're referring to `jdk1.1/src/java/awt/Graphics.java`. There are similar equivalents for other platforms. So let's get going!

This section contains three Java applets: `Movebar1.java`, `Movebar2.java` and `Movebar3.java`. The first applet introduces you to the basics of animation, and the last one contains everything you need to know to create a simple animation.

The subtle but significant variations between these programs highlight some important concepts of Java. The basic animation provided by applets in this section is illustrated with the following snapshots taken at different times in the animation. The best results, of course, can be viewed by running the program through an appletviewer or a browser.

The bar you see in the three images that make up Figure 2-2 is actually just one image. Its size is being modified by the Java applets to create the effect of an animation. To the uninitiated it would appear as some kind of magic wand that increases and decreases in size. Our attempt here is to uncover the magic for you and to teach you how you can create magic of your own.

2.2.1 Example: Moving Bar

Purpose of the Program
This program demonstrates how an animation can be built by using just one image. The bar shown in the three different snapshots below starts out very small, and grows to a maximum value. At that point it starts decreasing and the whole cycle is repeated continuously.

Important Concepts Covered in this Program
Movebar1.java provides the basic framework which is used for writing animation programs. We will expand this later to include more sophisticated techniques.

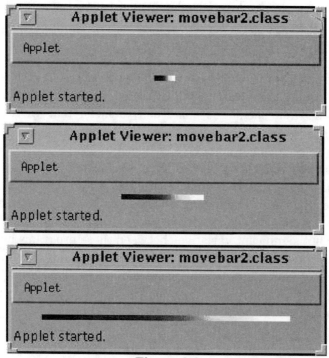

Figure 2-2

Source Code

HTML FILE: *Movebar1.htm*

```
<HTML>
<HEAD> </HEAD>
<BODY>
<applet codebase="http://myserver/HTML" code=Movebar1.class
width=300 height=20>
</applet>
</BODY> </HTML>
```

JAVA FILE: *Movebar1.java*

```
import java.awt.*;
import java.applet.Applet;
/ *Since we're constructing an animation, our applet needs
   to implement the Runnable interface so that we can make
   this class behave as a thread */

public class Movebar1 extends Applet implements Runnable
{
    Image fgImage1;
    /* We'll be creating a thread that will control the
       animation. Variable animThread1 is a placeholder for
       the thread */

    Thread animThread1;
    int i,j=0,k=0;

    /* This boolean becomes true when the starting point of
       the bar reaches near the center of the applet
       window. It will then be set to false so that the
       starting point starts moving to the edge */
    boolean centerReached=false;

    public void init()
    {
```

```
      fgImage1 = getImage(getCodeBase(),
      "GIF/rainbowline.gif");
   }
   public void start()
   {
      /* Create an instance of the Thread class. "this" is
         this instance of our applet */
      animThread1 = new Thread(this);

      /* Start the thread. This will give control to the
         run() method below */
      animThread1.start();
   }
   public void run()
   {
      /* Set the thread to a low priority so that it
         doesn't hog resources */
      Thread.currentThread().setPriority
      (Thread.MIN_PRIORITY);

      /* Repeat the code below until k's value changes to
         non-zero. Since no piece of code is doing that,
         this creates an infinite loop */
      while(k == 0)
        {
        if(animThread1 == null)
           break;
        /* Calling repaint() will explicitly invoke the
           paint() method */
        repaint();
        }

   }
   public void paint(Graphics g)
   {
      g.drawImage(fgImage1, j,10,(300 - 2*j),5,this);

      /* If the center has been reached, reduce the starting
         point of image display on the x-axis by 10, else
```

```
        increase it by 10. */
    if(centerReached)
        j-=10;
    else
        j+=10;

    if(j >= 150)
        centerReached=true;
    if(j <= 0)
        centerReached=false;
}
```

Implementation

This applet uses one of the most commonly used animation methods. The class Movebar1 is inheriting from the Applet class. At the same time it is making use of the Runnable interface: it is implementing a `run()` method, which can be used by a thread created in this class.

If at any point in this chapter you feel uncomfortable about threads, don't hesitate to glance through the threads chapter, especially the section on Runnable interface.

This class extends Applet because we're creating an applet. However, to achieve animation, we want it to behave as a thread, so we're implementing the Runnable interface. Runnable is an interface which allows a class to run in a distinct thread.

public class Movebar1 extends Applet implements Runnable

The image is loaded using the `getImage()` method in the `init()` method. The `init()` method, as we discussed in the previous section, is the initialization method.

The two variations of the **getImage()** method are documented in the **Applet.java** file, present in the **java.applet** directory of Java's source listing. First we declare a thread object:

Thread animThread1;

The `start()` method is invoked after `init()`. Normally we create threads and do other applet work in this method. In our example a thread is being created and started in the `start()` method:

```
animThread1 = new Thread(this);
animThread1.start();
```

The effect of these statements is that a new thread, whose name is `ani-mThread1`, is created and starts executing.

As you'll learn in the chapter on threads, when a thread is started, control goes to its `run()` method. Our classes can provide an implementation for this method.

Since the class Movebar1 itself is behaving as a thread because it's implementing the Runnable interface, when the thread created above is started, control goes to the `run()` method defined in this class.

The `run()` method first sets the priority of the thread to `Thread.MIN_PRIORITY`. The Thread class defines valid values to which the priority can be set. We are setting this to a low value as we don't want to upset other resources at the expense of our thread. However, at times you may want to set higher priorities for the thread if it needs to do some important work at a faster speed.

The Thread class and its methods are well documented in **java.lang.Thread.java** in Java's source listing.

Next, we put a `while` loop in the program:

```
while(k == 0)
```

This makes the thread run forever. To stop it, you will have to kill the applet. We will discuss in a later example how you can stop a thread at will.

In this loop we call the `repaint()` method. The effect of this is that the `paint()` method of the applet is called. `paint()` and `repaint()` are described by `java.awt.Component.java`.

But we have overloaded this method to provide our own implementation. It draws the image using the method `drawImage()`:

```
g.drawImage(fgImage1, j,10,(300 - 2*j),5,this);
```

Variations of `drawImage()` are explained in `java.awt.Graphics.java`.

The first parameter is the image to be drawn, and the second and third parameters determine the x and y positions of the image. The third and fourth parameters of the `drawImage()` method control the length and width of the image, respectively. The last parameter is used for determining the object in which the image is to be drawn. For most purposes, you will be specifying it as `this`, the current instance of the applet.

Here, the value of j is initially 0. So, in the first frame, the whole bar is drawn. In every call to the paint() method, the value of j is changed, so that the size of the bar is changed. Note that both the x position of the bar and its length are changed to get the desired effect.

2.2.2 Example: Moving Bar Stops and Restarts with Mouse Click

Purpose of the Program

This program is just an extension of Movebar1.java. In this example, we have added functionality so that the thread can be stopped/restarted by clicking a mouse button in the applet.

Concepts Covered in this Program

This program illustrates how a user can stop or restart an applet. It also introduces the mouseClicked() method.

The file **java.awt.Component.java** explains the **mouseClicked()** method.

Source Code

HTML FILE: *Movebar2.htm*

```
<HTML>
<HEAD></HEAD>
<BODY>
<applet codebase="http://myserver/HTML" code=Movebar2.class
width=300
height=20>
</applet>
</BODY>
</HTML>
```

JAVA FILE: *Movebar2.java*

```
/* This program is just an extension of Movebar1.java. In
this we have put functionality so that the thread can be
stopped/restarted by clicking a mouse button in the applet.
*/
```

```
import java.awt.*;
import java.applet.Applet;
import java.awt.event.*;
```

```
/* A mouse click is an "event" in Java's terminology. To
"catch" an event and to do some action on it, we need to
implement an interface whose methods are invoked when the
event occurs. The interface associated with mouse clicks is
the MouseListener, so we're implementing this interface */
```

```
public class Movebar2 extends Applet implements Runnable,
MouseListener
{
  Image fgImage1;
  Thread animThread1;
  int i,j=0,k=0;
  boolean frozen;
  boolean centerReached=false;

  public void init()
  {
     fgImage1 = getImage(getCodeBase(),
    "GIF/rainbowline.gif");
  }
  public void start()
  {
    frozen = false;
    /* The runtime system needs to be explicitly told that
       methods of the MouseListener interface should be
       invoked when the event occurs, and that this class
       contains implementation of those methods */
    addMouseListener(this);
    animThread1 = new Thread(this);
    animThread1.start();
  }
  public void run()
  {
    Thread.currentThread().setPriority(Thread.MIN_PRIORITY);
    while(k == 0)
```

```
    {
      if(animThread1 == null)
        break;
      repaint();
    }
  }
public void stop()
{
//Stop the animating thread. This will break the infinite
loop in run()
animThread1 = null;
}
/* These are the methods of the interface MouseListener.
   "mouseClicked()" will be invoked when the mouse is
   clicked on the applet window */
public void mousePressed(MouseEvent e){}
public void mouseReleased(MouseEvent e){}
public void mouseEntered(MouseEvent e){}
public void mouseExited(MouseEvent e){}
public void mouseClicked(MouseEvent e){}
{
  /* If the applet has already been frozen (possibly by a
     previous mouse click), restart it, else stop it */
  if (frozen)
  {
    frozen = false;
    start();
  }
  else
  {
    frozen = true;
    stop();
  }
}
public void paint(Graphics g)
{
  g.drawImage(fgImage1, j,10,(300 - 2*j),5,this);
  if(centerReached)
    j-=10;
```

```
   else
      j+=10;
   if(j >= 150)
      centerReached=true;
   if(j <= 0)
      centerReached=false;
 }
}
```

Implementation

The code for this program is the same as that of `Movebar1.java` except for the following additions:

It defines a variable "frozen", which is a boolean. This variable is initially set equal to false, to indicate that the thread is running.

The class also defines two more methods, namely **stop()** and **mouseClicked()**, besides some methods whose implementation is empty.

The method **mouseClicked()** is invoked every time the mouse is clicked. This is part of the event handling mechanism of GUI objects, which we will discuss in full detail in the GUI chapter.

Any object that wishes to receive events (such as mouse clicks, key presses, etc.) must register itself as an event listener. Distinct categories of event listeners have been created such as ActionListener, MouseListener, etc., which listen to different types of events.

The event handling classes are defined in `java.awt.event`, so we're importing this package:

```
import java.awt.event.*;
```

A class that needs to implement the functionality for handling the events implements the interface of that particular event. In the current example, we want to handle certain mouse events, to know when the mouse has been clicked. For this our class implements the MouseListener interface:

```
public class Movebar2 extends Applet implements Runnable,
MouseListener
```

Since this is an interface, we will need to define all methods of this interface, irrespective of whether we want to do something in them or not. The method of most interest to us is:

```
public void mouseClicked(MouseEvent e)
```

This method will be invoked every time the mouse is clicked. So we've put the event handling code inside this. All the same, to fulfill the condition of an interface, we need to provide dummy implementations of other methods of this interface such as mouseEntered().

But a class doesn't get methods simply by implementing the interface. It needs to register its objects with the required listeners. In this case, we wish to register the whole applet with the MouseListener so that any mouse click in the applet is handled:

```
addMouseListener(this);
```

If all this sounds like Greek to you (and if you know Greek, then Latin, and so on), don't worry — event handling is covered in great detail in the chapter on GUI.

When control enters mouseClicked() (i.e., when the mouse is clicked), it simply checks the value of **frozen**, and on the basis of this, it either calls the **start()** method (if the thread was previously stopped) or it calls the **stop()** method.

The stop() method is invoked when the user leaves the applet and moves to another page. This method should be overridden so that it breaks the animation loop, and so that resources are not wasted unnecessarily.

We have overridden the stop() method so it sets the value of the thread equal to null. The effect is that the while loop in the run() method is broken and control comes out of it, thus stopping the execution of the thread.

2.2.3 Example: Moving Bar with Different Background

Purpose of the Program
This program has been extended from Movebar2.jav. It shows how the default background can be overridden by another image. This type of functionality is often made use of for writing animation applets.

Concepts Covered in this Program
This program illustrates how two images can simultaneously exist in your animation, one of which is the foreground and the other is the background. It also explains an important concept known as double buffering which is used for making the animation smooth.

Source Code

HTML FILE: *Movebar3.htm*

```
<HTML>
<HEAD></HEAD>
<BODY>
<applet codebase="http://myserver/HTML" code=Movebar3.class
width=300
height=20>
</applet>
</BODY>
</HTML>
```

JAVA FILE: *Movebar3.java*

```
/* This example is the same as Movebar2.java except that
   instead of relying on a default background, the one
   drawn by the window manager, it paints a background
   image. The effect of this is that the default background
   is overridden */

import java.awt.*;
import java.awt.event.*;
import java.applet.Applet;
public class Movebar3 extends Applet implements Runnable,
MouseListener
{
  Image fgImage1;
  Image bgImage;
  Image offImage;
  Thread animThread1;
  Thread curThread;
  int i,j=0,k=0;
  boolean frozen;
  Graphics offGraphics;
  boolean centerReached=false;
  public void init()
```

```
{
  fgImage1 = getImage(getCodeBase(),
  "GIF/rainbowline.gif");
  bgImage = getImage(getCodeBase(),
  "GIF/BKGD/blue_bk.gif");
}
public void start()
{
  addMouseListener(this);
  animThread1 = new Thread(this);
  animThread1.start();
}
public void run()
{
  Thread.currentThread().setPriority(Thread.MIN_PRIORITY);
  while(k == 0)
  {
    if(animThread1 == null)
      break;
    repaint();
  }
}
public void stop()
{
  //Stop the animating thread.
  animThread1 = null;
}
public void mousePressed(MouseEvent e){}
public void mouseReleased(MouseEvent e){}
public void mouseEntered(MouseEvent e){}
public void mouseExited(MouseEvent e){}
public void mouseClicked(MouseEvent e){}
{
    if (frozen)
    {
      frozen = false;
      start();
    }
```

```
      else
      {
        frozen = true;
        stop();
      }
    }
    public void paint(Graphics g)
    {
      update(g);
    }
    public void update(Graphics g)
    {
      /* Create an empty image of size 300x50 */
      offImage = createImage(300,50);
      /* Get the Graphics Context of this image */
      offGraphics = offImage.getGraphics();

      /* Invoke the method paintFrame() which will paint
      the background to the dummy image we created above
      and will then paint the foreground image over this */
    paintFrame(offGraphics);

    /* Draw the image thus created */
    g.drawImage(offImage, 0, 0, 300, 50,this);
    }
  void paintFrame(Graphics g)
  {
    /* Draw the background image on the empty image. Then
      draw the foreground image on this */
    g.drawImage(bgImage, 0,0, 300, 20, this);
    g.drawImage(fgImage1, j,10,(300 - 2*j),5,this);
    if(centerReached)
      j-=10;
    else
      j+=10;
    if(j >= 150)
      centerReached=true;
    if(j <= 0)
      centerReached=false;
  }
}
```

Implementation

The code for this program is the same as that of `Movebar2.java` except that it loads a background image, overrides the `update()` method and introduces a new method `paintFrame()`. When the `repaint()` method is invoked, it first calls the method `update()`. This method simply repaints the screen with the default background color. Then the `paint()` method is invoked. This is the reason why in `Movebar1.java` and `Movebar2.java` only the latest image appears on the screen (as opposed to several images being superimposed on one another).

But what if you want another image to be painted in the background? Surprise, surprise — Java allows this. To handle this, we will be creating a composite image before making it available to the applet via the `drawImage()` method.

First of all a blank image is created, using the `createImage()` method:

```
offImage = createImage(300,50);
```

Next, we get the Graphics Context of this image using `getGraphics()`:

```
offGraphics = offImage.getGraphics();
```

By now you should have a fair idea where to look for the new methods we have introduced here: `createImage()` and `getGraphics()`. Oh well, you lazy bums, we will spoon-feed you one more time: look in the file **java.awt.Component.java**.

After that we call the method `paintFrame()`, which prepares the image to be drawn in the applet. This image is then drawn using `drawImage()`:

```
g.drawImage(offImage, 0, 0, 300, 50,this);
```

And this is how the `paintFrame()` method works: first, the background image, which was loaded in the `init()` method along with the foreground image, is drawn on the "virtual" Graphics Context derived in `update()`:

```
g.drawImage(bgImage, 0,0, 300, 20, this);
```

The foreground image is then imposed on top of this:

```
g.drawImage(fgImage1, j,10,(300 - 2*j),5,this);
```

The rest of the functionality is the same as that in previous examples, i.e., the value of `j` is changed to make the bar shrink or expand.

Now that the image `offImage` has been prepared, it is painted on the screen by the `update()` method.

Note that the `update()` method has been overridden in order to prevent the background from being repainted every time to the default, which is the normal behavior of this method.

The `paint()` method does not need to do anything, so it simply calls `update()`. You can also remove this method altogether and achieve the same functionality.

A question that might come to your mind is: why did we create a new image instead of drawing both the foreground and the background directly on the screen in the `update()` method? The reason for this is that, with that approach, sometimes the screen doesn't get updated all in one shot, especially in highly graphics-intensive applets. The approach we have used is known as *double buffering* and is one of the most commonly used approaches.

Double buffering is a technique used to reduce flicker in animations. As we've seen above, this is achieved by doing the drawing in a temporary area before the finished image is painted on the screen.

2.2.4 Example: Using Sleep in Animation

Purpose of the Program

This program is an extension of `Movebar3.java`. The only addition is that we make the thread sleep for 100 milliseconds at a time, so that consecutive frames are presented at a slower speed.

Concepts Covered in this Program

In this program we show how a thread can be put to sleep for an arbitrary period of time.

Source Code

HTML FILE: *MoveBar4.htm*

```
<HEAD>
</HEAD>
<BODY>
<applet codebase="http://myserver/HTML" code=Movebar4.class
```

```
width=300
height=20>
</applet>
</BODY>
```

JAVA FILE: *Movebar4.java*

```
/* This program is an extension of Movebar3.java. The only
addition in, this is that we make the thread sleep for 100
milliseconds at a time, so that the frames are presented at
a slower speed. */

import java.awt.*;
import java.awt.event.*;
import java.applet.Applet;
public class Movebar4 extends Applet implements Runnable,
MouseListener
{
  Image fgImage1;
  Image bgImage;
  Image offImage;
  Thread animThread1;
  Thread curThread;
  int i,j=0,k=0;
  boolean frozen;
  Graphics offGraphics;
  boolean centerReached=false;

  public void init()
  {
    fgImage1 = getImage(getCodeBase(),
    "GIF/rainbowline.gif");
    bgImage = getImage(getCodeBase(),
    "GIF/BKGD/blue_bk.gif");
  }
  public void start()
  {
    addMouseListener(this);
    animThread1 = new Thread(this);
    animThread1.start();
  }
```

```java
public void run()
{
  Thread.currentThread().setPriority(Thread.MIN_PRIORITY);
  while(k == 0)
  {
    if(animThread1 == null)
      break;
    repaint();
    /* Make the thread sleep for 100 milliseconds before the
    next repaint() is called */
    try
    {
    animThread1.sleep(100);
    } catch(InterruptedException e) {}
  }
}
public void stop()
{
  //Stop the animating thread.
  animThread1 = null;
}
public void mousePressed(MouseEvent e){}
public void mouseReleased(MouseEvent e){}
public void mouseEntered(MouseEvent e){}
public void mouseExited(MouseEvent e){}
public void mouseClicked(MouseEvent e){}
{
    if (frozen)
    {
      frozen = false;
      start();
    }
    else
    {
      frozen = true;
      stop();
    }
}
```

```
public void paint(Graphics g)
{
  update(g);
}
public void update(Graphics g)
{
  offImage = createImage(300,50);
  offGraphics = offImage.getGraphics();
  paintFrame(offGraphics);
  g.drawImage(offImage, 0, 0, 300, 50,this);
}
void paintFrame(Graphics g)
{
  g.drawImage(bgImage, 0,0, 300, 20, this);
  g.drawImage(fgImage1, j,10,(300 - 2*j),5,this);
  if(centerReached)
     j-=10;
  else
     j+=10;
  if(j >= 150)
     centerReached=true;
  if(j <= 0)
     centerReached=false;
}
}
```

Implementation

There are just four lines in addition to Movebar3.java in this program:

```
try
{
    animThread1.sleep(100);
} catch(InterruptedException e) {}
```

These have been added to the run() method. They make the thread sleep for 100 milliseconds before the next repaint() method is called.

But what is that weird-looking code which begins with a try? Here we're dealing with one of the concepts of Java you will be hearing a lot about: exceptions.

Exceptions are just another method of catching errors that might occur in your programs. Their advantage is that they make the code a lot cleaner and easier to understand and manage. For all methods for which an error can occur, there are one or more associated exceptions. For example, if you're trying to read a file, the possible errors are that the file itself is not present or there is some I/O error. There is an exception corresponding to both these error conditions. When any of these errors occurs, the corresponding exception will be raised. Your code needs to "catch" these. In other words, you need to write code that will tell the Java Virtual Machine what to do if such an error occurs.

All this is handled with the try-catch statements. If there is a method you're calling that can raise an exception, you enclose that within a pair of curly brackets ({.....}) with the reserved word "try" before the opening bracket. You need to put the "catch" reserved word after the closing bracket, in which you will supply the name of the exception that can be raised by this method. If there is more than one exception that can be raised by this method (or there are other methods being called between these curly brackets that can raise other exceptions), you can supply more than one "catch" statement to catch all of the exceptions.

The catch is followed by another pair of curly brackets in which you supply the code that should be executed when this exception comes up.

In the case of the `sleep()` method, the exception that can occur is `InterruptedException`. We're trying to catch this above.

However, since we don't want to do anything even if the exception is raised, we have a pair of curly brackets with no code in them after the "catch".

You can cut and paste this example to produce your own animation applet. Note that you can use multiple images in this framework to create the effect of an animated movie. The last section in this chapter gives an example of animation through multiple images.

If you haven't flipped through the pages of this section while sipping hot chocolate in your cozy bed and watching your favorite television program, you should now be able to write a simple animation. Next we go on to some text-based animation.

2.3 Animation: Using Text

Some of the least time-consuming animations are the ones that display moving text. In this section we will lead you through a set of examples that create text that moves horizontally. We will use some of the knowledge that you gathered in the previous section.

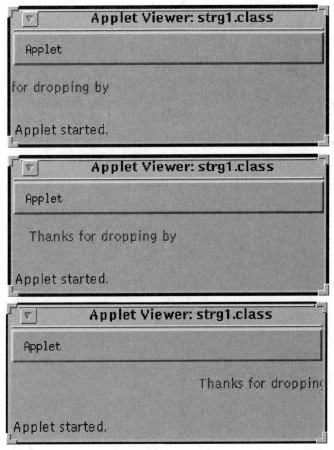

Figure 2-3

The first example demonstrates a simple text animation. As we go along we will be showing how you can use other fonts, find information about different fonts, change your background, and pass parameters from an HTML file to your Java program.

Read this section more seriously than you did the previous one as it will go a long way toward building your fundamental knowledge of animation. Besides, my psychic tells me that by reading between the lines of this page you can somehow figure out tomorrow's Super Lotto winning numbers.

2.3.1 Example: Scrolling Text String

Purpose of the Program

Strg1.java simply displays a text string which moves across the window, as shown in Figure 2-3. Once it goes out the right side, it comes back from the left side.

Concepts Covered in this Program

This program introduces you to text-based animation. It also shows how you can make your text choose its own font. You can cut and paste this program to make a text string that scrolls from left to right.

Source Code

HTML FILE: *Strg1.htm*

```
<HTML>
<HEAD> </HEAD>
<BODY>
<applet codebase="http://myserver/HTML" code=Strg1.class
width=300
height=50>
</applet>
</BODY>
</HTML>
```

JAVA FILE: *Strg1.java*

```
import java.lang.*;
import java.awt.*;
import java.awt.event.*;
import java.applet.Applet;
public class Strg1 extends Applet implements Runnable,
MouseListener
{
  Thread animThread1;
  int i,j,k=0;
  boolean frozen;
  int x=0;
```

```
String str = new String("Thanks for dropping by");
public void init()
{
}
public void start()
{
  frozen=false;
  addMouseListener(this);
  animThread1 = new Thread(this);
  animThread1.start();
}
public void run()
{
  Thread.currentThread().setPriority(Thread.MIN_PRIORITY);
  while(k == 0)
  {
    if(animThread1 == null)
      break;
    repaint();
    try
    {
      animThread1.sleep(80);
    } catch(InterruptedException e){}
  }
}
public void stop()
{
  //Stop the animating thread.
  animThread1 = null;
}
public void mousePressed(MouseEvent e){}
public void mouseReleased(MouseEvent e){}
public void mouseEntered(MouseEvent e){}
public void mouseExited(MouseEvent e){}
public void mouseClicked(MouseEvent e){}
{
  if (frozen)
  {
    frozen = false;
    start();
```

```
    }
    else
    {
       frozen = true;
       stop();
    }
}
public void paint(Graphics g)
{
    / *Inform the Graphics Context that we wish to use the
      color red for drawing our string */
    g.setColor(new Color(255,0,0));

    /* This method informs the Graphics Context that string
    should be drawn in the
    TimesRoman font, in bold text of size 20 */

    g.setFont(new Font("TimesRoman",Font.BOLD,20));

    /* Draw the string "str" which we've declared as an
       instance variable. Because of the above statement, it
       will be red in color */
    g.drawString(str, x,25);

    if(x >= 300)
       x=-180;
    else
       x+=5;
    }
}
```

Implementation

The applet follows the animation approach that we used in Movebar1.java. We want to print the string in the color red. To do this, we're using the setColor() method. This takes an object of the type Color as an argument. The Color class helps us create a color. Its constructor takes three arguments, each of which is an int that can range from 0 to 255 and specifies the amount of the primary colors (red, green and blue, respectively) that should be used for the Color object we want. So by using 255,0,0 we can get the color red while by specifying

0,255,0 we can go green with envy.

We want the string to be in red, so we tell the Graphics Context that all future drawing will be done using the red color unless another call to `setColor()` tells it otherwise.

```
g.setColor(new Color(255,0,0));
```

The new font is created and set in the Graphics Context just before the string is written on the display. The following line of code has been added in the paint method for this purpose:

```
g.setFont(new Font("TimesRoman",Font.BOLD,20));
```

There is a detailed description of fonts in `java.awt.Component.java` and `java.awt.Font.java`.

The text string is simply written at different positions on the x axis. The `update()` method has not been overridden, so every time `repaint()` is called, the screen is first refreshed and the previous frame is wiped out.

Also, this program allows the thread to be stopped and restarted by mouse clicks.

2.3.2 Example: Animation Without Flashing

Purpose of the Program

This program is an extension of `Strg2.java`. It eliminates the flashing that appears in `Strg2.java` by using the double buffering approach we saw in `Movebar3.java` in the previous chapter.

Concepts Covered in this Program

This program revisits the double buffering approach discussed earlier and shows how it is applicable to text-based animation.

Source Code

HTML FILE: *Strg3.htm*

```
<HTML>
<HEAD> </HEAD>
<BODY>
```

```
<applet codebase="http://myserver/HTML" code=Strg3.class
width=300
height=50>
</applet>
</BODY>
</HTML>
```

JAVA FILE: *Strg3.java*

```java
import java.lang.*;
import java.awt.*;
import java.awt.event.*;
import java.applet.Applet;
public class Strg3 extends Applet implements Runnable,
MouseListener
{
  Thread animThread1;
  int i,j,k=0;
  boolean frozen;
  int x=0;
  String str = new String("Thanks for dropping by");
  Graphics offGraphics;
  Image offImage;
  Image bgImage;
  public void init()
  {
    bgImage=getImage(getCodeBase(),
    "GIF/BKGD/yellowGreen.jpg");
  }
  public void start()
  {
    frozen=false;
    addMouseListener(this);
    animThread1 = new Thread(this);
    animThread1.start();
  }
  public void run()
```

```
{
  Thread.currentThread().setPriority(Thread.MIN_PRIORITY);
  while(k == 0)
  {
    if(animThread1 == null)
      break;
    repaint();
    try
    {
      animThread1.sleep(80);
    } catch(InterruptedException e){}
  }
}
public void stop()
{
  //Stop the animating thread.
  animThread1 = null;
}
public void mousePressed(MouseEvent e){}
public void mouseReleased(MouseEvent e){}
public void mouseEntered(MouseEvent e){}
public void mouseExited(MouseEvent e){}
public void mouseClicked(MouseEvent e){}
{
  if (frozen)
  {
    frozen = false;
    start();
  }
  else
  {
    frozen = true;
    stop();
  }
}
public void paint(Graphics g)
{
  update(g);
}
```

```
public void update(Graphics g)
{
   offImage = createImage(550,50);
   offGraphics = offImage.getGraphics();
   paintFrame(offGraphics);
   g.drawImage(offImage, 0, 0,this);
}
void paintFrame(Graphics g)
{
   g.drawImage(bgImage, 0, 0, 550,50,this);
   g.setColor(new Color(255,0,0));
   g.setFont(new Font("TimesRoman",Font.BOLD,20));
   g.drawString(str, x,25);
   if(x >= 300)
      x=-180;
   else
      x+=5;
}
}
```

Implementation

In this program we have simply added a background image and used the paintFrame() method that was introduced in Movebar3.java. The complete image is first prepared before being presented on the screen. See Movebar3.java for more details.

2.3.3 Example: Using a Filled Rectangle as Background

Purpose of the Program

This program behaves in the same way as Strg3.java except that instead of using an image as a background, it displays the moving text on a filled rectangle, as shown in Figure 2-4.

Concepts Covered in this Program

This program illustrates how you can use a different-colored rectangle as your background.

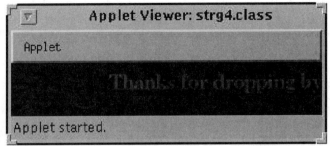

Figure 2-4

Source Code

HTML FILE: *Strg4.htm*

```
<HTML>
<HEAD> </HEAD>
<BODY>
<applet codebase="http://myserver/HTML" code=Strg4.class
width=300
height=50>
</applet>
</BODY>
</HTML>
```

JAVA FILE: *Strg4.java*

```
import java.lang.*;
import java.awt.*;
import java.awt.event.*;
import java.applet.Applet;
public class Strg4 extends Applet implements Runnable,
MouseListener
{
  Thread animThread1;
  int i,j,k=0;
  boolean frozen;
  int x=0;
  String str = new String("Thanks for dropping by");
  Graphics offGraphics;
```

```
Image offImage;
Image bgImage;
public void init()
{
  bgImage=getImage(getCodeBase(),
  "GIF/BKGD/yellowGreen.jpg");
}
public void start()
{
  frozen=false;
  addMouseListener(this);
  animThread1 = new Thread(this);
  animThread1.start();
}
public void run()
{
  Thread.currentThread().setPriority(Thread.MIN_PRIORITY);
  while(k == 0)
  {
    if(animThread1 == null)
      break;
    repaint();
    try
    {
      animThread1.sleep(80);
    } catch(InterruptedException e){}
  }
}
public void stop()
{
//Stop the animating thread.
animThread1 = null;
}
public void mousePressed(MouseEvent e){}
public void mouseReleased(MouseEvent e){}
public void mouseEntered(MouseEvent e){}
public void mouseExited(MouseEvent e){}
public void mouseClicked(MouseEvent e){}
{
```

```
   if (frozen)
   {
     frozen = false;
     start();
   }
   else
   {
     frozen = true;
     stop();
   }
}
public void paint(Graphics g)
{
   update(g);
}
public void update(Graphics g)
{
   offImage = createImage(550,50);
   offGraphics = offImage.getGraphics();
   paintFrame(offGraphics);
   g.drawImage(offImage, 0, 0,this);
}
void paintFrame(Graphics g)
{
   /* Create a filled rectangle of size 550x50 in the
      color black */
   g.setColor(new Color(0,0,0));
   g.fillRect(0, 0, 550,50);

   /* Now set the color to be used to red so that the
   string is displayed in red */
   g.setColor(new Color(255,0,0));

   g.setFont(new Font("TimesRoman",Font.BOLD,20));
   g.drawString(str, x,25);
   if(x >= 300)
     x=-180;
   else
```

```
        x+=5;
     }
   }
```

Implementation

For this, we have removed the line of code that painted the background image and replaced it with the following two lines:

```
g.setColor(new Color(0,0,0));
g.fillRect(0, 0, 550,50);
```

The `fillRect()` and `setColor()` methods are described in `awt/Graphics.java`.

2.3.4 Example: Moving String Going In and Out

Purpose of the Program

This program displays a moving text which starts rolling in from the left hand corner. Once the whole string has been displayed, it starts moving back to the left, where it came from. This continues forever until the program is terminated or the mouse is clicked.

Concepts Covered in this Program

This example shows you how parameters can be passed from an HTML file to a Java program. It also explains how information about a particular font can be gathered on the fly and used.

Source Code

HTML FILE: *Strg5.htm*

```
<HTML>
<HEAD> </HEAD>
<BODY>
<applet codebase="http://myserver/HTML" code=Strg5.class
width=300 height=40>
<param name=toDisplay value="Thanks for dropping by">
</applet>
```

```
</BODY>
</HTML>
```

JAVA FILE: *Strg5.java*

```java
import java.awt.*;
import java.awt.event.*;
import java.applet.*;
public class Strg5 extends Applet implements Runnable,
MouseListener
{
  Thread t1;
  int x;
  boolean textMoving;
  String str;
  int len;
  int width;
  boolean firstTime;
  boolean goingForward;
  Font f;
  public void init()
  {
    t1=null;
  }
  public void start()
  {
    addMouseListener(this);

    /* Create a Font object which will be used later */
    f = new Font("TimesRoman", Font.BOLD, 20);

    x=0;
    textMoving=true;
    goingForward=true;

    /* Get the value of the parameter "todisplay" as defined
       in the HTML file */

    str=getParameter("todisplay");
```

```
   len=str.length();

   /* If the parameter is not defined in the HTML file,
      str will be null, so we need to supply our own value
      */
   if(str == null)
   str = "This one needs a parameter";

   firstTime=true;
   if(t1 == null)
   {
      t1 = new Thread(this);
      if(t1 != null)
         t1.start();
   }
}
public void stop()
{
   t1 = null;
}
   public void mousePressed(MouseEvent e){}
   public void mouseReleased(MouseEvent e){}
   public void mouseEntered(MouseEvent e){}
   public void mouseExited(MouseEvent e){}
   public void mouseClicked(MouseEvent e){}
   {
      textMoving = !textMoving;
      if(textMoving == true)
         start();
      else
         stop();
   }
   public void run()
   {
      Thread.currentThread().setPriority(Thread.MIN_PRIORI
      TY);
      while(t1 != null)
      {
      repaint();
```

```
        try
        {
            t1.sleep(100);
        } catch(InterruptedException e){}
    }
}
public void paint(Graphics g)
{
    update(g);
}
public void update(Graphics g)
{
    g.setColor(new Color(0,0,0));
    g.fillRect(0,0,500,20);
    g.setFont(f);
    g.setColor(new Color(255,0,0));
    if(firstTime == true)
    {
        firstTime = false;
        /* Determine the maximum horizontal area that a
           string of this size with this font can occupy. We
           need to calculate this only once as the size of
           the string as well as its font are not changing
           through the execution of the program*/
        width = g.getFontMetrics(f).getMaxAdvance()*len;
        x = -width + 200;
    }
    g.drawString(str, x, 15);

        /* Depending upon the variable "goingForward" and the
           variable "x", determine the starting position on
           the x-axis where the string should start */
    if(goingForward == true)
    {
        if(x < 20)
            x+=5;
        else
            goingForward=false;
```

```
      }
      else
      {
         if(x > (-width + 200))
             x-=5;
         else
             goingForward=true;
      }
   }
}
```

Implementation

This program also follows the same animation principle that we have been using so far. However, it doesn't have any hard-coded display string. Instead, the string to be displayed can be passed as a parameter through the HTML file.

The advantage of this is that you can use the same Java program, without the need to recompile it, to display text that moves in and out of the display area. And this is how parameter passing is done:

In the HTML file, Strg5.html, we have the following line of code:

```
<applet codebase="http://myserver/HTML" code=Strg5.class
width=300 height=40>
<param name=toDisplay value="Thanks for dropping by">
</applet>
```

In the corresponding Java program, i.e., Strg5.java, we have the following:

```
String str;
str=getParameter("todisplay");
The method getParameter() belongs to java.applet.Applet.java
```

The effect of this is that value assigned to the parameter "todisplay" in the HTML file, using the tags param name= and value=, is passed to the Java program, and this is used for the display. So, our Java program displays "Thanks for dropping by".

You can change this to any other text you want to display without needing to recompile the Java file.

The only other thing that needs to be explained in this example is how we're determining the distance the text should travel forward before beginning its journey backward.

For this we need to know the width of each character. To save time, it is enough to know the maximum width any character in this font can occupy. In a later example, we show how to get the actual width being taken up by the font.

To get the maximum width value, we first need to get the metrics of the font, which will allow us to access specific information about the font.

The metrics are gathered by `g.getFontMetrics(f)`, where `g` is the Graphics Context and `f` is the name of the font which we created using :

```
f = new Font("TimesRoman", Font.BOLD, 20);
```

Now that we have a handle to the metrics we can easily determine the maximum space occupied by our string in this font, using the following line:

```
g.getFontMetrics(f).getMaxAdvance()
```

To determine the maximum horizontal space that will be required by this string, we have the following line of code:

```
width = g.getFontMetrics(f).getMaxAdvance()*len;
```

where `len` is the length of the string in number of characters.

So, did you find some clues to the Super Lotto? In this section we have revised our knowledge of animation. Also, by now you should be able to develop a pattern in your mind for searching the myriad methods offered by Java. For example, if it looks like Graphics-related stuff, the first place to look is the `awt` directory in the files `Graphics.java` and `Components.java`, and you should look in `java.applet.Applet.java` for something that is applet specific. You will build on this pattern as you go through more code.

In the next section we show more text animation, only this time it will grow not just horizontally, but also vertically.

2.4 More Animation Using Text

Imagine what you can do with text that grows in size both horizontally and vertically. The first thing that comes to mind is an animation that creates the effect of an object approaching you from a distance. Maybe you could create animated credits for a Star Wars movie using the concepts covered in this section.

We will be introducing several new concepts, not the least of which are arrays of fonts and images. We will show how you can increase the speed of your animation. We will also discuss some methods of the String class which you may find useful for these types of animations.

2.4.1 Example: Shrinking and Expanding Text Animation

Purpose of the Program

This program demonstrates a text animation, in which the text expands both vertically and horizontally until it reaches a maximum size (as shown in Figure 2-5), at which point it starts shrinking.

It also illustrates how an array of fonts can be created.

Concepts Covered in this Program

The key to this example is an array of fonts. We show how you can create and use an array of fonts to create an animation in which the font changes.

Source Code

HTML FILE: Grow1.htm

```
<HTML>
<HEAD>
</HEAD>
<BODY>
<applet codebase="http://myserver/HTML" code=Grow1.class
width=380
height=50>
</applet>
</BODY>
</HTML>
```

JAVA FILE: *Grow1.java*

```
/* This program illustrates text which expands and shrinks
both vertically and horizontally. It also illustrates how an
array of fonts can be created beforehand, so that minimum
work needs to be done inside the update() method.
*/
```

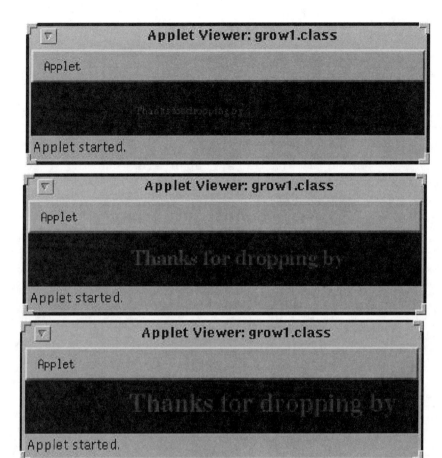

Figure 2-5

```java
import java.lang.*;
import java.awt.*;
import java.awt.event.*;
import java.applet.Applet;
public class Grow1 extends Applet implements Runnable,
MouseListener
{
  Thread animThread1;
  int i,j,k=0;
  boolean frozen;
  int x=0;
  int offset=0,count;
```

```
int strLen;
int size=10;
int initialSize;
int counter=0;
int height,width,initialHeight;
boolean stillDrawing=true;

boolean Growing;
  /* Create an array of fonts, capable of storing 4 Font
  objects */
  Font f[] = new Font[4];
  String temp;
  public void init()
  {
  }
  public void start()
  {
    addMouseListener(this);
    size=10;
    temp = getParameter("todisplay");
    if(temp == null)
      temp = "No parameter specified";
    strLen = temp.length();
    height = size+5;
    initializeValue();
    initialSize = size;
    initialHeight=height;
    counter=0;
    Growing=true;

    /* Create and store 4 fonts of increasing size in the
    array "f" we declared above */
    for(int i=0; i<4; i++)
    {
      f[i] = new Font("TimesRoman",Font.BOLD,size);
      size+=5;
    }

    animThread1 = new Thread(this);
```

```
    animThread1.start();
}
void initializeValue()
{
  offset=strLen/2;
  count=1;
  x=-200;
  width=5;
}
public void run()
{
  Thread.currentThread().setPriority(Thread.MIN_PRIORITY);
  while(k == 0)
  {
    if(animThread1 == null)
      break;
    repaint();
    try
    {
      animThread1.sleep(200);
    }catch(InterruptedException e){}
  }
}
public void stop()
{
  //Stop the animating thread.
    animThread1 = null;
}
public void mousePressed(MouseEvent e){}
public void mouseReleased(MouseEvent e){}
public void mouseEntered(MouseEvent e){}
public void mouseExited(MouseEvent e){}
public void mouseClicked(MouseEvent e){}
{
  if (frozen)
  {
    frozen = false;
```

```
      start();
   }
   else
   {
      frozen = true;
      stop();
   }
}
public void paint(Graphics g)
{
   update(g);
}
public void update(Graphics g)
{
   /* Depending upon the value of "counter", set one of
   the fonts from the array "f" as the font to be used
   for the current display */
   g.setFont(f[counter]);

   /* Change the value of counter so that the next time
   repaint() is called, a different font is used. */
   if(counter > 0 && (Growing == false))
   {
      counter--;
      if(counter==0)
         Growing=true;
   }
   else
   {
      if(counter < 3 && (Growing == true))
      {
         counter++;
         if(counter == 3)
            Growing=false;
      }
   }
   g.setColor(new Color(0,0,0));
   g.fillRect(0,0,500,60);
```

```
g.setColor(new Color(255,0,0));
g.drawString(temp, 100, 30);
size+=5;
if(size > 30)
   size=10;
}
}
```

Implementation

This program uses the approach of overriding the update() method to achieve animation.

It also gathers the string to be displayed as a parameter in the HTML file. A set of fonts with different sizes is stored in an array. The same string is displayed using these different fonts, with each new frame being presented at an interval of 200 milliseconds, thus giving the effect of text that grows and shrinks both horizontally and vertically.

The only important thing to be explained in this example is how the various fonts are created and stored in an array.

First, we declare an array of fonts:

```
Font f[] = new Font[4];
```

This prepares a placeholder for four fonts.

Then we fill up this array with fonts of different sizes. The code for this is:

```
for(int i=0; i<4; i++)
{
    f[i] = new Font("TimesRoman",Font.BOLD,size);
    size+=5;
}
```

Here, the initial value of size is 10. In the for loop, the value of size is incremented by 5, so that the fourth element in the array is of size 25.

In the update() method, a counter is maintained, which determines the font that is being used for the current display. It starts from the first font. Once the fourth font has been used for the display, the counter starts decreasing so that the next font which is used is the third element in the array and so on.

2.5 Animation: Using Multiple Images

This section shows two Java applets, `Dancers1.java` and `Dancers2.java`. The second one can be cut and pasted for performing animation. You can simply pick this program if you want to display an animation in which there are multiple images. For this, you need to name the images `p0.gif` through `pn.gif`. By simply changing the parameter `noOfImages` to the total number of images you have, you can easily achieve the desired animation. Of course, you can change the code to suit your needs.

    `Dancers2.java` introduces you to the MediaTracker class which can be used for making sure that images are loaded before being used.

2.5.1 Example: Java Dancers

Purpose of the Program
This program provides a ready-made animation program (shown in Figure 2-6) which can be easily modified for use in your applets.

Concepts Covered in this Program
This program is a recap of all you've learned up to now. It also shows how names can be constructed on the fly so that your program is easily extensible.

Source Code

HTML FILE: *Dancers1.htm*

```
<HTML>
<HEAD>
</HEAD>
<BODY>
<applet codebase="http://myserver/HTML" code=Dancers1.class
width=500
height=160>
</applet>
</BODY>
</HTML>
```

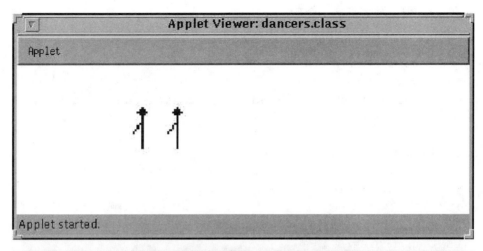

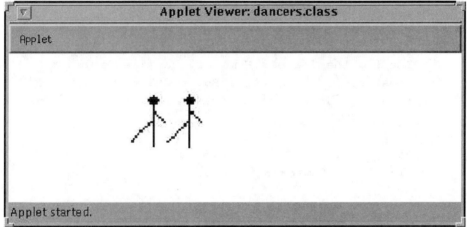

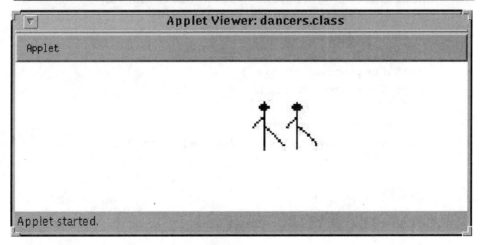

Figure 2-6

JAVA FILE: *Dancers1.java*

```
import java.applet.Applet;
import java.awt.*;
import java.awt.event.*;
public class Dancers1 extends Applet implements Runnable,
MouseListener
{
  Image[] imgs = new Image[20];
  Image im1;
  int noOfImages=10;
  Thread animThread1;
  int xPos, currentImage;
  boolean frozen;
  public void init()
  {
     int i;
     /* Loading the images. Name of the file is being
        constructed on the fly. For noOfImages equal to 2,
        this will load the following files - p0.gif, p1.gif
        */

     setBackground(new Color(255,255,255));
     for(i=0; i<noOfImages; i++)
     {
        /* Construct the name of the image to be loaded */
        StringBuffer gifBuffer = new StringBuffer();
        String gifFile;
        gifBuffer.append("GIF/p");
        gifBuffer.append(i);
        gifBuffer.append(".gif");
        gifFile = new String(gifBuffer);

        /* Load the image */
        imgs[i] = getImage(getCodeBase(), gifFile);
     }
  }
  public void start()
  {
```

```
      addMouseListener(this);
      frozen=false;
      currentImage = 0;
      xPos = 0;
      animThread1 = new Thread(this);
      animThread1.start();
   }
   public void stop()
   {
      //Stop the animating thread.
      animThread1 = null;
   }
   public void mousePressed(MouseEvent e){}
   public void mouseReleased(MouseEvent e){}
   public void mouseEntered(MouseEvent e){}
   public void mouseExited(MouseEvent e){}
   public void mouseClicked(MouseEvent e){}
   {
      if (frozen)
      {
         frozen = false;
         start();
      }
      else
      {
         frozen = true;
         stop();
      }
   }
   public void run()
   {
      int k=0;
      while(k==0)
      {
         if(animThread1 == null)
            break;
         repaint();
         try
         {
```

```
            animThread1.sleep(450);
        } catch(InterruptedException e){}
    }
  }
  public void paint(Graphics g)
  {
    g.drawImage(imgs[currentImage], xPos,30,this);

    /* Increment the variable "currentImage" so that in the
       next call to repaint(), the next image in this
       animation sequence is displayed */
    currentImage++;

    /* If the last image of the animation sequence has been
       displayed set currentImage equal to 0 so that the
       next time, the animation begins with the first image
       of the sequence */
    if(currentImage == noOfImages)
      currentImage=0;
    xPos+=5;
    if(xPos >= 510)
      stop();
  }


}
```

Implementation

The only point worth discussing here is the method we've used for creating a name on the fly. This method is the equivalent of using sprintf in C. Since we didn't want to hard code the names of the images in the program, we did the next best thing: the images were named starting with the letter "p", followed by an integer, which also determines the order in which the images should appear in the animation.

For this, we define a StringBuffer, to which "GIF/p" is appended. After this we append the current integer in the for loop, and there we go!

```
for(i=0; i<noOfImages; i++)
{
```

```
StringBuffer gifBuffer = new StringBuffer();
String gifFile;
gifBuffer.append("p");
gifBuffer.append(i);
gifBuffer.append(".gif");
gifFile = new String(gifBuffer);
imgs[i] = getImage(getCodeBase(), gifFile);
}
```

The result will be that p0.gif will be stored in imgs[0], p1.gif will be stored in imgs[1], and so on.

2.5.2 Example: Using MediaTracker to Improve Dancers

Purpose of the Program
Dancers1.java has an inherent problem. When you start the applet, the first few frames appear in a garbled way — either too slowly or too quickly. This program overcomes that problem.

Concepts Covered in this Program
This applet introduces you to the MediaTracker class. You can use this class to make sure that the images you require have been loaded before they are painted.

Source Code

HTML FILE: *Dancers2.htm*

```
<HTML>
<HEAD>
</HEAD>
<BODY>
<applet codebase="http://myserver/HTML" code=Dancers2.class
width=500
height=160>
</applet>
</BODY>
</HTML>
```

JAVA FILE: *Dancers2.java*

```java
import java.applet.Applet;
import java.awt.*;
import java.awt.event.*;
public class Dancers2 extends Applet implements Runnable,
MouseListener
{
  Image[] imgs = new Image[20];
  Image im1;
  int noOfImages=10;
  Thread animThread1;
  int xPos, currentImage;
  boolean frozen;
  MediaTracker tracker;
  public void init()
  {
    int i;

    /* Create an instance of the MediaTracker class. This
       will be used for tracking whether all the required
       images have been loaded or not. */
    tracker = new MediaTracker(this);

    /* Make the background white */
    setBackground(new Color(255,255,255));

    /* Loading the images. Name of the file is being
    constructed on the fly. For noOfImages equal to 2, this
    will load the following files - p0.gif, p1.gif */
    for(i=0; i<noOfImages; i++)
    {
      StringBuffer gifBuffer = new StringBuffer();
      String gifFile;
      gifBuffer.append("GIF/p");
      gifBuffer.append(i);
      gifBuffer.append(".gif");
      gifFile = new String(gifBuffer);
      imgs[i] = getImage(getCodeBase(), gifFile);
```

```
        /* Add all the images to the Media Tracker so that we
           can track whether they have been loaded or not */
        tracker.addImage(imgs[i], 0);
     }
     try
     {
        /* Make the program wait until all the images have
           actually loaded into memory. This is being done to
           prevent unnecessary flicker because of partially
           loaded images */
        tracker.waitForAll();
     } catch(InterruptedException e){return;}
  }
  public void start()
  {
     addMouseListener(this);
     frozen=false;
     currentImage = 0;
     xPos = 0;
     animThread1 = new Thread(this);
     animThread1.start();
  }
  public void stop()
  {
     //Stop the animating thread.
     animThread1 = null;
  }
  public void mousePressed(MouseEvent e){}
  public void mouseReleased(MouseEvent e){}
  public void mouseEntered(MouseEvent e){}
  public void mouseExited(MouseEvent e){}
  public void mouseClicked(MouseEvent e){}
  {
     if (frozen)
     {
        frozen = false;
        start();
     }
     else
```

```
    {
       frozen = true;
       stop();
    }
  }
  public void run()
  {
     int k=0;
     while(k==0)
     {
        if(animThread1 == null)
           break;
        repaint();
        try
        {
           animThread1.sleep(450);
        } catch(InterruptedException e){}
     }
  }
  public void paint(Graphics g)
  {
     g.drawImage(imgs[currentImage], xPos,30,this);
     currentImage++;
     if(currentImage == noOfImages)
        currentImage=0;
     xPos+=5;
     if(xPos >= 510)
        stop();
  }
}
```

Implementation

This applet instantiates the MediaTracker class. Information about this class can be found in `java.awt.MediaTracker.java`. All images that need to be loaded are added to this class, and then the `waitForAll()` method of this class is called, which puts the applet in a wait state until these images are actually loaded. The code for this is:

```
....
MediaTracker tracker;
....
tracker = new MediaTracker(this);
....
for(i=0; i<noOfImages; i++)
{
  ....
  tracker.addImage(imgs[i], 0);
}
try
{
  tracker.waitForAll();
} catch(InterruptedException e){return;}
....
```

Images are being added to the tracker in the `for` loop using its `addImage()` method. `waitForAll()` waits for all the images to be loaded. In the `addImage()` method, the second argument is an identification number. By assigning a different identification number to different images, you can track them independently. For this there is another MediaTracker method, `waitForID()`. There are quite a few methods implemented in the MediaTracker class which you should explore.

Now you know enough about animation to create your own cool little comic strips. The next thing you may want to learn is how you can combine sound with images in your applets.

But before stepping into the next dimension, how about a little exercise? The GIF directory in the CD accompanying this book contains `ball.gif`, a graphics image. Write an animation program that makes this ball behave like a bouncing ball. Set the applet size equal to 500 by 200 (by specifying the height and the width in your HTML file) and make the ball start from the upper left corner. It should rebound diagonally as soon as it touches one of the surfaces. Once it goes out of the screen on the right side, it should once again appear from the upper left corner. Also, you should be able to stop the applet when required by clicking the mouse button.

Also, just for fun, use the MediaTracker method we described in an earlier section to make sure your image is loaded before the painting begins.

2.6 All About Sound

So, what's been missing until now? Exactly. Your movies (or, as we're forced to call them, animations) belonged to the early 1900s; they lacked a basic ingredient: sound! In this section, we're going to show you how you can efficiently add sound to your applets. To save the examples from growing bigger than Mount Everest, we will show how sound and image can be combined together, without going into animations. With the knowledge of animation you've gathered in the previous pages, at the end of this section, integrating sound with animation is something that you will be able to do even while balancing a cone on your head (yes, with the flat base facing the sky!).

We are using ".au" files, which are Sun Audio files. These are supported on Sun Workstations. You can replace these with the format that is used on your system (e.g., Windows uses the ".wav" format). The important thing to note is that your Java program will remain the same (except for replacing "au" with "wav" or other formats).

2.6.1 Example: Loading Sounds in Java

Purpose of the Program
In this program, we demonstrate how you can load sounds and combine them with images in your applets. The applet first displays a string asking users to click the mouse. Also, the same message is played through an audio file. As users keep clicking on the screen, different images and audio clips start playing.

Concepts Covered in this Program
This program introduces you to the concept of sound in Java. In the next example we will show a more sophisticated way of loading and playing sounds.

Source Code

HTML FILE: *Sound1.htm*

```
<HTML>
<HEAD>
</HEAD>
<BODY>
<applet codebase="http://myserver/HTML" code=Sound1.class
width=300
```

```
height=350>
</applet>
</BODY>
</HTML>
```

JAVA FILE: *Sound1.java*

```java
import java.awt.*;
import java.awt.event.*;
import java.applet.*;
public class Sound1 extends Applet implements MouseListener
{
  /* The three sound files will be loaded in objects of the
     type AudioClip */
  AudioClip audioClip1;
  AudioClip audioClip2;
  AudioClip audioClip3;

  Image im1;
  Image im2;
  boolean displayLine=false;
  boolean displayRect=false;
  public void init()
  {
    addMouseListener(this);

    /* Load the 3 audio clips */
    audioClip1 = getAudioClip(getCodeBase(),
    "SOUND/click.au");
    audioClip2 = getAudioClip(getCodeBase(),
    "SOUND/line.au");
    audioClip3 = getAudioClip(getCodeBase(),
    "SOUND/rectangle.au");

    im1=getImage(getCodeBase(), "GIF/line.gif");
    im2=getImage(getCodeBase(), "GIF/rectangle.gif");
    /* Play the first audio clip */
    audioClip1.play();
  }
```

Figure 2-8

```
public void mousePressed(MouseEvent e){}
public void mouseReleased(MouseEvent e){}
public void mouseEntered(MouseEvent e){}
public void mouseExited(MouseEvent e){}
public void mouseClicked(MouseEvent e){}
{
   /* Depending upon whether a line is being displayed
   or a rectangle, play the right audio file */
   if(displayLine == false)
   {
      displayLine=true;
      displayRect=false;
      repaint();
      audioClip2.play();
   }
   else
   {
      displayLine=false;
      displayRect=true;
      repaint();
      audioClip3.play();
   }
}
public void paint(Graphics g)
{
   /* Depending upon the variables displayLine and
   displayRect draw the appropriate image */
```

```
if(displayLine == true)
   g.drawImage(im1, 20,20, this);
else
if(displayRect == true)
   g.drawImage(im2, 20,20, this);
else
{
   g.setColor(new Color(255,0,0));
   g.drawString("Click the mouse for more sound and
   images", 5, 20);
}
}
}
```

Implementation

Audio clips are stored in objects of the type AudioClip. We are storing our sound clip in the variable audioClip1. So the declaration of audioClip1 is:

AudioClip audioClip1;

There are three audio files being loaded: click.au, line.au and rectangle.au. The loading is being done in the init() method of the applet.

For loading, we use the getAudioClip() method:

audioClip1 = getAudioClip(getCodeBase(), "SOUND/click.au");

To play an audio clip, we use the play() method of AudioClip:

audioClip1.play();

In this example, the above line of code starts the audio file click.au, which plays the message "Click the mouse for more sound and images". Note that in the paint() method we are also writing this message on the screen. (In this way, you can create a "talking" book.)

We are using the mouseClicked() method to play audioClip2 or audioClip3 based on the boolean displayLine which determines whether a rectangle or a line is being displayed on the screen.

When the mouse is clicked for the first time, displayLine is false, so audioClip2 is played. Then displayLine is set to true and the repaint()

method is called, which causes the image of a line to be displayed on the screen. The net effect is that you hear a voice (via audioClip2.play()) saying "This is a line," and you see an image (via the paint() method).

When the mouse is clicked the next time, the variable displayLine has changed already, so now the code enters the else condition, causing a rectangle to be displayed and audioClip3 to be played.

2.6.2 Example: Loading Sounds Asynchronously

Purpose of the Program
This program shows how loading of audio files can be done asynchronously through another thread, and how audio files can be stored for future use.

Concepts Covered in this Program
This program introduces you to Hashtable, which can be used for storing objects. It also introduces you to more audio methods, such as loop() and stop(). The program also introduces you to the 1.1 Event Handling mechanism, which will be discussed in more detail in the GUI chapter.

Source Code

HTML FILE: *MyMusic.htm*

```
<HTML>
<HEAD></HEAD>
<BODY>
<applet codebase="http://myserver/HTML" code=MyMusic.class
width=500
height=80>
</applet>
</BODY>
</HTML>
```

JAVA FILES: *MyMusic.java*

```
import java.applet.*;
import java.awt.*;
```

```
import java.awt.event.*;

/* This program consists of three files. This class is the
top level of the applet. The other two are being used for
loading and storing the audio files for later use by this
class */
public class MyMusic extends Applet implements Runnable,
MouseListener
{
  /* The sounds will be stored by the class SoundStorage.
     That class has methods for retrieving and storing
     sounds */
  SoundStorage soundStorage;
  AudioClip soundClip;
  Thread t1;
  String str = new String("Welcome to the Sound Page");
  int r=0, gr=0, b=0;
  public void init()
  {
    t1=null;
    /* We create an instance of the SoundStorage class and
    ask it to load an audio clip */
    soundStorage = new SoundStorage(this, getCodeBase());
    soundStorage.loadClip("SOUND/whistle.au");
    addMouseListener(this);
  }
  public void start()
  {
    if(t1 == null )
    {
      t1 = new Thread(this);
      t1.start();
    }
    else
    {
      t1.resume();
    }
  }
```

```java
}
public void stop()
{
   /* Stop the audio clip and this thread */
   if(soundClip != null)
      soundClip.stop();
   t1.stop();
   t1 = null;
}
public void mouseClicked(MouseEvent e)
{
   System.out.println("MOUSE CLICKED");
   if(soundClip != null)
   {
      soundClip.stop();
      soundClip=null;
   }
   else
   {
      /* Get the sound clip we stored above by using the
         retrieveClip() method of SoundStorage */
      soundClip =
      soundStorage.retrieveClip("SOUND/whistle.au");

      /* Play the sound file continuously in a loop */
      soundClip.loop();
   }
   if(t1 == null)
      start();
   else
      stop();
}
public void mousePressed(MouseEvent e)
{
}
public void mouseEntered(MouseEvent e)
{
}
```

```
public void mouseReleased(MouseEvent e)
{
}
public void mouseExited(MouseEvent e)
{
}
public void paint(Graphics g)
{
   update(g);
}
public void update(Graphics g)
{
   g.setColor(new Color(0,0,0));
   g.fillRect(0,0,500,40);
   g.setColor(new Color(255,0,0));
   g.setFont(new Font("TimesRoman", Font.BOLD, 25));
   g.drawString(str, 100, 30);
}
public void run()
{
   Thread.currentThread().setPriority(Thread.MIN_PRIORITY);
   soundClip = null;
   int k=0;
   while(k == 0)
   {
     if(t1 == null )
        break;
     if(soundClip == null)
     {
             soundClip =
               soundStorage.retrieveClip
               ("SOUND/whistle.au");
     }
     if(soundClip != null)
     {
        soundClip.loop();
        break;
     }
   }
```

```
      }
    }
  }
```

SoundStorage.java

```
import java.util.*;
import java.applet.*;
import java.net.URL;

  /* SoundStorage inherits a Hashtable in which the sound
     clip(s) will be stored */
class SoundStorage extends Hashtable
{
  Applet origApplet;
  URL origURL;
  static AudioClip audioClip;

  public SoundStorage(Applet app, URL theURL)
  {
    super(5); /* Initialize the Hashtable so that five
    elements can be stored in it */
    origURL = theURL;
    origApplet = app;
  }

  /* The method loadClip() causes the specified clip to be
     loaded using the SoundThread */
  public void loadClip(String relativeURL)
  {
    new SoundThread(origApplet, this, origURL, relativeURL);
  }

  /* The method storeClip() stores the specified audio clip
     in the Hashtable */
  public void storeClip(String key, AudioClip clip)
  {
    put(key, clip); // key being used to enter and retrieve
    elements
```

```java
}

/* The method retrieveClip() retrieves the specified clip
   from the Hashtable and returns it to the calling method
   */
public AudioClip retrieveClip(String key)
{
    audioClip=(AudioClip)get(key);
    return (AudioClip)audioClip;
}
}
```

SoundThread.java

```java
/* This class is used for loading a sound clip */
import java.applet.*;
import java.net.URL;
class SoundThread extends Thread
{
 Applet applet;
 SoundStorage soundStorage;
 URL origURL;
 String key;

 /* The constructor needs handles to the applet as well as
    to SoundStorage. The applet is required as we want to
    use the getAudioClip() method of Applet to load an
    audio file. SoundStorage instance is required as we
    want to use its method storeClip() to store the audio
    clip */
public SoundThread(Applet applet, SoundStorage
soundStorage,
   URL origURL, String key)
{
   this.applet = applet;
   this.soundStorage = soundStorage;
   this.origURL = origURL;
```

```
   this.key = key;
   setPriority(MIN_PRIORITY);
   start();
}
public void run()
{
   /* Load the sound file by using the getAudioClip()
   method of applets */
   AudioClip audioClip = applet.getAudioClip(origURL, key);

   /* Store the audio clip in the Hashtable using the
   storeClip() method of SoundStorage */
   soundStorage.storeClip(key, audioClip);
}
}
```

Implementation

This program makes use of three Java files: MyMusic.java, SoundThread.java and SoundStorage.java.

MyMusic.java is the top level routine which extends Applet. A thread is started in this program which is used for playing the sound file.

Yet another thread is being used for loading the sound. This is SoundThread.java. The storage of the audio file is done in SoundStorage.java. This file contains a class which extends a Java library class, Hashtable.

The overall picture is like this: MyMusic creates an instance of SoundStorage. SoundStorage immediately creates the SoundThread and starts it. SoundThread starts loading the audio file. Once that's done, it sends the audio file to SoundStorage, which stores it in a Hashtable. When MyMusic requires the audio file it simply retrieves it from SoundStorage by a method provided by SoundStorage for the purpose.

Now let's go to the actual implementation:

MyMusic.java

The SoundStorage class is instantiated and asked to load the audio file whistle.au which resided in the SOUND directory (relative to the code base):

```
soundStorage = new SoundStorage(this, getCodeBase());
soundStorage.loadClip("SOUND/whistle.au");
```

`addMouseListener()` is part of the Java 1.1 Event Handling Mechanism enhancement. This has been discussed in `Movebar2.java` in brief. It is discussed at length in the chapter on GUI.

The current thread is then started.

The `stop()` method for this thread calls `soundClip.stop()`, which is used for stopping the audio clip:

soundClip.stop();

The `update()` method is used for drawing a string on the applet. If you don't know how this works, you must have read the last few pages of this chapter sleepily in front of the fireplace.

The `run()` method, which is the heart of the thread, retrieves the clip and plays it:

soundClip = soundStorage.retrieveClip("SOUND/whistle.au");
. . . .
soundClip.loop();

Here `retrieveClip()` is a method implemented in `SoundStorage()`. `soundClip.loop()` is being used for putting the sound clip in a loop — that is, it plays forever unless stopped (by killing the applet, clicking the mouse button, etc.):

SoundStorage.java

This class extends Hashtable. It is being used for storing the audio file. It also provides methods for retrieving the sound.

It first creates a Hashtable with a capacity of 5:

super(5);

The method `loadClip()` creates a `SoundThread()`. The strings `origURL` and relative URL combined together give the full path of the audio file.

The method `storeClip()` calls the `put()` method of the Hashtable. This stores the audio clip "clip" in the Hashtable. Here "key" is a unique String which is being used for identifying which object is being stored in the Hashtable. This will be used for retrieval. For example, if you store five different audio files in this Hashtable, at the time of retrieval you would like to know which one is which. For this, each entry is associated with a key. In this case, we're using the name of the audio file as a key.

```
put(key, clip);
```

Similarly, for retrieving the audio file, the method `retrieveClip()` uses this key as an argument to the `get()` method of Hashtable, which retrieves the audio file:

```
audioClip=(AudioClip)get(key);
```

SoundThread.java

SoundThread is a simple thread. The only thing to be discussed about this thread is how it interacts with SoundStorage. The audio file is loaded in the `run()` method:

```
AudioClip audioClip = applet.getAudioClip(origURL, key);
```

Once the clip is loaded (i.e., when `getAudioClip()` returns), the `storeClip()` method of SoundStorage is called for storing the clip in the Hashtable:

```
soundStorage.storeClip(key, audioClip);
```

Note that the key is the name of the audio file and that the same will be used by any method that tries to retrieve the file from the Hashtable.

This completes our tour of the world of applets. At this point, you should have a fair idea of how you can create applets, and how you can add sound, images and animation to them. Also, small concepts that have been dealt with in the preceding examples should be firmly rooted in your mind.

In other words, you are now ready to leave the framework offered by appletviewers or browsers, and enter the world of applications. As we discussed earlier, applications are not bound to a browser — you don't need to write those teeny-weeny HTML files in order to run your program.

But before we move on, there's one more topic that is of interest to people who really like playing with graphics: image filters.

2.7 Image Filters

In this section we will show you how to obliterate the image of a person from the face of the earth — and what better image to choose than one of the authors! The example in this chapter visits one of the esoteric areas of Java: image filters. It shows you how you can get pixel data of an image and modify it in order to create a new image.

2.7.1 Example: Fading Image

Purpose of the Program

This program loads an image in an applet. When the mouse is clicked in this applet, pixels are overwritten at random, causing the face to disappear gradually.

Concepts Covered in this Program

This example shows how image filters work and how you can write one of your own. It also introduces you to the MemoryImageSource class, as well as an animation enhancement introduced in Java 1.1 whereby you can make a Memory-ImageSource an animated object.

Source Code

HTML FILE: *FilterExample.htm*

```
<HTML>
<HEAD></HEAD>
<applet codebase="http://myServer/HTML"
code=FilterExample.class
height=160 width=250>
</applet>
</HTML>
```

JAVA FILES: *FilterExample.java*

```
import java.applet.*;
import java.awt.*;
import java.awt.event.*;
import java.awt.image.*;
public class FilterExample extends Applet implements
```

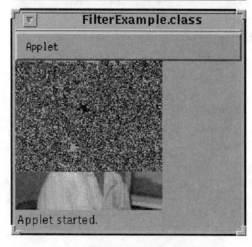

Figure 2-8

```
Runnable, MouseListener
{
    /* raster will be used for storing the pixel values of
       each pixel that constitutes the image we're trying to
       modify */
    public static int[] raster = new int[80000];
    public static int dstH, dstW;
    public static boolean ArrayCopied = false;
    Thread anim;
    MediaTracker tracker;

    /* MemoryImageSource is being used to create an image in
       memory which will be manipulated before being written
       out */
    MemoryImageSource imgsrc;
    Image memimg;
    Image memimg2;
    Image vivImage;
    int firstTime = 1;

    public void init()
    {
        /* Load the image and make a copy of it. This is the
        initial image which will be displayed. The animation
        will start when the mouse is clicked*/
        vivImage = getImage(getCodeBase(), "GIF/vsharma.jpg");
        memimg = vivImage;

        addMouseListener(this);
    }
    public void mousePressed(MouseEvent e){}
    public void mouseReleased(MouseEvent e){}
    public void mouseEntered(MouseEvent e){}
    public void mouseExited(MouseEvent e){}
    public void mouseClicked(MouseEvent e){}
    {
        Image output;
        /* Create an instance of our filter */
        ImageFilter filter = new BasicFilter();
```

```
/* Pass the image as well as the filter to an
   ImageProducer object. The ImageProducer loads the
   image pixel by pixel. As the image is being loaded
   it will call methods which are actually meant for
   the image consumer. Image consumer is the one that
   creates the final image to be displayed. However,
   our filter has overridden those methods. So it
   will intercept those methods, do its work, and
   then invoke the corresponding methods of the image
   consumer. This way, the filter can, if it wants,
   manipulate the image before it reaches the image
   consumer. Our filter is a very simple one. It
   doesn't manipulate the image. It just stores the
   pixel data of the image in an array which will be
   manipulated later to produce frames of the
   animation. */
```

ImageProducer producer = new
  FilteredImageSource(vivImage.getSource(), filter);

```
/* We now reconstruct the image using the producer.
   Since the filter didn't manipulate the image at
   all, the original image will be created once again
   and we'll display this as the first shot of our
   animation sequence */
```
memimg = createImage(producer);
```
repaint();
startThread();
}
public void startThread()
{
   anim.start();
}
public void start()
{
   anim = new Thread(this);
}
public synchronized void stop()
```

```
{
  anim = null;
  notify();
}
public synchronized void run()
{
  /* Wait for a 1000 ms */
  try {wait(1000);} catch (InterruptedException e)
  {return;}

  /* Wait until ArrayCopied is set equal to true. It
     will be set to true by the filter once it has
     copied the pixel data of the original image to the
     raster array defined in this class */
  while(ArrayCopied == false)
  {
  try {wait(100);} catch (InterruptedException e)
  {return;}
  }

  /* We construct an image in the memory using the
     raster array into which pixel data of the original
     image has been stored by the filter. At this point
     this image will be a replica of the original
     image. The reason why we're creating a
     MemoryImageSource is that this image can be
     manipulated in the memory for our animation. */
  imgsrc = new MemoryImageSource(dstW,
     dstH,ColorModel.getRGBdefault(), raster, 0, dstW);

  /* The setAnimated() method tells that this memory
     image is an animated image which will change */
  imgsrc.setAnimated(true);

  /* Using this memory image create an object of the
     type Image which can be displayed by paint() */
  memimg2 = createImage(imgsrc);
```

```
/* We set firstTime equal to 0 so that the paint
   method now uses memimg2 as the image to be
   displayed. Until now it had been using memimg. */

firstTime = 0;

while (Thread.currentThread() == anim)
{
  int x,y;
  /* Generate a random number. The pixel
     corresponding to this location will be modified
     */
  x = (int)(Math.random() * dstW);
  y = (int)(Math.random() * dstH);
  int i;
  /* Modify 80 consecutive pixels in the raster array
     */
  for(i=0; i<80; i++)
  {
      if((y*100 +x +i) < 80000)
          raster[y * 100 + x + i] =
          ((int) (Math.random() * 0xffffff)) |
          (0xff<<24);
  }
  /* Inform the runtime system that pixels of the
  memory image have been modified. We don't need to
  recreate memimg2 as that has been created from
  imgsrc, which is an animated memory image */
  imgsrc.newPixels(x, y, 5, 5);
  repaint();
  try {wait(1);} catch (InterruptedException e)
  {return;}
  }
}
public void paint(Graphics g)
{
  if(firstTime == 1)
  {
    g.drawImage(memimg, 0, 0, this);
```

```
      }
      else
        g.drawImage(memimg2, 0, 0, this);
  }
}
```

BasicFilter.java

```java
import java.awt.image.ColorModel;
import java.awt.image.ImageFilter;
import java.util.Hashtable;
import java.awt.Rectangle;

public class BasicFilter extends ImageFilter
{
  private static ColorModel defaultRGB =
  ColorModel.getRGBdefault();

  public static int raster[];
  private int pixData[];
  private int xoffset, yoffset;
  private int srcW, srcH;
  public static int dstW, dstH;

  public BasicFilter()
  {
  }

  /* These are the methods which we want to intercept before
     they reach the image consumer. */
  public void setDimensions(int width, int height)
  {
    srcW = width;
    srcH = height;
    dstW = width;
    dstH = height;
    raster = new int[srcW * srcH];
    pixData = new int[srcW * srcH];
```

```
   consumer.setDimensions(width, height);
}
public void setColorModel(ColorModel model)
{
   consumer.setColorModel(defaultRGB);
}
public void setHints(int hintflags)
{
   consumer.setHints(TOPDOWNLEFTRIGHT
        | COMPLETESCANLINES
        | SINGLEPASS
        | (hintflags & SINGLEFRAME));
}

public void setPixels(int x, int y, int w, int h,
ColorModel model,
        byte pixels[], int off, int scansize)
{
   int srcOffset = off;
   int dstOffset = y * srcW + x;
   for (int yy = 0; yy < h; yy++)
   {
      for (int xx = 0; xx < w; xx++)
      {
         raster[dstOffset++] =
             model.getRGB(pixels[srcOffset++] &0xff);
      }
         srcOffset += (scansize - w);
         dstOffset += (srcW - w);
   }
}

public void setPixels(int x, int y, int w, int h,
ColorModel model, int pixels[], int off, int scansize)
{
   int srcOffset = off;
   int dstOffset = y * srcW + x;
   if (model == defaultRGB)
   {
```

```
        for (int yy = 0; yy < h; yy++)
        {
           System.arraycopy(pixels, srcOffset, raster,
           dstOffset, w);
           srcOffset += scansize;
           dstOffset += srcW;
        }
     }
     else
     {
        for (int yy = 0; yy < h; yy++)
        {
           for (int xx = 0; xx < w; xx++)
           {
               raster[dstOffset++] =
               model.getRGB(pixels[srcOffset++]);
           }
           srcOffset += (scansize - w);
           dstOffset += (srcW - w);
        }
     }
  }
  public void imageComplete(int status)
  {
     int i;
     FilterExample.dstH = dstH;
     FilterExample.dstW = dstW;
     for(i=0; i<dstW*dstH; i++)
     {
        pixData[i] = raster[i];
        /* Store the pixel data of the image in the raster
           array of defined in the applet */
        FilterExample.raster[i] = pixData[i];
     }
     FilterExample.ArrayCopied = true;
     consumer.setPixels(0, 0, dstW, dstH, defaultRGB,
     pixData, 0, dstW);
     consumer.imageComplete(status);
  }
}
```

Implementation

First a bit of theory. After an image is loaded and before it's displayed, it can be intercepted for manipulation. The piece that loads is the image producer; the one that displays it is the image consumer. Another piece, called the image filter, can be inserted between these layers for manipulating the image.

When an image is being loaded by your applet, you can specify that it pass through an image filter which will modify it (depending upon how the image filter has been implemented) before it comes to the screen. You can use existing image filters, or if you're more of an adventurer you can write one of your own.

Another concept is that of creating an image in the memory. For this you can instantiate MemoryImageSource. This allows you to create an image in the form of an array of pixels, which can be modified to form the image.

In Java 1.1 there is another feature which allows the pixels in the Memory image to be modified, i.e., the image can itself be made animated. In other words, you don't need to create new sets of images; the same image can be modified at runtime and displayed as it's modified.

This example consists of two Java files: one (FilterExample.java) is the applet itself while the other (BasicFilter.java) is the image filter.

We begin by declaring an array of int which will be used for storing the pixel data of the image once it's been loaded. We also declare an object of the type MemoryImageSource:

```
public static int[] raster = new int[80000];
MemoryImageSource imgsrc;
```

The image GIF/vsharma.jpg is loaded using getImage(). Another image, memimg, is set equal to this image — this is the one that displays before the animation starts. The real action begins when the mouse is clicked.

First, our image filter is instantiated:

```
ImageFilter filter = new BasicFilter();
```

Its source data is then gathered by the method getSource(). This will be used by the ImageProducer for pixelizing the image data. This source along with the image filter we created is passed to a new object of the type FilteredImageSource. This is the image producer which will act on the image:

```
ImageProducer producer = new FilteredImageSource
                         (vivImage.getSource(), filter);
```

The image producer, as it loads the image, makes calls that are meant for the image consumer. However, our filter intercepts those calls to get the pixel data of the image. Once it has received all the information required and has modified whatever it needs to, the image filter sends the data to the image consumer. In our example, the filter is being used just for gathering the pixel data. The actual modification will be done using the MemoryImageSource.

Finally the image (after modification, if any, by the image filter) is created by using the producer:

```
memimg = createImage(producer);
```

Once the image filter (BasicFilter) has completed its job of gathering all the pixel data and storing it in the `raster` array of our applet, it sets a variable ArrayCopied equal to true.

Inside the `run()` method of the applet, we wait until this variable has been set to `true`. This is very important because it's an indication that the whole image has been loaded in the memory and its pixel data is available for modification.

```
while(ArrayCopied == false)
{
   try {wait(100);} catch (InterruptedException e)
   {return;}
}
```

Here we see another method, `wait()`. This is similar to `sleep()`, but is much broader. However, for our purposes, we're using it just like `sleep()`.

After the data has been gathered in memory, we create a new image in the memory:

```
   imgsrc = new MemoryImageSource(dstW,
dstH,ColorModel.getRGBdefault(),
             raster, 0, dstW);
```

```
memimg2 = createImage(imgsrc);
```

Here `raster` is the array into which pixel data of our image has been copied by the image filter. `dstW` and `dstH` are the width and height of the image as determined by the image filter.

We also use a new Java 1.1 method to specify that this image is animated — that is, its pixel data will be changed at runtime:

```
imgsrc.setAnimated(true);
```

Inside the thread's `while` loop, we modify pixels of the pixel array at random:

```
raster[y * 100 + x + i] = ((int) (Math.random() *
Oxffffff)) |
(Oxff<<24);
```

The method `newPixels()` is then called, which causes the image to be updated with this new array. After this, the `repaint()` method is called, which causes the newly created frame to be displayed:

```
imgsrc.newPixels(x, y, 5, 5); repaint();
```

Now let's look at the image filter. This is created by extending the Image-Filter class. The methods of this class are never directly called. Instead, they are invoked by the image producer as it sends pixel data.

Through these methods the image filter comes to know all the information about the image, and can store and modify individual pixels.

For example, when the producer invokes the `setDimensions()` method, it passes the width and height of the image. Using this, we create an array of the size `width*height`, which will be used for storing the pixel data that comes through other methods:

```
public void setDimensions(int width, int height)
{
   . . . . . .
   raster = new int[srcW * srcH];
}
```

Every method that gets called needs to be propagated to the actual consumer, which has to display the image. To do this, we invoke the method in the following way:

```
consumer.setDimensions(width, height);
```

Here `consumer` is a handle to the actual consumer and is already declared and defined in the ImageFilter; we can directly use it.

Similarly, there are methods that can be used for determining the color model to be used (`setColorModel()`), to determine in what order pixels will come (`setHints()`), etc.

One method of importance to us is `setPixels()`. In this method, the actual pixels are sent. Our image filter simply stores them in the array raster which was created earlier:

```
raster[dstOffset++] = model.getRGB(pixels[srcOffset++] &
0xff);
```

Once all the data has been sent, the `imageComplete()` method is called. Here we can modify the pixels before calling the consumer's `imageComplete()`. The image will not be drawn by the consumer until this method is called.

In our example, we're simply copying this data to the array in our FilterExample class because our only purpose was to gather data. The modification is being handled in FilterExample:

```
for(i=0; i<dstW*dstH; i++)
{
  pixData[i] = raster[i];
  FilterExample.raster[i] = pixData[i];
}
```

The variable ArrayCopied is set to true to indicate to the applet that all the pixel data has been gathered.

Finally the consumer's `imageComplete()` method is called and the image gets drawn.

Now that you've successfully eliminated Vivek Sharma, you can try your hand on any other voodoo dolls lying around your house. Meanwhile, we move on to applications.

## CHAPTER 3

THREADS

A thread is a basic element used for construction of our clothes. Sorry, for a moment we forgot that we are software developers and that our dictionaries have changed from what Miss Daisy taught us in Grade 1. Threads, native language, the letter C — everything has taken on a new meaning.

3.1 Introduction to Threads

For us, a thread can be perceived as a program that is running simultaneously with other programs, all of which have originated from the same parent, trying to do a job. It has its own beginning and ending.

However, a thread is not exactly a program in itself. It does not run on its own; there is a parent process which starts up one or more threads to do a piece of work.

Threads help you do jobs concurrently instead of sequentially (which is how non-thread-based programs work). For example, if you write a program that needs to read two different files, modify their outputs and write them back, the traditional approach to this would be: read the first file, modify its data and write it out, then repeat the same process with the next file. With threads, the parent program would start off two threads, each one of which would read, modify and write one file, thus working concurrently.

To understand threads, try to correlate them with the concept of timesharing. With timesharing, the computer seems to be running a large number of errands simultaneously, even if it has the capability of running only one job at a time. This is managed by doing one job for a short period of time, then doing the second job, the third job, then returning to the first job, and so on. This way, one job doesn't tie down the system. You can ask the computer to run a number of programs and go off for a siesta instead of waiting for one to finish before giving it the next job.

Threads extend this concept. You can write a multithreaded program. Each of the threads of this program will run "simultaneously." Threads help programs make more than one thing happen at once.

A common example of thread usage is your web browser. You may have noticed that if you're downloading a web page with lots of images, you can use the scrollbar to scroll down the page even as the images are being loaded. This is because there are different threads that control the downloading of the image and everything else.

There are essentially two ways in which threads can be created in a Java program: by extending the Thread class or by implementing the Runnable interface. We made extensive use of the Runnable interface in the chapter on applets. In this chapter, we're going to concentrate on the other method, which is normally used for Java applications. In the end, however, we do revisit the Runnable interface with a very small animation example.

3.1.1 Example: Introduction to Threads

Purpose of the Program
This program introduces you to threads. It displays a few strings on the screen generated by a thread.

Concepts Covered in this Program
This program is an introduction to threads. It shows how a thread can be constructed. It also introduces you to the `run()` method of the thread.

Source Code

```
/* Class Main1 creates a thread and starts it */
```

Main1.java

```
public class Main1
{
  /* Declare a Thread variable */
  public static Thread1 t1;

  public static void main(String args[])
  {
    /* Create a thread */
    t1 = new Thread1();

    /* Start the thread */
    t1.start();

    /* Now that the thread has been started, it's on its
       own. This program can now do whatever it wants
       without bothering about the thread. The thread
       will run independently alongside this program */
  }
}
```

Thread1.java

```
/* This class extends the Thread class so it will have
   all the properties of threads. When the thread object
   created above is started (using the start() method of
   Thread), the run() method defined in this class will be
   invoked */

class Thread1 extends Thread
{
  public void run()
  {
    int noOfLines = 0;

    /* Control comes to the run() method when the thread
       is started. Here we've put the thread in a loop
       which executes five times and prints out a string.
```

```
        Once this is done, there is nothing more to be
        done in the run() method, so the thread dies. */

    while(noOfLines < 5)
    {
        System.out.println("This is your first thread");
        noOfLines++;
    }
  }
}
```

Implementation

The program consists of two Java files: `Main1.java` and `Thread1.java`. `Main1.java` is the top level file containing the `main()` method. The thread has been declared in this file:

public static Thread1 t1;

Inside the `main()` method, the thread is created:

t1 = new Thread1();

And it's started:

t1.start();

The thread itself has been defined in `Thread1.java`. Here we're extending the Threads class to form our own class called Thread1:

class Thread1 extends Thread

Thread1 is the thread that was instantiated in `Main1.java`.

When a thread is started, it causes the `run()` method of the thread to be invoked. By overloading this method (i.e., by defining this method in our class) we can take control of the thread and make it do whatever we want.

The line `t1.start()` in `Main1.java` causes the `run()` method of the thread to be invoked. We have already provided our own implementation of the same:

```
public void run()
{
    ......
}
```

The run() method is the heart and soul of any thread. This is where all the action takes place. Once all the activity has been completed in this method, the thread dies. You can write normal code inside the run() method to achieve any desired output. You can even make calls to other functions and create loops inside the run() method.

In our program, we've created a while loop which cycles five times, and each time it prints out: "This is your first thread". Once it's done this five times, control goes out of the while loop. Since there's nothing happening after that, the thread dies.

3.1.2 Example: Two Threads

Purpose of the Program
In this program we create two threads, each of which prints a message on the screen.

Concepts Covered in this Program
This program introduces you to the concept of multiple threads. It also describes the sleep() method.

Source Code

```
/* This program creates and starts two threads, each of
   which runs independently alongside the main program */
```

Main3.java

```
public class Main3
{
    public static Thread3_1 t1;
    public static Thread3_2 t2;
    public static void main(String args[])
```

```
    {
       t1 = new Thread3_1();
       t2 = new Thread3_2();
       t1.start();
       t2.start();
    }
}
```

Thread3_1.java

```
class Thread3_1 extends Thread
{
   public void run()
   {
      int noOfLines = 0;
      while(noOfLines < 5)
      {
         System.out.println("This is the thread: Thread3_1");
         noOfLines++;

         /* We want the thread to take a rest for 200
            milliseconds. The thread will give up the
            control it had acquired over the system, and the
            system is free to allocate resources to other
            threads/programs. After 200 milliseconds, the
            thread will wake up and try to reclaim these
            resources and continue its execution from the
            point where it left to take a nap. */

         try
         {
            sleep(200);
         } catch(InterruptedException e){}
      }
   }
}
```

Thread3_2.java

```java
class Thread3_2 extends Thread
{
  public void run()
  {
    int noOfLines = 0;
    while(noOfLines < 5)
    {
      System.out.println("This is the thread: Thread3_2");
      noOfLines++;
      try
      {
          sleep(200);
      } catch(InterruptedException e){}
    }
  }
}
```

Implementation

Here we extend what we learned in `Main1.java` in order to create two threads. The two threads are created: they're first declared, then instantiated, then started. The same approach we followed to create one thread is repeated.

Each of the threads exists in separate Java files, `Thread3_1.java` and `Thread3_2.java`. Their implementation is also the same as that of `Thread1.java`.

However, there's one new thing that's been introduced here: threads can be made to sleep, i.e., you can ask a thread to not do anything for a specified period of time. This is done through the `sleep()` method:

sleep(200);

This causes the thread to sleep for 200 milliseconds. The variations of the `sleep()` method are all discussed in `java.lang.Thread.java`.

However, you must remember that 200 milliseconds is not guaranteed to be the exact time for which your thread will sleep. Efforts will be made by the system to make this as close as possible, but it all depends upon several factors, such as the time-slicing mechanism of the processor, the priority of the thread, etc.

If you look at the `sleep()` method in `java.lang.Thread.java`, you'll realize that it can raise an exception, called InterruptedException. We need to catch this, otherwise our code will give compilation errors:

```
try
{
    sleep(200);
} catch(InterruptedException e){}
```

3.1.3 Example: Two Interacting Threads

Purpose of the Program
In this program there are two threads again. However, one of the threads stops the other thread once its own work is done.

Concepts Covered in this Program
This program introduces you to the stop() method, which can be used for stopping a thread's execution.

Source Code
```
/* Here again two threads are being created. The second
   thread is such that if left to itself it will continue
   executing forever. The first thread makes sure this
   doesn't happen by explicitly stopping the thread after
   some time */
```

Main4.java

```
public class Main4
{
    public static Thread4_1 t1;
    public static Thread4_2 t2;
    public static void main(String args[])
    {
        t1 = new Thread4_1();
        t2 = new Thread4_2();
        t1.start();
        t2.start();
    }
}
```

Thread4_1.java

```
class Thread4_1 extends Thread
{
  public void run()
  {
    int noOfLines = 0;
    while(noOfLines < 20)
    {
      System.out.println("This is the thread: Thread4_1");
      noOfLines++;
      try
      {
        sleep(200);
      } catch(InterruptedException e){}
    }

    /* After looping 20 times, this thread stops the
       second thread by using the stop() method of
       Thread. */

    Main4.t2.stop();
  }
}
```

Thread4_2.java

```
class Thread4_2 extends Thread
{
  public void run()
  {
    int noOfLines = 0;

    /* If left to itself, this thread will continue
       forever because of the while(true) loop */

    while(true)
    {
      System.out.println("This is the thread: Thread4_2");
      noOfLines++;
      try
```

```
    {
        sleep(200);
    } catch(InterruptedException e){}
  }
 }
}
```

Implementation

In this example, we create two different threads by instantiating the classes Thread4_1 and Thread4_2. The threads are also started in the same way as previous examples.

Now let us look at the threads themselves. Thread4_2 has been implemented in the same way that earlier threads have been implemented, with one significant difference: this thread can continue indefinitely. This is because the `while` loop will go on forever:

```
while(true)
{
  ......
}
```

The thread simply prints This is the thread: Thread4_2 repeatedly forever.

Looking at this, you may think, "This thread is never going to end, and will eat my system resources forever!" Relax; Java allows you to kill a thread, using a method called `stop()`. In `Thread4_1.java`, we're creating the thread in the normal fashion. Here the `while()` loops 20 times. Once control comes out of the loop, we are explicitly killing the other thread:

```
Main4.t2.stop();
```

This method causes the thread to die.

There are other methods that can be used for suspending the thread temporarily and then resuming it after some time. These are `suspend()` and `resume()`, and they are documented in `java.lang.Thread.java`.

Note that to get a handle to the thread we've declared `t2` as static in `Main4.java`:

```
public static Thread4_2 t2;
```

This means that we can reference t2 using the class name Main4. As you may recall, static methods are shared by all the instances of a class and are not tied down to one instance. So we don't need an instance of Main4 to access t4. We can directly refer to it by using Main4 as our handle.

The output of the program looks like this:

```
This is the thread: Thread4_1
This is the thread: Thread4_2
This is the thread: Thread4_1
. . . . .
```

However, you cannot be sure that the same sequence will be repeated — the output of one thread may come consecutively, depending on which thread gets control of the system.

3.1.4 Example: Two Threads Using One Class

Purpose of the Program

This program also creates two threads which print a message on the screen. However, here we're using just one class which is being instantiated twice to make the threads.

Concepts Covered in this Program

We show how the same class can be instantiated more than once to create multiple threads. We also show how you can distinguish one such thread from another by introducing you to the getName() method.

Source Code

```
/* In this program we're creating two threads by
   instantiating the same class twice */
```

Main5.java

```
public class Main5
{
  public static Thread5 t1;
  public static Thread5 t2;
  public static void main(String args[])
```

```
   {
      t1 = new Thread5("First Thread");
      t2 = new Thread5("Second Thread");
      t1.start();
      t2.start();
   }
}


class Thread5 extends Thread
{
   public Thread5(String str)
   {
      /* We're invoking the super(String) constructor of
         Thread, which assigns the name supplied in the
         argument to the thread */

      super(str);
   }
   public void run()
   {
      int noOfLines = 0;
      while(noOfLines < 5)
      {
         /* getName() returns the name of the thread. This
            is the name that was given to the thread when
            it was constructed. */

         System.out.println("This is the thread: " +
         getName());

         noOfLines++;
         try
         {
            sleep(200);
         } catch(InterruptedException e){}
      }
   }
}
```

Implementation

In this example, we're creating two threads by instantiating the same class, Thread5, twice. The two threads are t1 and t2:

```
public static Thread5 t1;
public static Thread5 t2;
```

The threads are created and started in the normal fashion. However, the constructor is being passed an argument, which is the name of the thread.

Now look at Thread5.java. Here the constructor Thread5() has been defined so that it takes a string argument:

```
public Thread5(String str)
```

In the body of this method we have super(str). The super() method essentially calls the constructor of the parent class, in this case, the Thread class. The constructor of the Thread class that accommodates a string as a parameter saves that string as the name of the thread. This name can later be retrieved by the getName() method which we're using in our screen output:

```
System.out.println("This is the thread: " + getName());
```

Here getName() will return First Thread if t1 is used, and Second Thread if t2 is used.

The output of the program looks like this:

```
This is the thread: First Thread
This is the thread: Second Thread
This is the thread: First Thread
This is the thread: Second Thread
.....
```

Note that both threads have the same priority, i.e., the system doesn't give one preference over the other. However, a thread can set its priority. By setting a high priority the thread can take more control over the system's resources. The priority can be lowered if the thread is not too time-critical. To set the priority of a thread, you can use the setPriority() method. This method is explained in java.lang.Thread.java. The priority can range from Thread.MIN_PRIORITY to Thread.MAX_PRIORITY.

3.2 Using Multiple Threads

The most challenging part of using threads lies in synchronizing multiple threads running simultaneously. Let's say there are two threads, one of which is generating some data while the other is using that data, both of them running simultaneously. Now, if the second thread tries to access the data while the first one is still modifying it, there could be data corruption. Java provides methods to avoid scenarios like this one and also many other complex irritants such as deadlocks (where multiple threads are waiting for one another, bringing the entire operation to a halt). In this section, we will show how multiple threads can follow the principle of peaceful co-existence. If only we could use the same principles to alleviate the problems of the world that we live in!

3.2.1 Example: Threads Reading and Writing Files

Purpose of the Program
This program is a skeleton in which two threads run, one of which is supposed to read data from one file while the other one is supposed to write the data to another file. We haven't included the actual file reading/writing part, to prevent the program from growing unwieldy.

Concepts Covered in this Program
Through this program we introduce the concept of synchronization of multiple threads. We introduce you to a monitor object that will ensure that the various threads are in sync with each other and don't lead to data corruption.

Source Code

```
/* When there are multiple threads running, synchronizing
   them  becomes important, especially if they interact
   with one another or try to access the same piece of
   data together.

   In this program, one thread simulates reading a file
   while another simulates writing the data read by the
   first thread to a second file. Obviously there would
   be chaos if the second thread attempts to write before
   the first one has finished reading.
```

The problem is solved by using a monitor object which contains the read and write methods. A thread has to get hold of the monitor to invoke the read or the write method and only one thread at a time can access this monitor. So, while reading is being done, writing cannot be done, and vice versa. */

MainFile1.java

```
class MainFile1
{
  public static ThreadMonitor1 m;
  public static ReadThread1 r;
  public static WriteThread1 w;
  public static void main(String[] args)
  {
    /* Create the thread monitor and pass it to the two
       threads as they'll be using it for reading/writing
       */
    m = new ThreadMonitor1();
    r = new ReadThread1(m);
    w = new WriteThread1(m);

    r.start();
    w.start();
  }
}
```

ReadThread1.java

```
class ReadThread1 extends Thread
{
  private ThreadMonitor1 tm;
  public ReadThread1(ThreadMonitor1 tm)
  {
    this.tm = tm;
  }
  public void run()
  {
    int i;
```

```
      /* Instead of putting readFile() in this thread, we
         have defined this method in the monitor */
      for(i=0; i<5; i++)
        tm.readFile();
    }
  }
```

WriteThread1.java

```
  class WriteThread1 extends Thread
  {
    private ThreadMonitor1 tm;
    public WriteThread1(ThreadMonitor1 tm)
    {
      this.tm = tm;
    }
    public void run()
    {
      int i;
      for(i=0; i<5; i++)
        tm.writeFile();
    }
  }
```

ThreadMonitor1.java

```
  class ThreadMonitor1
  {
    /* This variable is true so long as the read thread has
       control of the monitor */
    private boolean goingToReadFile = true;

    String data;
    ThreadMonitor1()
    {
    }

    /* This is a synchronized method, which means that only
       a thread that is currently holding the monitor can
       invoke this method */
```

```
public synchronized void readFile()
{

   while(!goingToReadFile)
   {
      /* If goingToReadFile is false, the monitor is
      being controlled by another thread, so this thread
      has to wait */
      try
      {
         wait();
      } catch(InterruptedException e){}
   }
   System.out.println("Inside readFile");
   // Read data into the string

   /* After doing its work, this thread must set
      goingToReadFile to false so that writeFile()
      doesn't get stuck in its while() loop */
   goingToReadFile = false;

   /* Inform the system that the monitor is being
      released and may be assigned to another thread */
   notify();

   return;
}
public synchronized void writeFile()
{
   while(goingToReadFile)
   {

      try
      {
         wait();
      } catch(InterruptedException e){}
   }
   System.out.println("Inside writeFile");
```

```
    //Write data from the String
    goingToReadFile = true;
    notify();
    return;
  }
}
```

Implementation

This program is split over four Java files: MainFile1.java, ReadThread1.java, WriteThread1.java and ThreadMonitor1.java.

As you may have guessed, MainFile1.java is the top level file which contains the main() method. Here we create a monitor object, a read thread and a write thread. The read and write threads will use methods which are implemented in the monitor. These methods are synchronized, which means that as long as a thread is executing that method, no other thread can take hold of the monitor. In other words, while a thread is executing a method of this monitor, other threads cannot execute a method of the same monitor. In this example, our objective is that, while reading is being done, no writing should be done. This would be required in a scenario where the reader is filling up a buffer and the writer should proceed only when the buffer is filled (this will be determined by a flag set by the reader). Similarly, while the buffer is being written out, the reader should not update the buffer with new data. So, how do we achieve this? Read on.

The threads and the monitor are instantiated in MainFile1.java. The threads are passed a handle to the monitor which will be used by the threads to invoke the methods required by that particular thread:

```
m = new ThreadMonitor1();
r = new ReadThread1(m);
w = new WriteThread1(m);
```

Then the threads are started.

Note that the same instance of the monitor must be used by both threads. This is because each instance of a monitor can lock a piece of data. If you use multiple monitors in these two threads, there will be no synchronization.

In both the threads, the constructor accepts an argument of the type Thread-Monitor1. The ThreadMonitor which was passed as a parameter during the construction of the thread is stored as a private object:

```
private ThreadMonitor1 tm;
public ReadThread1(ThreadMonitor1 tm)
{
   this.tm = tm;
}
```

The same is also being done for the write thread.

The major component here is the monitor. In Java, a monitor is a class that has one or more synchronized methods in it. It is used for locking a data item so that other methods cannot access this data until the lock is released. Every method that needs to modify this data must first obtain a lock on the monitor. We are achieving this here by defining the functions that modify and access the data in the monitor. Our read and write threads invoke these methods through the instance of the monitor that was passed to them from the main program.

In our monitor, ThreadMonitor1, we first define a boolean goingToRead-File, which is initially set to true. When the value of this is true, it means that the read thread is currently working or is about to start reading a file. When the value is false, it's the write thread that is active.

```
private boolean goingToReadFile = true;
```

We don't need to do anything in the constructor, so the body of the constructor is empty.

Our first synchronized method is readFile(). Here "synchronized" is a reserved word. The synchronized word suggests that while a thread is executing this method, no other thread can invoke any other synchronized method of this object:

```
public synchronized void readFile()
```

First we check the variable goingToReadFile to make sure that it's appropriate for this method to do something. The first time around, since the variable is true, this part will be skipped, i.e., it will break out of the while loop and print out Inside readFile. Then, if we had implemented the code fully, it would have read data from the file and stored it in the string called data. Note that at this point in time our ReadThread has taken control of the monitor, so the WriteThread cannot do anything until the ReadThread releases the monitor. So we set the variable goingToReadFile to false. This will be used by

WriteThread. Then we call the method `notify()`. This method sends out a notification that the monitor is now free for use by other threads:

```
notify();
```

The `notify()` method works in conjunction with the `wait()` method, which we'll explain in a while. When the `notify()` method is called, it wakes up one of the threads that are waiting for this monitor to be released by the current thread. However, you should note that there is no guarantee as to which thread will actually get activated.

Once the return is encountered, all the functionality within the `readFile()` method has been completed, and the thread gives up control of the monitor.

Now, if you look at the code of the read and write threads, you will note that they repeatedly call the `readFile()` and `writeFile()` methods. What if somehow the read thread again gains control of the monitor and once again `readFile()` is invoked? This is where we make use of the `wait()` method. At this point, the variable `goingToReadFile` will be `false`. Thus the code will go into the `while()` loop:

```
while(!goingToReadFile)
```

Here we have put the `wait()` method. When a thread calls the `wait()` method, it goes into a sleep which lasts until `notify()` is called by another thread and wakes it up. There is a variation of `wait()` which makes it sleep for a specified period of time. So, coming back to our example, due to the `wait()` method, the read thread goes to sleep until it receives a notification to wake up, the end result being that it doesn't do anything. Also, since we have put this in a `while` loop which will break only when `goingToReadFile` becomes `true`, we don't have to worry about the fact that it may again get control of the monitor — it won't be able to do anything until the variable `goingToReadFile` has been set to `false` by our `writeFile()` method. The `wait()` method can raise the InterruptedException, so here is how we call it:

```
try
{
    wait();
} catch(InterruptedException e){}
```

Now, since the read thread has gone to sleep, the monitor is once again free. It can now be taken over by the write thread. The `writeFile()` method also implements its functionality in the same way.

The output of the program looks like this:

```
Inside readFile
Inside writeFile
Inside readFile
Inside writeFile
. . . . .
```

3.2.2 Example: Synchronization Between Three Threads

Purpose of the Program

This example is just an extension of `MainFile1.java`. Here there are three threads being synchronized. The first one is for reading a file, the second one is for modifying its data, while the third one is for writing the data to another file. Once again, we haven't added the code which actually reads/changes/writes the data.

Concepts Covered in this Program

The program extends the idea presented in the first example and shows how it can be applied to more than two threads. It also introduces the `notifyAll()` method.

Source Code

```
/* In this program we have three threads which compete for
   a monitor */
```

MainFile2.java

```
class MainFile2
{
  public static ThreadMonitor2 m;
  public static ReadThread2 r;
  public static WriteThread2 w;
  public static ChangeThread2 c;
  public static void main(String[] args)
```

```
   {
     m = new ThreadMonitor2();
     r = new ReadThread2(m);
     w = new WriteThread2(m);
     c = new ChangeThread2(m);
     r.start();
     w.start();
     c.start();
   }
}
```

ReadThread2.java

```
class ReadThread2 extends Thread
{
  private ThreadMonitor2 tm;
  public ReadThread2(ThreadMonitor2 tm)
  {
    this.tm = tm;
  }
  public void run()
  {
    int i;
    for(i=0; i<5; i++)
      tm.readFile();
  }
}
```

WriteThread2.java

```
class WriteThread2 extends Thread
{
  private ThreadMonitor2 tm;
  public WriteThread2(ThreadMonitor2 tm)
  {
    this.tm = tm;
  }
  public void run()
```

```
  {
    int i;
    for(i=0; i<5; i++)
       tm.writeFile();
  }
}
```

ChangeThread2.java

```
class ChangeThread2 extends Thread
{
  private ThreadMonitor2 tm;
  public ChangeThread2(ThreadMonitor2 tm)
  {
    this.tm = tm;
  }
  public void run()
  {
    int i;
    for(i=0; i<5; i++)
       tm.changeFile();
  }
}
```

ThreadMonitor2.java

```
class ThreadMonitor2
{
  /* Here the monitor uses an int, currentStatus, to
     determine which thread has control of the monitor at
     this point in time */

  public static int currentStatus = 0;

  ThreadMonitor2()
  {
  }
  public synchronized void readFile()
```

```
{
   while(currentStatus != 0)
   {
     try
     {
        wait();
     } catch(InterruptedException e){}
   }
   System.out.println("Inside readFile");
   currentStatus = 1;

   /* Tell everybody that the monitor is going to be
      freed and any thread can grab hold of it. */
   notifyAll();

   return;
}
public synchronized void changeFile()
{
   while(currentStatus != 1)
   {
     try
     {
        wait();
     } catch(InterruptedException e){}
   }
   System.out.println("Inside changeFile");
   currentStatus = 2;
   notifyAll();
   return;
}
public synchronized void writeFile()
{
   while(currentStatus != 2)
   {

     try
     {
```

```
            wait();
        } catch(InterruptedException e){}
    }
    currentStatus = 0;
    System.out.println("Inside writeFile");
    notifyAll();
    return;
    }
}
```

Implementation

Implementation is the same as that of `MainFile1.java`, except that there is a new thread, ChangeThread2. The only new thing in this is the method `noti-fyAll()` which we're using in our monitor.

When `notifyAll()` is invoked, it sends a message to all the threads in this monitor that the monitor is up for grabs. These threads then compete among themselves to gain control of the monitor, as opposed to `notify()`, in which case the runtime system picks up one of the waiting threads and gives it the monitor. The thread that wins gains control of the monitor, and the others go back to their cozy little beds for a nap.

The output of this program looks like this:

```
Inside readFile
Inside changeFile
Inside writeFile
Inside readFile
Inside changeFile
Inside writeFile
. . . . .
```

3.3 Threads Using the Runnable Interface

As we mentioned in the introduction, threads can also be constructed using the Runnable interface. This approach is normally made use of in threads in applets. Here, for a moment, we take you back to applets in order to explain how the Runnable interface works.

3.3.1 Example: Moving String

Purpose of the Program

This is an applet in which there is a text string that moves from the top of the applet's screen to its bottom.

Concepts Covered in this Program

This program shows how the Runnable interface can be used for creation of a thread.

Source Code

HTML FILE

```
<HTML>
<HEAD><TITLE>THREADS</TITLE></HEAD>
<applet codebase="http://myServer/HTML" code=Thread6.class
height=160
width=500>
</applet>
</HTML>
```

JAVA FILE *Thread6.java*

```
/* This class itself implements a Runnable interface. It
   means that this  program can run as a thread. If a
   thread is created and started here, control will go to
   the run() method defined in this class */

import java.awt.*;
import java.applet.*;
public class Thread6 extends Applet implements Runnable
{
  Thread t1;
  int i;
  public void start()
  {
    t1 = new Thread(this);
    t1.start();
  }
```

```
public void run()
{
   for(i=0;  i<150;  i+=10)
   {
      repaint();
      try
      {
         t1.sleep(100);
      }catch(InterruptedException e){}
   }
}
public void paint(Graphics g)
{
      g.drawString("String coming from a thread", 0,
                   i+20);
}
}
```

Implementation

The program imports the `java.awt.*` and `java.applet.*` classes, as these will be required by our applet:

```
import java.awt.*;
import java.applet.*;
```

Since we're going to start a thread in this applet, we make this class implement the Runnable interface:

```
public class Thread6 extends Applet implements Runnable
```

Inside this class, we declare an object of the type Thread:

```
Thread t1;
```

In the `start()` method, we create the thread and start it:

```
t1 = new Thread(this);
t1.start();
```

Since we're implementing the Runnable interface, we need to define the run() method, because this is the method that is called when the thread is started. Our run() method has a for loop in which the value of the variable "i" is incremented from 0 in steps of 10 until it reaches 150:

```
for(i=0; i<150; i+=10)
```

Inside the loop, we call the repaint() method, which invokes the paint() method and causes the string to be displayed at a coordinate whose location on the y axis is the current value of "i". The thread also sleeps for 100 milliseconds between each iteration of the for loop:

```
t1.sleep(100);
```

Once the for loop is over, the thread dies automatically as all the action in the run() method is complete. We used more complex examples showing how threads can be stopped and restarted in the chapter on applets.

That brings to an end our discussion of threads. You should now be in a position to knit and weave your own programs making efficient use of threads. You should try to fill in the blanks in our examples on multiple threads to get a more hands-on feeling for threads. Writing code to do actual file reading/changing/writing would be a good exercise. We also suggest that you play around with thread priorities: change priorities of various threads and see how they hog the system, or, if they have a very low priority, how the runtime system treats them like the scum of society.

CHAPTER 4

GUI

Until not too long ago software developers were accustomed to writing horizontal lines using "_", vertical lines using "|", and the "#" or "*" characters were used for adding aesthetics to screens. Rip Van Winkle, if he were to wake today, would start wondering how we've managed to create the pretty pictures in this chapter using those characters. Welcome to the world of graphical user interface (GUI).

Java allows you to create prettier-than-thou graphical user interfaces for your programs. And with the ease of the programming paradigm that has been followed, especially the radically different approach of version 1.1, it's very easy to generate a(n) (inter)face adorned with lipstick and mascara.

This chapter will teach you how you can build and use your GUI. We will discuss everything from major GUI components to layout managers. We'll also cover a new feature of Java, the clipboard.

4.1 Basic GUI Concepts

With the vast range of basic GUI components that Java offers, it's very easy to create almost anything you want. These components include buttons, text fields (which are single-line text entry fields), text areas (which are multi-line text entry fields), menus, popup menus, labels, and many more.

It's also very easy to catch the users' inputs/actions (better known as events) on these components so that your program can respond in whatever way it wants. Events are things such as a mouse click, the Return key being pressed in a text area, and so on.

In JDK 1.1, the event handling mechanism has been separated from the rest of the GUI. This allows the building of much better-organized code. Special interfaces have been defined containing methods that will be invoked depending on the kind of event that has occurred.

Every event has an event listener associated with it. And every event listener has an interface associated with it. When an event occurs, one of the methods of this interface is invoked.

If you want to handle events occurring on a component to be handled by one of your methods, you need to do a couple of things: a) you must provide an implementation for the method which will handle the event, and b) you must let Java know which class contains this method.

This is where event listeners and interfaces come into play. For every type of event the event listener will invoke one of the predefined methods (all these methods are listed in the chart at the end of this chapter). There are interfaces that contain declaration of these methods. To handle an event, your program needs to implement an interface that contains the method(s) to be invoked when that event occurs. The implementation of this method can contain whatever action you want to take when the event occurs.

Since Java allows you to separate event handling code from the rest of the GUI, the listener that takes care of the interface you're implementing has to be informed of the object that contains the event handling code.

Let's say there's a button. An event will be generated every time the user clicks on the button. If you want to do something every time this button is clicked, you'll need to implement the interface that contains the method that will be invoked when this button is clicked. You'll also need to provide an implementation for this method, either in the same class that generated the button or in another class. Also, you will have to inform the event listener associated with this interface of the object that contains the event handling method you wrote above.

There are essentially two ways in which event handling can be done:

1. The class that creates the GUI can implement the required interface(s) itself.

2. A separate class can be created for implementing the interface(s).

The class that implements the interface needs to be specified to the listener. There is a unique method for this for each type of listener. For example, for the ActionListener, you need to use the method `addActionListener` (`<object_that_will_handle_the_events>`).

Every component that wishes its events to be handled by your program needs to register itself with the appropriate listener. If it doesn't, the events are not passed to your program.

Our attempt here is not to explain everything in a few words; we've only built a theory base you'll find useful as you go through the next few examples.

4.2 First UI: Button and Text Field

4.2.1 Example: UI with Button and Text Field

Purpose of the Program

This is the first GUI program. Here we show how you can create a GUI with one button and one text field (as shown in Figure 4-1).

Concepts Covered in this Program

This example introduces you to the basic building blocks of a GUI. We show how elements are added to a GUI and how we can respond to users' actions.

Source Code

FirstUI.java

```java
import java.awt.*;
public class FirstUI
{
   public static void main(String[] args)
   {
      /* Create an instance of the class TheUI */
      TheUI myUI = new TheUI();

      /* Set the size of the GUI window 450x450 */
      myUI.setSize(450,450);
```

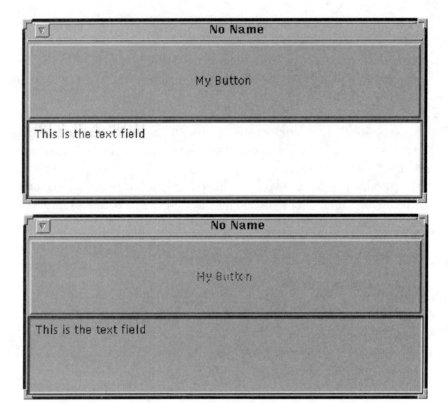

Figure 4-1

```
    /* Show the GUI window */
    myUI.show();
  }
}
```

TheUI.java

```
import java.awt.*;
import java.awt.event.*;

public class TheUI extends Frame implements ActionListener
{
  /* This GUI will display a button and a text field */
  Button b;
```

```
TextField t;

TheUI()
{
    /* Divide screen into two rows and one column. Every
       component that is added to the GUI should go to
       one of these cells. */
    setLayout(new GridLayout(2,1));

    /* Create a button */
    b = new Button("My Button");

    /* Add the button to the GUI window */
    add(b);

    /* Inform event handling mechanism that event
       handling code for the button is written in this
       class itself */
    b.addActionListener(this);

    /* Create and add a text field */
    t = new TextField(10);
    add(t);

    /* Inform event handling mechanism that event
       handling code for the text field is written in
       this class itself */

    t.addActionListener(this);

    validate();
}

/* This method will be called by the runtime system
   when the button is clicked or Return is pressed in
   the text field. This is the event handling code. */

public void actionPerformed(ActionEvent e)
```

```
{
        /* Determine the object that generated the event */
        Object arg = e.getSource();

        /* Check whether the event was generated from a
           Button or a TextField and accordingly call the
           appropriate method */

        if(arg instanceof Button)
        {
           handleButtons(arg);
        }
        if(arg instanceof TextField)
        {
           handleTextFields(arg);
        }
}
public void handleTextFields(Object arg)
{
   /* If the event was generated from the text field "t",
      make "t" uneditable */

      if(arg == t)
      {
         t.setEditable(false);
      }
}
public void handleButtons(Object arg)
{
      /* If the event was generated from the button "b",
         disable "b". */

      if(arg == b)
      {
         b.setEnabled(false);
      }
   }
}
```

Implementation

The top level class, FirstUI, creates an instance of the class TheUI and displays it in a window of size 450x50. Addition of components (button and text field) is being handled by TheUI.

TheUI adds a button and a text field to the GUI window. It also listens for events occurring on this window such as a mouse click and a Return being pressed in the text field.

Initially, a button and a text field appear in the window. If you click the button, it will be disabled, i.e., the text will be grayed out and the button will be nonfunctional.

You can write in the text field, but once you've pressed the Return key, the text field will also be disabled and won't allow you to enter more text.

So how did we achieve this? Read on!

We're using approach 1 described above, i.e., the class TheUI which creates the GUI is itself handling events occurring on its components.

The main action is in `TheUI.java`. It begins by importing some necessary packages. You've used `awt` before—this class needs a new one, `java.awt.event`, which contains classes that handle events:

```
import java.awt.event.*;
```

Next, we declare the TheUI class. This class extends the Frame class. The Frame class creates a window when it's instantiated. We can then add components in this window to create our GUI. So, when this class is instantiated in FirstUI, a window is created.

Also, we want to handle events generated in this window. We will be adding a button and a text field, and the only events we're interested in are a button click and Return pressed in the text field.

Now look at the chart given at the end of this chapter to see which event listeners will get notified when the above two events occur. Look at the kinds of events generated by Buttons and TextFields. There's only one listener that responds to events generated by Buttons and TextFields: the ActionListener. And the method that will be invoked when any of these events occurs would be `actionPerformed`. So, in order to catch the events, we need to implement the interface ActionListener and define the method `actionPerformed`.

Armed with the knowledge that it's the ActionListener that will listen to these events, we declare our class so that it implements this interface:

```
public class TheUI extends Frame implements ActionListener
```

Then we declare two objects, a Button and a TextField:

```
Button b;
TextField t;
```

Classes implementing these are defined in `java.awt`.

Just before we add the components, we would like to indicate the positions at which the components should be present. To do this layout we make use of something known as the layout manager. Java offers a variety of layout managers, one of which is GridLayout. Using this, we specify the number of rows and columns into which the GUI window should be divided. Then, as we keep on adding components, each of them goes into one cell, starting from the topmost cell.

Here we want the text field to be below the button, so we define the layout to consist of two rows and one column.

```
setLayout(new GridLayout(2,1));
```

Then we create the button. We can pass a string to the constructor of the Button class. This will be displayed as a label on the button:

```
b = new Button("My Button");
```

Then we add the button to the GUI window:

```
add(b);
```

Note that since we're using a layout with two rows and one column, the button goes to row 0 column 0.

We also want to catch the event that occurs when this button is clicked. And since this class (TheUI) itself implements the required interface, we add it to the action listener for this button:

```
b.addActionListener(this);
```

What this means is that whenever the mouse is clicked on this button, the method `actionPerformed`, which is defined in this class, should be invoked. We create and add the text field in a similar way, and add TheUI class to the action listener.

Since we're implementing the ActionListener interface, we need to define its methods in our class. There's just one method that belongs to this interface: `actionPerformed`. As you may recall, this method is going to be called every time the user clicks on the button or presses Return in the text field:

```
public void actionPerformed(ActionEvent e)
```

A question that might have come to mind is: if this method is going to be called for both the button and the text field, how will I know where the event occurred? The answer lies in the argument that is passed to the method: Action-Event. You can use the `getSource()` method on ActionEvent to determine what was the source of the event:

```
Object arg = e.getSource();
```

You can directly compare this with a component to see which component it came from. But if you have 10 buttons and 20 text fields and you do all the compares, your code will get messy. There's an easy way out. You can use the `instanceof` operator to see what type of component the event has come from (i.e., a button, a text field, or something else). Once this classification has been done, you can narrow it down to the exact component that generated the event:

```
if(arg instanceof Button)

{
    handleButtons(arg);
}
```

So, in our case, if the mouse is clicked, `(arg instanceof Button)` will be true and the method `handleButtons()` will be invoked. Similarly, if the text field is clicked, `handleTextFields()` will be invoked.

Inside these specific methods we can do another check to see which specific instance the event was generated in. In our example, if Return is pressed, we want the text field to become non-editable. For this we make use of the method `setEditable()` which is defined in TextComponent (in `java.awt.TextComponent.java`). Note that TextField extends TextComponent so methods defined in TextComponent can be used by TextField:

```
t.setEditable(false);
```

Similarly, we wish to disable the button if it is clicked. So we use the method setEnabled(), which is applicable to buttons. This method is defined in java.awt.Component.java, but is available for use by Button because the Button class (java.awt.Button.java) has been derived from the Component class:

b.setEnabled(false);

As we've seen in this example, it's very easy to create a GUI and to handle events. Using these basic principles, we can create more complex user interfaces. But for that, we need to know some basic components offered by Java, and that's what we're going to explore in the next few sections.

4.2.2 Example: UI with Button, Text Field and Choice Menu

Purpose of the Program

This program creates a GUI consisting of a button, a text field and a choice menu. It handles events generated in any of these.

Concepts Covered in this Program

Here we show how multiple event listeners can be accommodated in one class. We also show how you can use the Choice menu.

Source Code

Ex1.java

```
import java.awt.*;
public class Ex1
{

   public static void main(String[] args)
   {
     UI1 myUI = new UI1();
     myUI.setSize(450,450);
     myUI.show();
   }
}
```

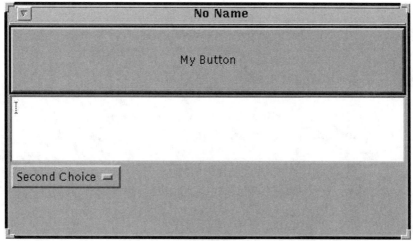

Figure 4-2

UI1.java

```
import java.awt.*;
import java.awt.event.*;

public class UI1 extends Frame implements ActionListener,
ItemListener
{
    Button b;
    TextField t;
    Choice c;
    UI1()
    {
        setLayout(new GridLayout(3,2));
        b = new Button("My Button");
        add(b);
        b.addActionListener(this);
        t = new TextField(10);
        add(t);
        t.addActionListener(this);

        /* Invoke our method addChoice() which will create a
           choice and add it to the GUI window */
```

```
        addChoice();

        validate();
    }
    public void addChoice()
    {
        /* Create an instance of Choice */
        c = new Choice();

        /* Add four items to the choice object. These will be
           the four choices from which the user can select
           one at a time */

        c.addItem("First Choice");
        c.addItem("Second Choice");
        c.addItem("Third Choice");
        c.addItem("Fourth Choice");

        /* Inform the runtime system that events for this
           choice will be handled by code written in this
           class */

        c.addItemListener(this);

        /* Add the choice to the GUI window */
        add(c);
    }

    /* This method is invoked by the event handling
       mechanism of Java when an event occurs on the choice
       */

    public void itemStateChanged(ItemEvent e)
    {
        Object arg = e.getSource();
        if(arg instanceof Choice)
        handleChoice(arg);
    }
    public void actionPerformed(ActionEvent e)
```

```java
{
   Object arg = e.getSource();
   if(arg instanceof Button)
   {
      handleButtons(arg);
   }
   if(arg instanceof TextField)
   {
      handleTextFields(arg);
   }
}
public void handleChoice(Object arg)
{
   String value;
   /* If the event has occurred on the choice "c",
      determine which of its items was selected by the
      user */

   if(arg == c)
   {
      /* getSelectedIndex() returns the index position of
         the selected item. getItem() returns the string
         associated with this index position */

      value = c.getItem(c.getSelectedIndex());

      System.out.println("Selected :" + value);
   }
}
public void handleTextFields(Object arg)
{
   String textWritten;
   if(arg == t)
   {
      textWritten = t.getText();
      System.out.println("Text entered in text field :" +
                          textWritten);
   }
}
```

```
public void handleButtons(Object arg)
{
   if(arg == b)
   {
      b.setEnabled(false);
   }
}
}
```

Implementation

This example is an extension of the previous example. It has one more UI component in it, the Choice menu. This is a type of menu in which you can select only one item. Look at Figure 4-2 to see how it looks: like a button with text on it. If you click on it, a menu appears from which you can select one item. The name of the selected item will be displayed as the new text on the choice button.

If you look at the chart at the end of this chapter, you'll notice that a Choice menu isn't handled by an ActionListener. Events here are listened to by ItemListener. And since we're doing event handling for buttons and text fields also within the class UI1, we need to implement two interfaces, so that events for all three types of components are handled. So the declaration of the class looks like this:

public class UI1 extends Frame implements ActionListener,
ItemListener

The Choice menu is defined in the class Choice. Its implementation is in `java.awt.Choice.java`. So we first declare an object of the type Choice:

Choice c;

Next, we change our layout to accommodate this new component. Our window will now be divided into three rows and two columns:

setLayout(new GridLayout(3,2));

Now we add the button and the text field, and then we create the Choice menu and add it. This is being handled by `addChoice()`:

public void addChoice()

We first create an instance of the Choice class:

```
c = new Choice();
```

Our Choice menu has four choices. We add each of them:

```
c.addItem("First Choice");
c.addItem("Second Choice");
c.addItem("Third Choice");
c.addItem("Fourth Choice");
```

Since the class UI1 itself is the event handler, we add it to the ItemListener's list:

```
c.addItemListener(this);
```

Now, if there's any event occurring in the Choice menu, the appropriate method of the ItemListener interface will be invoked. Take a look at `java.awt.event.ItemListener.java`. This interface also has just one method, itemStateChanged. This method is invoked if you select an item from the Choice menu.

In our example, every time the user selects an item from the Choice menu, we'd like to print it on the standard output. So we've created our own implementation of the method:

```
public void itemStateChanged(ItemEvent e)
```

This one is passed an ItemEvent Object from which we can derive the actual source of the event using the `getSource()` method. Then we call `handleObject()`, which prints out the selected item:

```
value = c.getItem(c.getSelectedIndex());
System.out.println("Selected :" + value);
```

To determine which of the choices was selected we first get the index of the selected choice (i.e., whether it's the first item from the top or the second, and so on). This is done by using the `getSelectedIndex()` method of Choice. We derive the label associated with this item using the `getItem()` method. This is then printed on the standard output.

If you take a look at `Button.java`, `Choice.java` or `Text.java`, you'll see that there are a lot of methods defined in these classes which allow us to do a lot of operations on them. For every basic GUI object you should thoroughly study the Java file in which it is defined to see what all capabilities are offered by it.

4.2.3 Example: Panels and Popup Menus

Purpose of the Program
This program shows how you can create panels and popup menus.

Concepts Covered in this Program
We show how panels can be used to split your GUI window into smaller windows, each of which is separately controlled. We also show how you can add popup menus to your GUI.

Source Code

Ex2.java

```java
import java.awt.*;
public class Ex2
{

  public static void main(String[] args)
  {
    UI2 myUI = new UI2();
    myUI.setSize(450,450);
    myUI.show();
  }
}
```

UI2.java

```java
/* Here UI2 itself is not adding anything directly to the
   GUI window except for two panels. It is these panels
   which add the visible components such as the button and
   the text field */
```

```java
import java.awt.*;
import java.awt.event.*;

public class UI2 extends Frame
{
   public Button b;
   public TextField t;
   public FirstPanel p1;
   public SecondPanel p2;
   Choice c;
   UI2()
   {
      setLayout(new GridLayout(2,1));

      /* Create the first panel. */
      p1 = new FirstPanel(this);

      /* Add the first panel to the GUI window */
      add(p1);

      p2 = new SecondPanel(this);
      add(p2);
      validate();
   }
}

class FirstPanel extends Panel implements ActionListener
{
   UI2 myUI;
   public PopupMenu pm1;
   public PopupMenu pm2;
   public MenuItem pm1_1, pm1_2, pm2_1, pm2_2;
   FirstPanel(UI2 myUI)
   {
      this.myUI = myUI;
      createTheGUI();
   }
   public void createTheGUI()
   {
```

```
/* Create instances of two PopupMenu classes. The
first one will have "First Menu" on the title bar */

pm1 = new PopupMenu("First Menu");

pm2 = new PopupMenu("Second Menu");

/* Add items to the menus. For example, if the user
   clicks on "First Menu", two choices will be
   displayed, out of which one can be selected. These
   choices are "First Menu First Choice" and "First
   Menu Second Choice" */

pm1_1 = new MenuItem("First Menu First Choice");

pm1_2 = new MenuItem("First Menu Second Choice");

pm2_1 = new MenuItem("Second Menu First Choice");
pm2_2 = new MenuItem("Second Menu Second Choice");

/* Events are associated with menu items. We're
   informing the system that if an event occurs on
   any of these menu items the appropriate methods in
   this class should be invoked and they will handle
   it. */

pm1_1.addActionListener(this);
pm1_2.addActionListener(this);
pm2_1.addActionListener(this);
pm2_2.addActionListener(this);

/* Make the second menu item of the second menu
   disabled. It will be grayed out and users won't be
   able to select it */
pm2_2.setEnabled(false);

pm1.add(pm1_1);
pm1.add(pm1_2);
pm2.add(pm2_1);
```

```
      pm2.add(pm2_2);
      pm1.addActionListener(this);
      pm2.addActionListener(this);

      /* Add the popup menus to the GUI window. Note that
         they won't be visible yet. */

      add(pm1);
      add(pm2);
   }
   /* This method will be invoked when a menu item is
      selected */

public void actionPerformed(ActionEvent e)
{
   Object source = e.getSource();
   if(source instanceof MenuItem)
   {
      handleMenuItems(e, (MenuItem)source);
   }
}
public void handleMenuItems(ActionEvent e, MenuItem
source)
{
   /* Get the String corresponding to the selected menu
      item and print it on the standard output */

   String selected = source.getLabel();
   System.out.println("String Selected is : " +
   selected);
   }
}

class SecondPanel extends Panel implements ActionListener
{
   UI2 myUI;
   public Button b;
   SecondPanel(UI2 myUI)
```

```
        {
            this.myUI = myUI;
            createTheGUI();
        }
        void createTheGUI()
        {
            /* Add a button to the second panel */

            b = new Button("Click to see a Popup Menu");
            add(b);
            b.addActionListener(this);
        }


        /* This method will be invoked when the button of the
           second panel is clicked. In this case we will make
           the two popup menus visible */

        public void actionPerformed(ActionEvent e)
        {

            /* Show the first popup menu at location 0,0 */
            myUI.p1.pm1.show(myUI.p1, 0, 0);

            /* Show the second popup menu at location 180,0 */

            myUI.p1.pm2.show(myUI.p1, 180, 0);
        }
}
```

Implementation

Frame UI2 is split into two parts, each containing a panel. The popup menu is being added to the first panel, while a button is being added to the second panel.

A popup menu is a menu which is not initially available — it pops up in response to a user action, and once an item has been selected from it, the popup menu disappears.

A panel is a class that allows you to split your main GUI window into smaller sections. Each of these sections can use its own layout manager.

In our program, a button gets displayed in the second panel. If this button is clicked, the popup menu is displayed in the first panel. The item which is selected from this popup menu is written on the standard output.

At the top of UI2, we're creating the panels. (Note that this class doesn't implement any of the Listener interfaces. This is because event handling is being done in the individual panels):

```
p1 = new FirstPanel(this);
....
p2 = new SecondPanel(this);
```

We have created classes FirstPanel and SecondPanel, which extend Panel. Their instances are being created above and added to our Frame UI2.

Now let's take a look at the individual panels.

FirstPanel, as you can see, extends the Panel class. We're going to add the popup menu to this. The events generated by the popup menu are handled by the ActionListener, so we make this class implement the ItemListener interface:

```
class FirstPanel extends Panel implements ActionListener
```

We're creating two popup menus: pm1 and pm2. Each of these menus has two items in it. pm1 has pm1_1 and pm1_2, and pm2 has pm2_1 and pm2_2. To create the popup menu, we instantiate the PopupMenu class:

```
pm1 = new PopupMenu("First Menu");
```

A new popup menu item is created by instantiating MenuItem:

```
pm1_1 = new MenuItem("First Menu First Choice");
```

Events will be occurring on these menu items rather than on the popup menu. So we register the menu item with the action listener, specifying that this panel will be handling the events (i.e., the panel implements the required interface):

```
pm1_1.addActionListener(this);
```

Then the item is added to the popup menu:

```
pm1.add(pm1_1);
```

These steps are repeated for each of the menu items. Then the popup menus are themselves added to the panel:

```
add(pm1);
```

In addition, we're disabling pm2_2 just to show that a menu item can be disabled:

```
pm2_2.setEnabled(false);
```

Note that the popup menu will not yet be visible. Some other method needs to explicitly instruct the Java runtime system to make it visible.

To handle the events, we have implemented the interface ActionListener. In the implementation of actionPerformed(), which will be invoked if a menu item is selected, we check to see if the event source is a MenuItem and, if it is, handleMenuItems() is called.

This method gets the label associated with the menu item and prints it on the standard output:

```
String selected = source.getLabel();
```

The second panel contains a button. The panel is added to the ActionListener associated with it. When the button is clicked, we cause the menu to be shown by invoking the show() method:

```
myUI.p1.pm1.show(myUI.p1, 0, 0);
```

Here myUI is a handle to the instance of the UI2 class in which the panels are defined. p1 is the panel in which the popup menus are present. pm1 is the first popup menu. So the above statement means "display the menu pm1 which belongs to the panel p1 that is part of the frame myUI". 0,0 are the coordinates at which the popup menu appears, relative to the top left corner of the panel to which it is attached. We're showing the second popup menu at location 180, 0.

4.3 More GUI Components

Let us now look at some more GUI components. Once you start writing your GUIs you will find these examples very useful.

4.3.1 Example: Some GUI Components

Purpose of the Program
In this example we're creating quite a few GUI components, such as checkboxes, labels, radio buttons and lists.

Concepts Covered in this Program
We introduce some more GUI components in this example.

Source Code

Ex3.java

```
import java.awt.*;
public class Ex3
{

   public static void main(String[] args)
   {
     UI3 myUI = new UI3();
     myUI.setSize(450,450);
     myUI.show();
   }
}
```

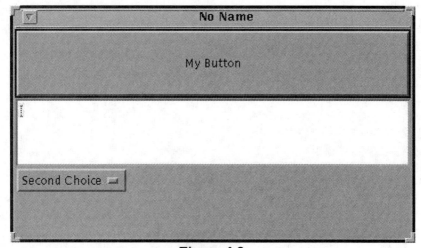

Figure 4-3

UI3.java

```java
import java.awt.*;
import java.awt.event.*;
public class UI3 extends Frame
{
  public FirstCBPanel cb1;
  public SecondCBPanel cb2;
  public ListPanel l1;
  UI3()
  {
    setLayout(new GridLayout(3,1));
    cb1 = new FirstCBPanel(this);
    cb2 = new SecondCBPanel(this);
    add(cb1);
    add(cb2);
    l1 = new ListPanel(this);
    add(l1);
    validate();
  }
}


/* This class will add two checkboxes to the GUI and will
   also manage events occurring on them */

class FirstCBPanel extends Panel implements ItemListener
{
  UI3 myUI;
  public Checkbox c1, c2;
  FirstCBPanel(UI3 myUI)
  {
    this.myUI = myUI;
    createTheGUI();
  }
  void createTheGUI()
  {
    /* Create a label and add it to the panel */
    add(new Label("Multiple Select"));
```

```
/* Create and add two checkboxes and inform the
   system that event handling code is written in this
   class itself. The first box will have the name
   "First Choice". */

c1 = new Checkbox("First Choice");
add(c1);
c2 = new Checkbox("Second Choice");
add(c2);
c1.addItemListener(this);
c2.addItemListener(this);
}

/* This method is invoked when one of the checkboxes is
   selected or deselected */

public void itemStateChanged(ItemEvent e)
{
   Object source = e.getSource();
   if(source instanceof Checkbox)
   {
      Checkbox localC;
      localC = (Checkbox)source;
      String str = "";

      /* The getState() method tells us whether the
         checkbox was selected or deselected */

      if(localC.getState() == true)
         str = "Checked";
      else
         str = "Unchecked";

      /* getLabel() returns the name of the checkbox */

      System.out.println("Current state of : " +
                         localC.getLabel()+ " is: " +
                         str);
   }
}
}
```

```
/* This class will also add two checkboxes. Unlike the
   checkboxes in the previous class which can both be
   selected together, in this case only one box can be
   selected at a time. If one is selected, the other is
   automatically deselected. This is radio button
   behavior. */

class SecondCBPanel extends Panel implements ItemListener
{
  UI3 myUI;
  public Checkbox c1, c2;
  public CheckboxGroup c;
  SecondCBPanel(UI3 myUI)
  {
    this.myUI = myUI;
    createTheGUI();
  }
  void createTheGUI()
  {
    add(new Label("Single Select"));

    /* Create a CheckBoxGroup. This will be passed as an
       argument to the constructor of the checkbox to
       indicate that the checkbox belongs to this group
       */

    c = new CheckboxGroup();

    /* Create a checkbox with the name "Choice 1" which
       belongs to the group "c". It is selected when the
       group first appears in the GUI window because the
       last parameter is "true". If another box of this
       group is selected by the user, it will
       automatically be deselected */

    c1 = new Checkbox("Choice 1", c, true);
    add(c1);

    c2 = new Checkbox("Choice 2", c, false);
    add(c2);
```

```
      c1.addItemListener(this);
      c2.addItemListener(this);
    }
  public void itemStateChanged(ItemEvent e)
  {
      Object source = e.getSource();
      if(source instanceof Checkbox)
      {
        Checkbox localC;
        localC = (Checkbox)source;
        String str = "";
        if(localC.getState() == true)
            str = "Checked";
        else
            str = "Unchecked";
        System.out.println("Current state of : " +
                        localC.getLabel() + " is: " +
                        str);
      }
    }
}


/* This will add a list to the GUI. The user can select
   any number of items from this list by clicking the
   mouse on the desired item. It will also add an exit
   button. If this button is clicked the program will
   exit.
*/

class ListPanel extends Panel implements ItemListener,
ActionListener
{
  UI3 myUI;
  public List theList;
  public Button Exit;
  ListPanel(UI3 myUI)
  {
      this.myUI = myUI;
      createTheGUI();
  }
```

```
void createTheGUI()
{
   setLayout(new GridLayout(1,2));

   /* Create a list with two items in it. "true"
      indicates that more than one item can be selected
      at a time */

   theList = new List(2, true);

   theList.add("First List Choice");
   theList.add("Second List Choice");
   add(theList);
   theList.addItemListener(this);
   Exit = new Button("EXIT");
   add(Exit);
   Exit.addActionListener(this);
}
public void itemStateChanged(ItemEvent e)
{
   Object source = e.getSource();

   /* If an item of the list is selected or deselected,
      the getItem() method of ItemEvent will return an
      integer object that can tell the index position of
      the item */

   Object it = e.getItem();

   if(source instanceof List)
   {
      String sel = "";
      String item = "";
      List localL = (List)source;
      if(it instanceof Integer)
      {
         Integer pos = (Integer)it;

         /* intValue() gives the int value of pos which
```

```
                  is passed to getItem(). This returns the
                  name of the item on which the event
                  occurred. */

             item = locaL.getItem(pos.intValue());
        }
        int change = e.getStateChange();
        if(change == ItemEvent.SELECTED)
            sel = "Selected";
        else
            sel = "Deselected";
        System.out.println("Item " + item + " was " + sel);
    }
}
public void actionPerformed(ActionEvent e)
{
    Object source = e.getSource();
    if(source instanceof Button)
    {
        Button ex = (Button)source;
        if(ex == Exit)
            handleExitButton();
    }
}
/* This method is called when the exit button is
clicked */
void handleExitButton()
{
    int[] fromList;
    String sel = "selected";
    String unsel = "unselected";

    /* getSelectedIndexes() returns the list of indexes
       of items which are selected at this point of time
       */

    fromList = theList.getSelectedIndexes();

    System.out.println("*********************************");
```

```
System.out.println("Items Selected from List are :");
try
{
    int i;
    for(i=0; i< 20; i++)
    {
        /* Get the names of items that have been
            selected */
        System.out.println(theList.getItem(fromList[i]));
    }
} catch(ArrayIndexOutOfBoundsException e){};
System.out.println("*********************************");
System.exit(1);
    }
}
```

Implementation

If you've studied the previous examples carefully, this one will be quite easy to follow (even though it looks intimidating). The only things we'll discuss here are the new things.

The frame has been divided into three sections, each of which is a panel. The first panel contains checkboxes. The second panel contains radio buttons. The difference between checkboxes and radio buttons is that you can select multiple checkboxes but only one radio button.

In the third panel we've put a list and a button. A list displays a number of items, one or more of which can be selected. Unlike the choice menu, it displays all the elements (or as many as it is allowed to), and you can select one or more items (this is modifiable by your program). When you press the exit button of this program, it displays the items selected from the list and exits.

So let's look at some of the newer pieces. In the first panel a label is created by instantiating the Label class. The string which is passed to it is displayed as a label:

```
add(new Label("Multiple Select"));
```

Then we create two checkboxes:

```
c1 = new Checkbox("First Choice");
```

The first panel needs to listen to events occurring on these checkboxes, so it implements the ItemListener interface. Inside the method `itemState-Changed`, we check which checkbox has been clicked, and we display its name and the state it is in:

```
if(localC.getState() == true)
.....
System.out.println("Current state of : " +
                   localC.getLabel() + " is: " + str);
```

The method `getState()` returns `true` if the checkbox is selected, otherwise it returns `false`. `getLabel()` gets the name of the checkbox. Note that our first checkbox is called "First Choice", and the second one is "Second Choice".

Radio buttons are also created using the Checkbox class. However, since we want only one to be selected out of many, we group all such checkboxes together in a CheckboxGroup:

```
c = new CheckboxGroup();
```

At the time of creation of the checkbox, we use the constructor of the Checkbox class, which allows us to specify which group the checkbox belongs to:

```
c1 = new Checkbox("Choice 1", c, true);
```

Here "c" is the checkbox group, "Choice 1" is the name of the checkbox, and `true` indicates that it is selected by default. Event handling for this is the same as that for the multiple select checkboxes of the first panel.

In the third panel, we're creating a list and a button. We first declare the list:

```
public List theList;
```

An empty list is then created:

```
theList = new List(2, true); // multiple select
```

`true` indicates that this is a multiple select list, i.e., you can select more than one item.

Elements of the list are then added to the list:

```
theList.add("First List Choice");
```

The panel is added to the ItemListener:

```
theList.addItemListener(this);
```

The method `itemStateChanged()` is invoked when an element of the list is selected or deselected. We can get a lot of information from the ItemEvent object that is passed as an argument to this method.

We first get the source of the event. This would be the list itself. Then we get the item that caused the event using `getItem()`:

```
Object it = e.getItem();
```

The item in this case would be an Integer object that reflects the position of the item which was selected or deselected. We're making use of the `intValue()` method of Integer to convert this to an `int` which we can use in the `getItem()` method of the list — this will give us the string corresponding to the item selected or deselected:

```
item = localL.getItem(pos.intValue());
```

We can also determine from the list whether the item was selected or deselected. This information is available by using the method `getStateChange()`:

```
int change = e.getStateChange();
```

Its value will be `ItemEvent.SELECTED` if a selection was made. Otherwise it was deselected.

In the event handler of the button we're using the method `getSelectedIndexes()` of a list. This returns the index of all the items that are selected at this point in time:

```
fromList = theList.getSelectedIndexes();
```

As you can see, the result is returned into an array of integers.

We then traverse this array of integers and print the string associated with the selected items. This is done by using the `getItem()` method, which takes the index of the required item as an argument and returns the string to which the item is tied:

```
System.out.println(theList.getItem(fromList[i]));
```

4.4 Dialog Boxes

Another important GUI component is the dialog box. This section teaches you how to create and use dialog boxes.

4.4.1 Example: Dialog Box

Purpose of the Program
This program shows how to create dialogs.

Concepts Covered in this Program
Here we show what a dialog box is and how one can be created/used.

Source Code

Ex4.java

```
import java.awt.*;
public class Ex4
```

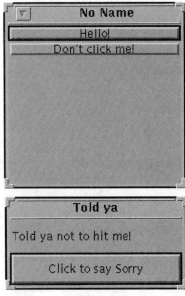

Figure 4-4

```
{
    public static void main(String[] args)
    {
        UI4 myUI = new UI4();
        myUI.setSize(200,200);
        myUI.show();
    }
}
```

UI4.java

```
import java.awt.*;
import java.awt.event.*;
public class UI4 extends Frame implements ActionListener
{
    public Button b1;
    public Button b2;
    public Warning w;
    UI4()
    {
        setLayout(new GridLayout(10,2));
        b1 = new Button("Hello!");
        add(b1);
        b2 = new Button("Don't click me!");
        add(b2);
        b1.addActionListener(this);
        b2.addActionListener(this);
        validate();
    }
    public void actionPerformed(ActionEvent e)
    {
        Object source = e.getSource();
        if(source instanceof Button)
        {
            Button b = (Button)source;

            /* If the first button is clicked, print a message
               else to bring up the dialog */
```

```
    if(b == b1)
        System.out.println("You clicked the Hello button");
    else
    {
        if(w == null)
        {
            /* If "w" is null, i.e., an instance of
               Warning  has not been created,
               instantiate it */

            w = new Warning(this, "Told ya");
        }

        /* Make the dialog box visible */
        w.show();
    }
}
}
}
```

Warning.java

```
import java.awt.*;
import java.awt.event.*;
public class Warning extends Dialog implements
ActionListener
{

    public Button b;
    Warning(UI4 par, String titleString)
    {
        /* super() invokes the constructor of Dialog.
           titleString is the string which will be displayed
           in the title bar. The last parameter is "true",
           indicating the dialog box is modal */

        super(par, titleString, true);

        setLayout(new GridLayout(2,1));
```

```
    /* Add a label and a button to the dialog window */

    add(new Label("Told ya not to hit me!"));
    b = new Button("Click to say Sorry");
    add(b);
    b.addActionListener(this);

    /* Set the size of the dialog window 200x100 */
    setSize(200,100);
  }

/* This method will be invoked when the button in the
   dialog window is clicked. When this button is
   clicked, our code will hide the dialog window. */

public void actionPerformed(ActionEvent e)
{
    Object source = e.getSource();
    if(source instanceof Button)
    {
        /* Hide the dialog window */
        if(source == b)
            setVisible(false);
    }
  }
}
```

Implementation

A dialog box is a window that normally comes up in response to a user action, as shown in Figure 4-4. For example, a warning dialog box may come up if the user has done something illegal, or a window with a text entry field may come up under certain circumstances. The bottom line is that normal dialog boxes are those windows you wish to display temporarily only under certain circumstances.

Let us see how and when our program creates a dialog box. The code is present in three Java files: Ex4.java, UI4.java, and Warning.java. Ex4.java is the top level file which instantiates our GUI frame. The frame is created in UI4.java. We're adding two buttons here. If you click the first button a message is printed on the standard output. If you click the second button, a dialog window is brought up.

The dialog box is implemented in `Warning.java`. This contains a button. If you click this button the dialog box disappears. The dialog window is declared in `UI4.java`:

```
public Warning w;
```

Here Warning is our class, which we've created by extending the Dialog class. If you look at the snapshot of this GUI shown in Figure 4-4, you'll notice that the buttons are thinner. The reason for this is that in our layout we're splitting the window into ten rows and one column. Each button goes into one row, and since the row heights are very small, the buttons also appear to be thinner:

```
setLayout(new GridLayout(10,1));
```

When the "Don't click me" button is clicked, we create an instance of the Warning class. Before that we make sure that we haven't already created the instance earlier — this is checked by seeing whether "w" is null or not. When no instance has been created, "w" will be null. Once we create an instance, "w" will point to it and will no longer be null:

```
if(w == null)
{
   w = new Warning(this, "Told ya");
}
```

Here, "Told ya" is the string that will be displayed in the title bar of the Warning window. The window created thus needs to explicitly show:

```
w.show();
```

This statement makes the window appear on the screen. The implementation of the Warning window is done in `Warning.java`. Note that this is like any other window. It has a size which is being set by using `setSize()`. It has a button in it. It also responds to button clicks.

However, we're creating the window by extending the Dialog class instead of the Frame class, as this is a transient window:

```
public class Warning extends Dialog implements
ActionListener
```

Our constructor takes two arguments: instance of the parent window (in this case an instance of UI4) and the title bar string. It then calls the constructor of the parent class (i.e., Dialog):

```
super(par, titleString, true); // Modal
```

"super" is a keyword which is used for calling the constructor of the parent of a derived class. In this case, the constructor `Dialog(Frame,String, boolean)` of the Dialog class will be invoked.

The last argument to this determines whether the dialog box is going to be modal or not. A modal dialog box is one which hogs the focus, i.e., you cannot do anything in the parent window until this dialog box is dismissed. If it's not modal, both the dialog box and the parent window (which created the dialog box) will be active at the same time.

In our case, we're creating a modal dialog box. So, while the dialog box is visible, you cannot do anything in the original window. Next, we're setting the layout of this window. It will contain one label and one button, so we create a layout with two rows and one column:

```
setLayout(new GridLayout(2,1));
```

Then the button and the label are added just like they are added to frames or panels.

The class is also added to the ActionListener. The window is then resized to 200x100 — so when this window is displayed, its size will be 200x100.

Since this class is catching events by implementing the ActionListener interface, it has to implement the `actionPerformed()` method. We want the dialog box to disappear when the user clicks the "..Sorry" button. We're handling this with the `setVisible()` method. This method hides the dialog box. If it's a modal window (like our example), control will return to the parent window:

```
if(source == b)
  setVisible(false);
```

4.5 Menu Bars

4.5.1 Example: Menu Bars and Mouseless Operation

Purpose of the Program
This program creates a GUI containing a menu bar, a list and a button. One of
the elements of the menu has a hot key associated with it.

Concepts Covered in this Program
In this program, we show how you can create menu bars and how a hot key can
be associated with menu items for mouseless operation.

Source Code

Ex6_6.java

```java
import java.awt.*;
public class Ex6_6
{

  public static void main(String[] args)
  {
    UI6_6 myUI = new UI6_6();
    myUI.setSize(450,450);
    myUI.show();
  }
}
```

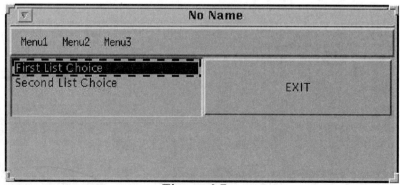

Figure 4-5

UI6_6.java

```
import java.awt.*;
import java.awt.event.*;
public class UI6_6 extends Frame implements ActionListener
{
  public ListPanel l1;
  MenuBar mb;
  Menu m1, m2, m3;
  MenuItem m1_1, m1_2, m1_3, m1_4;
  MenuItem m2_1, m2_2;
  UI6_6()
  {
    createMenu();
    l1 = new ListPanel(this);
    add(l1);
    validate();
  }

/* This method creates a menu. This is different from a
   popup menu because this menu is always attached to the
   GUI window (instead of popping up in response to an
   event) */

public void createMenu()
{
  /* For this type of menu you first need to create a
     menu bar. The menus will be added to the bar. The
     actual menu items will be added to the menus */

  mb = new MenuBar();
  setMenuBar(mb);

  /* Create a menu and add it to the menu bar */

  m1 = new Menu("Menu1", false);
  mb.add(m1);

  /* Add menu items to the menu */
```

```
m1_1 = new MenuItem("Menu1 Choice1");
m1_1.addActionListener(this);
m1.add(m1_1);
```

```
/* Choice 2 of menu 1 is being made sensitive to a
   hot key. If a modifier key and the "s" key are
   pressed, the effect will be the same as selecting
   this option using the mouse */
```

```
m1_2 = new MenuItem("Menu1 Choice2", new
MenuShortcut('s'));
```

```
m1_2.addActionListener(this);
m1.add(m1_2);
m1_3 = new MenuItem("Menu1 Choice3");
m1_3.addActionListener(this);
m1.add(m1_3);
m1_4 = new MenuItem("Menu1 Choice4");
m1_4.addActionListener(this);
m1.add(m1_4);

m2 = new Menu("Menu2", false);
mb.add(m2);
m2_1 = new MenuItem("Menu2 Choice1");
m2_1.addActionListener(this);
m2.add(m2_1);
m2_2 = new MenuItem("Menu2 Choice2");
m2_2.addActionListener(this);
m2.add(m2_2);

m3 = new Menu("Menu3", false);
mb.add(m3); // No Items in this menu

validate();
}
public void actionPerformed(ActionEvent e)
{
    Object source = e.getSource();
    if(source instanceof MenuItem)
```

```
       {
          MenuItem m = (MenuItem)source;

          /* Print the name of menu item selected */
          System.out.println("Selected " + m.getLabel());
       }
    }
}


class ListPanel extends Panel implements ItemListener,
ActionListener
{
  UI6_6 myUI;
  public List theList;
  public Button Exit;
  ListPanel(UI6_6 myUI)
  {
     this.myUI = myUI;
     createTheGUI();
  }
  void createTheGUI()
  {
     setLayout(new GridLayout(1,2));
     theList = new List(2, true); // multiple select
     theList.add("First List Choice");
     theList.add("Second List Choice");
     add(theList);
     theList.addItemListener(this);
     Exit = new Button("EXIT");
     add(Exit);
     Exit.addActionListener(this);
  }
  public void itemStateChanged(ItemEvent e)
  {
     Object source = e.getSource();
     Object it = e.getItem();
     if(source instanceof List)
     {
        String sel = "";
```

```
    String item = "";
    List localL = (List)source;
    if(it instanceof Integer)
    {
        Integer pos = (Integer)it;
        item = localL.getItem(pos.intValue());
    }
    int change = e.getStateChange();
    if(change == ItemEvent.SELECTED)
        sel = "Selected";
    else
        sel = "Deselected";
    System.out.println("Item " + item + " was " + sel);
    }
}
public void actionPerformed(ActionEvent e)
{
  Object source = e.getSource();
  if(source instanceof Button)
  {
    Button ex = (Button)source;
    if(ex == Exit)
        handleExitButton();
  }
}
void handleExitButton()
{
  int[] fromList;
  String sel = "selected";
  String unsel = "unselected";
  fromList = theList.getSelectedIndexes();
  System.out.println("*********************************");
  System.out.println("Items Selected from List are :");
  try
  {
    int i;
    for(i=0; i< 20; i++)
    {
        System.out.println(theList.getItem(fromList[i]));
```

```
      }
   } catch(ArrayIndexOutOfBoundsException e){};
   System.out.println("********************************")
   ;
   System.exit(1);
  }
 }
```

Implementation

In this example we're creating a menu which is attached to the top of the frame. We're also adding a list and a button to this GUI. A menu is different from a popup menu bar because it is permanently attached to the frame (instead of popping up in response to a particular user action).

When you select a menu item, a message is printed on the standard output, saying which menu item was selected. If you select or deselect a list item, again a message is printed. If the exit button is pressed, all the items that were selected from the list are printed out.

A complete menu consists of the following three components: a menu bar, menus which are attached to the menu bar, and menu items, which are actual selectable items of the menu.

Our program first declares variables which will hold these items:

```
MenuBar mb;
Menu m1, m2, m3;
MenuItem m1_1, m1_2, m1_3, m1_4;
MenuItem m2_1, m2_2;
```

The menu bar will automatically attach to the top of the frame. We're creating a list through the class ListPanel.

Let's see how the menu is created. We first create an instance of the menu bar:

```
mb = new MenuBar();
```

And then inform the system that we're using this menu bar:

```
setMenuBar(mb);
```

Next we create two menus and add them to this menu bar:

```
m1 = new Menu("Menu1", false);
mb.add(m1);
```

These menus need to get items. We create these using the MenuItem class:

```
m1_1 = new MenuItem("Menu1 Choice1");
```

When a menu item is clicked, the ActionListener is invoked. Using this we can determine which item was selected. Each menu item needs to register with the ActionListener. In this case, the class UI6_6 is going to handle events on the menu, so we're adding it to the listener:

```
m1_1.addActionListener(this);
```

The menu item is then added to the menu:

```
m1.add(m1_1);
```

But for menu item 2 of the first menu we're using a hot key, "s". This means that this menu item can be selected by pressing a set of keys (it will work through a mouse click also, but the approach we're using allows mouseless operation):

```
m1_2 = new MenuItem("Menu1 Choice2", new
MenuShortcut('s'));
```

Here, by supplying the argument MenuShortcut('s'), we're telling the system that if the user simultaneously presses a modifier key and the key representing the letter "s" on the keyboard, this menu item should be selected.

So which key is the modifier key? It varies depending on the system you're using. In Motif and Windows, it's Control, whereas on Macs it's Command. This means that if you're running this program on Motif and press Control-s, this menu item will be selected.

Then we add the remaining menus and menu items. It's not necessary to add items to a menu. The third menu has no items in it. When a menu item is clicked, the method actionPerformed() is invoked. Using the getSource method, we can get the menu item from which the event was generated.

Menu items have a method called `getLabel()` which returns the label associated with the menu item. We're using this to print our "Selected..." message:

```
System.out.println("Selected " + m.getLabel());
```

Next, we're creating a button and a list in a panel. You've already learned about these two components, so we won't go into the details.

4.6 Event Handling

Haven't you seen one too many GUI components? In this section we digress a little bit to show how you can separate the event handling code.

4.6.1 Example: Separating UI from Event Handling

Purpose of the Program
This program shows how you can separate the code for event handling from the rest of your GUI.

Concepts Covered in this Program
Here we show how event handling can be separated from the rest of the GUI. This is very useful in developing large applications. It also introduces you to the concept of adapters.

Source Code

MainUI.java

```
import java.awt.*;
public class MainUI
{

  public static void main(String[] args)
  {
    UIWindow myUI = new UIWindow();
    myUI.setSize(450,450);
    myUI.show();
  }
}
```

UIWindow.java

/* This class creates the GUI window and adds all the
   components to it. However, it doesn't do any event
   handling. Event handling is being done by other
   classes, ActionEvt and FocusEvt. This class needs to
   make it clear to the event listeners that handling is
   being done by ActionEvt or FocusEvt, so it creates an
   instance of that class and passes it as a parameter
   when event listeners are being added for individual
   components. */

```
import java.awt.*;
import java.awt.event.*;

public class UIWindow extends Frame
{
   public Button b1;
   public Button b2;
   public TextField t1;
   public TextField t2;
   FocusEvt eListener;
   ActionEvt aListener;
   UIWindow()
   {
      /* Create instances of the classes ActionEvt and
         FocusEvt which implement the interfaces of the
         ActionListener and the FocusListener. */

      aListener = new ActionEvt(this);
      eListener = new FocusEvt(this);

      setLayout(new GridLayout(10,2));
      b1 = new Button("First Button");
      add(b1);

      /* Tell the FocusListener and ActionListener of "b1"
         that event handling code is present in eListener
         and aListener, respectively. */
```

```
    b1.addFocusListener(eListener);
    b1.addActionListener(aListener);

    b2 = new Button("Second Button");
    b2.addFocusListener(eListener);
    b2.addActionListener(aListener);
    add(b2);
    t1 = new TextField(10);
    add(t1);
    t1.addActionListener(aListener);
    t2 = new TextField(10);
    add(t2);
    t2.addActionListener(aListener);
    validate();
  }
}
```

ActionEvt.java

```
/* This class implements the ActionListener and handles
   all the events listened to by the ActionListener. */

import java.awt.event.*;
import java.awt.*;
public class ActionEvt implements ActionListener
{
  UIWindow myUI;

  /* We need to store a handle to UIWindow as all the
     variables containing handles to the components are
     defined in that class. We'll need these to perform
     actions on those components such as disabling a
     particular button, etc. */

  ActionEvt(UIWindow myUI)
  {
    this.myUI = myUI;
  }
  public void actionPerformed(ActionEvent e)
```

```
{
   Object source;
   source = e.getSource();
   if(source instanceof Button)
   {
      Button b = (Button)source;
      if(b == myUI.b1)
      {
         System.out.println("First Button clicked");
      }
      if(b == myUI.b2)
      {
         System.out.println("Second Button clicked");
      }
   }
   if(source instanceof TextField)
   {
      TextField t = (TextField)source;
      if(t == myUI.t1)
      {
         /* Print the text currently displayed by text
            field "t" */

         System.out.println("Text set in first field is :
         " + t.getText());
      }
      if(t == myUI.t2)
      {
         System.out.println("Text set in second field is
         : " + t.getText());
      }
   }
}
}
}
```

FocusEvt.java

```
/* This class implements the FocusListener and handles all
   the events listened to by the FocusListener. */
```

```java
import java.awt.*;
import java.awt.event.*;
public class FocusEvt extends FocusAdapter
{
   public UIWindow myUI;
   FocusEvt(UIWindow myUI)
   {
      this.myUI = myUI;
   }
   public void focusGained(FocusEvent e)
   {
      Object source = e.getSource();
      if(source instanceof Button)
      {
         Button b = (Button)source;
         /* Print label(name) of the button which has just
            gained focus */
         System.out.println("Focus gained by Button: " +
                                    b.getLabel());
      }
   }
   public void focusLost(FocusEvent e)
   {
      Object source = e.getSource();
      if(source instanceof Button)
      {
         Button b = (Button)source;
         System.out.println("Focus lost by Button: " +
                                    b.getLabel());
      }
   }
}
```

Implementation

Separating event handling code from the rest of the GUI is of great use when you're creating large applications and want your code to be well organized. In fact, we're making use of this approach in our complete example (in the chapter with the same name).

As you can see, the implementation spreads across four files: MainUI.java,

UIWindow.java, ActionEvt.java and FocusEvt.java. MainUI.java is the usual top level file which instantiates our frame. UIWindow.java creates the UI. The difference is that this UI itself is inert and the class defined in this file won't respond to any user event. The event handling is left up to two new classes, ActionEvt and FocusEvt, which we've created in the files ActionEvt.java and FocusEvt.java, respectively.

UIWindow creates two buttons and two text fields. It also declares variables for storing the ActionListener and the FocusListener that we'll be using (implemented in ActionEvt and FocusEvt):

```
FocusEvt eListener;
ActionEvt aListener;
```

Instances of these listeners are created:

```
aListener = new ActionEvt(this);
eListener = new FocusEvt(this);
```

The buttons and text fields are added to the frame by setting the layout to a grid layout with ten rows and two columns.

Next we invoke the addFocusListener() method for all the buttons and the addActionListener() method for all the text fields as well as the buttons. But we're not passing "this" as a parameter. This is because the class UIWindow is not handling the events (it doesn't implement any EventListener's interface). Instead, we're passing handles to FocusEvt and ActionEvt, as these are the classes that will be doing event handling:

```
b1.addFocusListener(eListener);
b1.addActionListener(aListener);
.....
t1.addActionListener(aListener);
.....
```

What this means is that all "Focus" events will be handled by the instance eListener and all "Action" events will be handled by the instance aListener. Note that the buttons are using both the FocusListener and the ActionListener.

Now let's take a look at the classes FocusEvt and ActionEvt. The class ActionEvt is defined in ActionEvt.java:

```
public class ActionEvt implements ActionListener
```

The constructor of this class takes one argument: the instance of the class UIWindow which is instantiating it. This is being stored for future reference:

```
this.myUI = myUI;
```

Here `this.myUI` is the instance variable `myUI` which is declared in this class. We can refer to instance variables using the "this" keyword. It is helpful in cases like this one where you have an argument whose name is the same as that of an instance variable and you want to distinguish which one is which. So, `this.myUI` means the instance variable `myUI`, and `myUI` is the argument that was passed to this method.

We've implemented `actionPerformed()`. When the user presses Return in the text fields, control will go to the ActionListener, which will route it to the method `actionPerformed()` in this class, ActionEvt.

Inside this, we check to see if the source was a button or a text field:

```
if(source instanceof Button)
{
    .....
}
if(source instanceof TextField)
{
    .....
}
```

If the first button is clicked, we need to display the message "First Button clicked". If the second button is clicked, we have to display "Second Button clicked". This means that we need to find out exactly which button caused the event. Here we'll make use of `myUI`, the handle to the instance of UIWindow that we stored above. Using this, we'll compare the source "b" with the buttons that are defined in UIWindow to see which one of them is the same as "b" and print the appropriate message:

```
if(b == myUI.b1)
{
    System.out.println("First Button clicked");
}
```

```
if(b == myUI.b2)
{
   System.out.println("Second Button clicked");
}
```

We're doing a similar thing for the text fields also. Take a look at FocusEvt now. Here we show another method in which an event handler can be defined. There is nothing too complex or too different about this from the method that we've been using all along. In this, instead of implementing an interface, we extend another class, known as an adapter, which implements the required interface.

So our class is declared as:

public class FocusEvt extends FocusAdapter

Note that we could as easily write "public class FocusEvt implements Focus-Listener". So what's the advantage of having adapters? If you're implementing an interface, you have to give an implementation (even if it's empty) for every method declared in the interface. This sometimes becomes cumbersome. For example, if you want to use the focus listener, but are interested in only the "Focus Gained" events and not in the "Focus Lost" events, you'd like to write code only for the "Focus Gained" events. But if you're using the FocusListener interface, you'll have to write a dummy focusLost() which doesn't do anything. This just makes the code messy.

However, in an adapter, dummy code has already been written. You can simply extend this class and provide implementation for only the methods you're interested in.

Look at java.awt.event.FocusAdapter.java to get a better understanding of what we're talking about here. Then look at java.awt.event.Mouse-Adapter.java to see an adapter containing several methods. In such cases, you may be more inclined to use an adapter rather than implementing the interface.

The rest of the implementation is along the same lines as before. We're storing the instance of UIWindow in an instance variable through the constructor. We've implemented the methods focusGained() and focusLost(), which will be invoked every time one of our buttons gains focus or loses it. We're printing a message telling whether focus has been gained or lost by the button. The name of the button is displayed by using the getLabel() method:

```
System.out.println("Focus gained by Button: " +
                b.getLabel());
```

4.7 Images in Applications

We've seen how images can be displayed in an applet. But there are times when you may want to use an image in an application. For example, you may want to add a background image to the GUI of your applications. (For instance, if you're a millionaire working for fun, in a demo prepared for the vice president of the company you could put the image of your boss dozing off in his office). This chapter shows how you can embark upon such ventures.

4.7.1 Example: Using Canvas for Displaying an Image

Purpose of the Program
This program shows how you can use Canvas in your GUI.

Concepts Covered in this Program
We show how you can create and use the Canvas class. We also show how an image can be loaded and displayed in a canvas.

Source Code

Ex5.java

```java
import java.awt.*;
public class Ex5
{

  public static void main(String[] args)
  {
    UI5 myUI = new UI5();
    myUI.setSize(200,200);
    myUI.show();
  }
}
```

UI5.java

```java
/* This class creates a GUI window containing two buttons.
   If the first button is clicked, an instance of another
   class (SplashScreen) which extends a Frame is created.
```

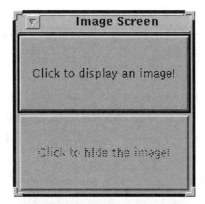

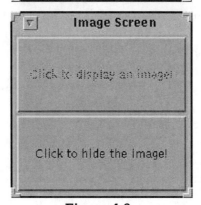

Figure 4-6

The splash screen creates an instance of a class (ImgCanvas) which extends Canvas. This class causes an image to be painted in the Frame of the splash screen. */

```
import java.awt.*;
import java.awt.event.*;
public class UI5 extends Frame implements ActionListener
{
  public Button b1;
  public Button b2;
  public SplashScreen s;
  UI5()
  {

    /* Set the title bar of the GUI window to "Image
       Screen" */

    this.setTitle("Image Screen");

    setLayout(new GridLayout(2,1));
    b1 = new Button("Click to display an image!");
    add(b1);
    b1.addActionListener(this);
    b2 = new Button("Click to hide the image!");
    add(b2);
    b2.addActionListener(this);
    b2.setEnabled(false);
    validate();
  }
  public void actionPerformed(ActionEvent e)
  {
    Object source = e.getSource();
    if(source instanceof Button)
    {
      Button b = (Button)source;

      /* If button "b1" has been clicked, display the
         splash screen which contains the canvas, disable
         "b1" and enable "b2". If "b2" has been clicked,
```

```
        hide the splash screen, disable "b2" and enable
        "b1" */

    if(b == b1)
    {
        if(s == null)
        {
            s = new SplashScreen();
        }
        s.setVisible(true);
        b2.setEnabled(true);
        b1.setEnabled(false);
    }
    else
    {
        s.setVisible(false);
        b1.setEnabled(true);
        b2.setEnabled(false);
    }
        }
    }
}

/* This class creates an instance of the canvas and adds
   the canvas to itself */

class SplashScreen extends Frame
{
  public ImgCanvas c;
  SplashScreen()
  {
    this.setTitle("Our Image Canvas");
    setLayout(new GridLayout(1,1));
    c = new ImgCanvas();
    add(c);
    c.setSize(ImgCanvas.width, ImgCanvas.height);
    setSize(ImgCanvas.width, ImgCanvas.height);
    c.setVisible(true);
  }
}
```

ImgCanvas.java

```java
/* This class extends a canvas to which an image will be
   painted */

import java.awt.*;
class ImgCanvas extends Canvas
{
  public static Image im1;
  public static int width;
  public static int height;
  ImgCanvas()
  {
    /* Load the image that we wish to display in this
       canvas */

    im1 = Toolkit.getDefaultToolkit().getImage("rajiv.jpg");

    width = 190;
    height = 210;
  }
  public void update(Graphics g)
  {
    paint(g);
  }
  public void paint(Graphics g)
  {
    g.drawImage(im1, 0,0, width, height,this);
  }
}
```

Implementation

A canvas is simply a drawing surface. This can be used by GUIs for drawing images, writing strings, etc., as shown in Figure 4-6.

This program's implementation is split into three Java files: Ex5.java, Img-Canvas.java and UI5.java.

Ex5.java contains the main() method and it creates our frame, UI5. In UI5 we're creating two buttons. If the first button is clicked, an image will be displayed and the button will be grayed out, and the second button will be activated. Now if you click the second button, the image will disappear, the button will get deactivated, and the first button will again be activated.

Actually, when the first button is clicked, a new frame is created. This frame instantiates the canvas which is defined in `ImgCanvas.java`. The image is then drawn on this canvas. The other frame (which will contain the canvas) is defined in the class SplashScreen and is present in `UI5.java`. We first declare a variable "s" of this type:

```
public SplashScreen s;
```

Then we set the title bar of the main frame (which contains the two buttons):

```
this.setTitle("Image Screen");
```

The buttons are then added in a grid layout of two rows and one column. The second button is disabled.

The juicy part comes in `actionPerformed()`. When the first button is clicked we first check whether an instance of the SplashScreen has been created:

```
if(s == null)
```

If not, we create this instance:

```
s = new SplashScreen();
```

The splash screen is then displayed (this in turn will display the image). The second button is now enabled and the first one is disabled:

```
s.setVisible(true);
b2.setEnabled(true);
b1.setEnabled(false);
```

But if the second button is clicked, the splash screen is hidden:

```
s.setVisible(false);
```

The splash screen is nothing more than another frame. Here we declare a variable "c" of the type ImgCanvas, our class that extends the Canvas class:

```
public ImgCanvas c;
```

The title bar of this frame is set, and a new canvas is created and added to it:

```
c = new ImgCanvas();
add(c);
```

The canvas is resized and so is the frame itself. The size is determined on the basis of static variables "width" and "height" which are defined in ImgCanvas:

```
c.setSize(ImgCanvas.width, ImgCanvas.height);
setSize(ImgCanvas.width, ImgCanvas.height);
```

The frame then calls the setVisible() method of Canvas. However, note that this will have no effect until the frame itself is shown (by UI5, when the first button is clicked). ImgCanvas simply extends the Canvas class.

We're defining static variables "width" and "height" which will contain the width and height to which the canvas should be resized by SplashScreen:

```
public static int width;
public static int height;
```

Inside the constructor, we're loading the image. For this we're using the getImage() method of Toolkit (java.awt.Toolkit.java). Since this is a public non-static method, we need to get an instance of the Toolkit for using this method. For this purpose we're using another Toolkit method, getDefault-Toolkit() which returns a handle to the default Toolkit:

```
im1 = Toolkit.getDefaultToolkit().getImage("rajiv.jpg");
```

A canvas is very much like an applet in that it has a painting surface. It uses the methods paint() and update() pretty much as they're used in applets.

In our paint() method, we're drawing the image loaded above at location 0,0:

```
g.drawImage(im1, 0,0, width, height,this);
```

4.8 Layout

In this section we show how you can lay out your screens as you want. We introduce you to the most powerful layout manager, GridBagLayout. We also show

how this can be used in conjunction with another layout manager to achieve the best results.

In GridBagLayout we specify the position of a component by applying some constraints on it. For example, there are ways of specifying that the component should be left-aligned, or it should be to the right and bottom of another component, etc. Each of these constraints has a keyword associated with it.

We explain some of the main constraints in the paragraphs that follow. Don't worry if you don't understand them right away. Each of them is dealt with in the following examples. As you're going through the examples you should refer to this section so as to understand what each constraint means.

gridx and **gridy**: These are used to specify the row and column at the upper left of the component. The leftmost column and topmost row has gridx = 0 and gridy = 0. In the examples that follow, this constraint will be widely used.

gridwidth and **gridheight**: This is used to specify the number of columns and rows the component should occupy. By default they take up one row/column.

ipadx and **ipady**: This specifies the minimum size that the component will have. These values determine how much bigger than the default minimum size the component should be. If we specify ipadx = x and ipady = y, the minimum height will be (default minimum height + 2*y) and minimum width will be (default minimum width + 2*x).

weigthx and **weighty**: These mainly determine how the components are distributed. Their values range from 0 to 1. A 0 value will force the components to be clustered at the center, while a 1 will push them outward toward the edges of the screen.

anchor: This is used to determine which direction the component should be closer to — north, south, east, etc.

fill: This is used to specify how the component should adjust itself if the window is resized.

With this knowledge it should be easier to follow the examples. So, on with the show!

4.8.1 Example: First GridBagLayout Example

Purpose of the Program

This is an introduction to a powerful layout manager, GridBagLayout.

Concepts Covered in this Program

In this example we introduce you to GridBagLayout, which is a very flexible manager for layout of components on your GUI window.

Source Code

Ex6_1.java

```java
import java.awt.*;
public class Ex6_1
{

  public static void main(String[] args)
  {
    UI6_1 myUI = new UI6_1();
    myUI.setSize(400,200);
    myUI.show();
  }
}
```

UI6_1.java

```java
import java.awt.*;
public class UI6_1 extends Frame
{
  TextField t1,t2;
  UI6_1()
  {

    createText();

    /* Create an instance of the GridBagLayout manager
       and specify that this is the layout manager to be
       used. */
```

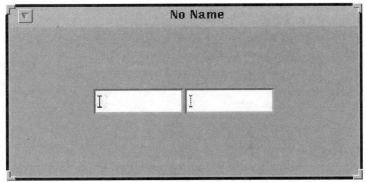

Figure 4-7

```
GridBagLayout g = new GridBagLayout();
setLayout(g);
```

```
/* Create an instance of GridBagConstraints which
   will be used for setting constraints that will
   help determine where a component is to be placed.
   */
```

```
GridBagConstraints g1 = new GridBagConstraints();
```

```
add(t1);
add(t2);
g1.weightx = 0.0;
g1.weighty = 0.0;
g1.gridx = 0;
g1.gridy = 0;
```

```
/* Specify that the constraints' list to be used for
   the placement of "t1" is in the instance "g1" */
```

```
g.setConstraints(t1, g1);
```

```
g1.gridwidth = GridBagConstraints.REMAINDER;
   // So its last component in row
g1.gridx = 1;
g.setConstraints(t2, g1);
```

```
    }
    void createText()
    {
        t1 = new TextField(10);
        t2 = new TextField(10);
    }
}
```

Implementation

Like all our programs until now, there is one class which instantiates the GUI window; in this case, it is Ex6_1. The GUI itself is created in UI6_1.

The GUI window contains two text fields, adjacent to each other in the same row, as shown in Figure 4-7. The text fields are at the center of the window. We could have used a GridLayout with two columns and one row. However, making the fields go to the center of the window would not have been possible. For this we're making use of another layout manager, GridBagLayout.

First, the text fields are created using a method defined in this class:

```
createText();
```

Next, we create an instance of the GridBagLayout class:

```
GridBagLayout g = new GridBagLayout();
```

And we inform the system that we're going to use this as our layout manager:

```
setLayout(g);
```

GridBagLayout is implemented in `java.awt.GridBagLayout.java`. Next, we create an instance of the constraints class. This will be used for adding the constraints to the components so that they can be placed as we want:

```
GridBagConstraints g1 = new GridBagConstraints();
```

The components are then added to the window. Note that they are still not displayed because we haven't `validate()`ed them. This means that we still have a chance of specifying the constraints. And that's exactly what we're doing next. We want our components to be clustered toward the center, so we specify `weightx` and `weighty` as 0:

```
g1.weightx = 0.0;
g1.weighty = 0.0;
```

The first text field should be below and to the right of the upper left corner. So its `gridx` and `gridy` are 0:

```
g1.gridx = 0;
g1.gridy = 0;
```

These are the only things we require for the first text field. So we set the constraints constructed above on it:

```
g.setConstraints(t1, g1);
```

Now look at the second text field. We want it to be clustered in the center. So we don't change `weightx` and `weighty`. But we want this to be the last component in this row. So we use a constant defined in GridBagConstraints — `GridBagConstraints.REMAINDER`. If `gridwidth` is set equal to this, it means that this should be the last component in this row. In other words, if another component is added after this, it can't come to the right of this component:

```
g1.gridwidth = GridBagConstraints.REMAINDER;
```

Note that you can set `gridheight` also equal to this to indicate that the component should be the last one in this column. We want the component to be in the column to the right of the first text field. This means that its `gridy` is still 0, but its `gridx` is 1:

```
g1.gridx = 1;
```

Now we attach the constraints to this component:

```
g.setConstraints(t2, g1);
```

Because of these constraints, the component appears as shown in the figure. Next, we vary some of the constraints to see how the constraints affect a component's placement.

4.8.2 Example: Playing with gridy, weightx and weighty

Purpose of the Program

This program varies some of the constraints set in the above example and shows how they affect component placement.

Concepts Covered in this Program

We're modifying `weightx`, `weighty` and `gridy` to show how these constraints affect the appearance.

Source code:

Ex6_2.java

```
import java.awt.*;
public class Ex6_2
{

   public static void main(String[] args)
   {
     UI6_2 myUI = new UI6_2();
     myUI.setSize(400,200);
     myUI.show();
   }
}
```

UI6_2.java

```
import java.awt.*;
public class UI6_2 extends Frame
```

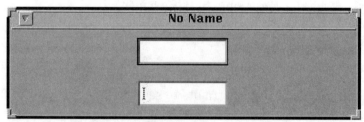

Figure 4-8

```
{
  TextField t1, t2;
  UI6_2()
  {
    createText();
    GridBagLayout g = new GridBagLayout();
    setLayout(g);
    GridBagConstraints g1 = new GridBagConstraints();

    add(t1);
    add(t2);

    /* Setting weightx and weighty to 1.0 pushes
       components toward the edges of the screen */

    g1.weightx = 1.0;
    g1.weighty = 1.0;

    g1.gridx = 0;
    g1.gridy = 0;
    g.setConstraints(t1, g1);

    g1.gridy = 1;
    g.setConstraints(t2, g1);
  }
  void createText()
  {
    t1 = new TextField(10);
    t2 = new TextField(10);
  }
}
```

Implementation

The code here looks similar to the previous example. So how come Figure 4-8 looks different than Figure 4-7? The answer lies in the constraints associated with the two text fields.

In this example, we don't want the components to be clustered in the center, we want them to be near the edges of the window. So we're setting weightx and weighty equal to 1:

```
g1.weightx = 1.0;
g1.weighty = 1.0;
```

Also we want the second text field to come below the first text field. This means that its `gridx` should be 0 (it's in the first column), but its `gridy` should be 1 (it's in the second row):

```
g1.gridy = 1;
```

4.8.3 Example: Using ipadx and ipady

Purpose of the Program
This one shows how the padding of a component can be modified.

Concepts Covered in this Program
In this example we show how `ipadx` and `ipady` can be used for modifying the size of a component.

Source Code

Ex6_3.java

```java
import java.awt.*;
public class Ex6_3
{

  public static void main(String[] args)
  {
    UI6_3 myUI = new UI6_3();
    myUI.setSize(400,200);
    myUI.show();
  }
}
```

UI6_3.java

```java
import java.awt.*;
public class UI6_3 extends Frame
```

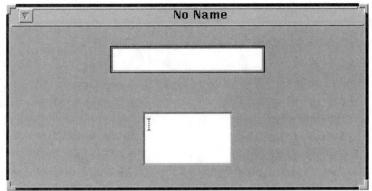

Figure 4-9

```
{
  TextField t1, t2;
  UI6_3()
  {

    createText();
    GridBagLayout g = new GridBagLayout();
    setLayout(g);
    GridBagConstraints g1 = new GridBagConstraints();

    add(t1);
    add(t2);

    g1.weightx = 1.0;
    g1.weighty = 1.0;
    g1.gridx = 0;·
    g1.gridy = 0;

    /* We're increasing the horizontal size of "t1" using
       ipadx */
    g1.ipadx = 70;

    g.setConstraints(t1, g1);

    g1.ipadx = 0;
    g1.gridy = 1;
```

```
      /* We're increasing the vertical size of "t2" using
         ipady */
      g1.ipady = 30;

      g.setConstraints(t2, g1);
    }
    void createText()
    {
      t1 = new TextField(10);
      t2 = new TextField(10);
    }
  }
```

Implementation

The implementation of this one follows the same lines as the previous example. But the first text field has increased in length while the second one has increased in height, as shown in Figure 4-9. To achieve this, we've used the ipadx and ipady constraints.

If you remember from the discussion of these constraints above, the numeric value assigned to these is multiplied by 2, and the resulting number of pixels is added to the default minimum size of the component.

In our example, for the first text field we're setting ipadx equal to 70. This means that its length will increase by 140 (70*2) pixels:

```
  g1.ipadx = 70;
```

For the second text field we want the length to be the original one, but its height should increase by 60 pixels. So we're setting ipady equal to 30 and ipadx equal to 0:

```
  g1.ipadx = 0;
  g1.ipady = 30;
```

4.9 Placing Components

In this section, we see more constraints that can be used for optimally placing components on your GUI window, including fill and insets.

4.9.1 Example: Using fill

Purpose of the Program
Here we display a text field which will fill the entire window horizontally.

Concepts Covered in this Program
This example demonstrates the use of the fill constraint.

Source Code

Ex6_4.java

```
import java.awt.*;
public class Ex6_4
{

  public static void main(String[] args)
  {
    UI6_4 myUI = new UI6_4();
    myUI.setSize(400,200);
    myUI.show();
  }
}
```

UI6_4.java

```
import java.awt.*;
```

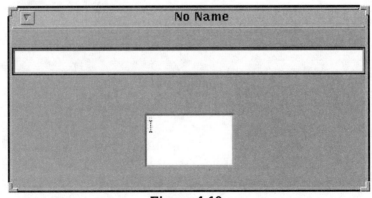

Figure 4-10

```
public class UI6_4 extends Frame
{
  TextField t1, t2;
  UI6_4()
  {

    createText();
    GridBagLayout g = new GridBagLayout();
    setLayout(g);
    GridBagConstraints g1 = new GridBagConstraints();

    add(t1);
    add(t2);

    g1.weightx = 1.0;
    g1.weighty = 1.0;
    g1.gridx = 0;
    g1.gridy = 0;

    /* The fill constraint is being used so that "t1"
       fills the entire screen horizontally */

    g1.fill = GridBagConstraints.HORIZONTAL;

    g.setConstraints(t1, g1);

    /* Resetting "fill" so that "t2" is not affected */

    g1.fill = GridBagConstraints.NONE;

    g1.gridy = 1;
    g1.ipady = 30;
    g.setConstraints(t2, g1);
  }
  void createText()
  {
    t1 = new TextField(10);
    t2 = new TextField(10);
```

```
    }
}
```

Implementation

In this example we want the first text field to fill the screen horizontally. If the window is resized, the text field should occupy the entire length. For this we set the `fill` constraint equal to `GridBagConstraints.HORIZONTAL`. This means that the text field should fill the window fully in the horizontal direction. This applies even when the window is resized:

`g1.fill = GridBagConstraints.HORIZONTAL;`

But we don't want the second text field to behave in this way. It should not fill the screen horizontally and should appear as it appeared in the previous example, as shown in Figure 4-10. So we need to reset the `fill` parameter back to the default:

`g1.fill = GridBagConstraints.NONE;`

If you want the component to cover the area both horizontally and vertically, you can use `GridBagConstraints.BOTH`. Now we extend the same example to show how the `insets` constraint can be used.

4.9.2 Example: Using Insets

Purpose of the Program

This program creates a GUI similar to the previous one, except that the first text field doesn't touch the screen's edges.

Concepts Covered in this Program

In this example we show how insets can be used.

Source Code

Ex6_5.java

```
import java.awt.*;
public class Ex6_5
```

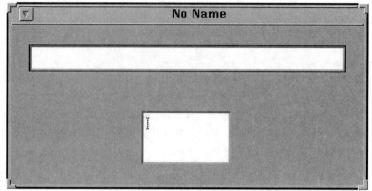

Figure 4-11

```
    {

    public static void main(String[] args)
    {
        UI6_5 myUI = new UI6_5();
        myUI.setSize(400,200);
        myUI.show();
    }
    }
```

UI6_5.java

```
    /* This one is different from Ex6_4.java because of the
       insets. Note that the first text field still covers
       most of the screen horizontally, but it doesn't touch
       the edges. This is because we have specified some
       padding for it using insets. */

import java.awt.*;
public class UI6_5 extends Frame
{
    TextField t1, t2;
    UI6_5()
    {

        createAndText();
```

```
GridBagLayout g = new GridBagLayout();
setLayout(g);
GridBagConstraints g1 = new GridBagConstraints();

add(t1);
add(t2);

g1.weightx = 1.0;
g1.weighty = 1.0;
g1.gridx = 0;
g1.gridy = 0;
g1.fill = GridBagConstraints.HORIZONTAL;

/* To provide a padding around "t1" so that it
   doesn't flow to the edges */

g1.insets = new Insets(20,20,20,20);

g.setConstraints(t1, g1);

g1.fill = GridBagConstraints.NONE;
g1.gridy = 1;
g1.ipady = 30;
g.setConstraints(t2, g1);
}
void createAndText()
{
  t1 = new TextField(10);
  t2 = new TextField(10);
}
}
```

Implementation

Looking at Figure 4-10 and Figure 4-11, it would take a connoisseur to determine the difference between the two. If you look carefully at Figure 4-11, you'll notice that although the first text field tries to fill the screen horizontally, it stops a few pixels short. It doesn't touch the edges of the window as the text field in the previous example did.

We're achieving this by using insets. Insets are specified by making use of the Insets class. An instance of Insets is created by passing the padding required above, below and to the sides of the component as constructor arguments.

Insets is defined in `java.awt.Insets.java`, and this is how the constructor looks:

```
public Insets(int top, int left, int bottom, int right)
```

In our example we want 20 pixels to be padded in all four directions. So we're creating an instance of the Insets class using these values and assigning it to the `insets` constraint for the text fields:

```
g1.insets = new Insets(20,20,20,20);
```

This prevents the fields from clinging to the edges.

4.10 Summary

This is a wrap-up of a lot of things we've learned up to now. Here we make use of a number of GUI components and two different layout managers to create a complex GUI window that looks like Figure 4-12.

410.1 Example: A Complex GUI Example

Purpose of the Program
This program combines a lot of things we've learned to show how various pieces can be integrated to achieve the desired output.

Concepts Covered in this Program
This program shows how we can use more than one layout manager to achieve better results. It also introduces you to another GUI component, the TextArea.

Source Code

Ex6_Final.java

```
import java.awt.*;
```

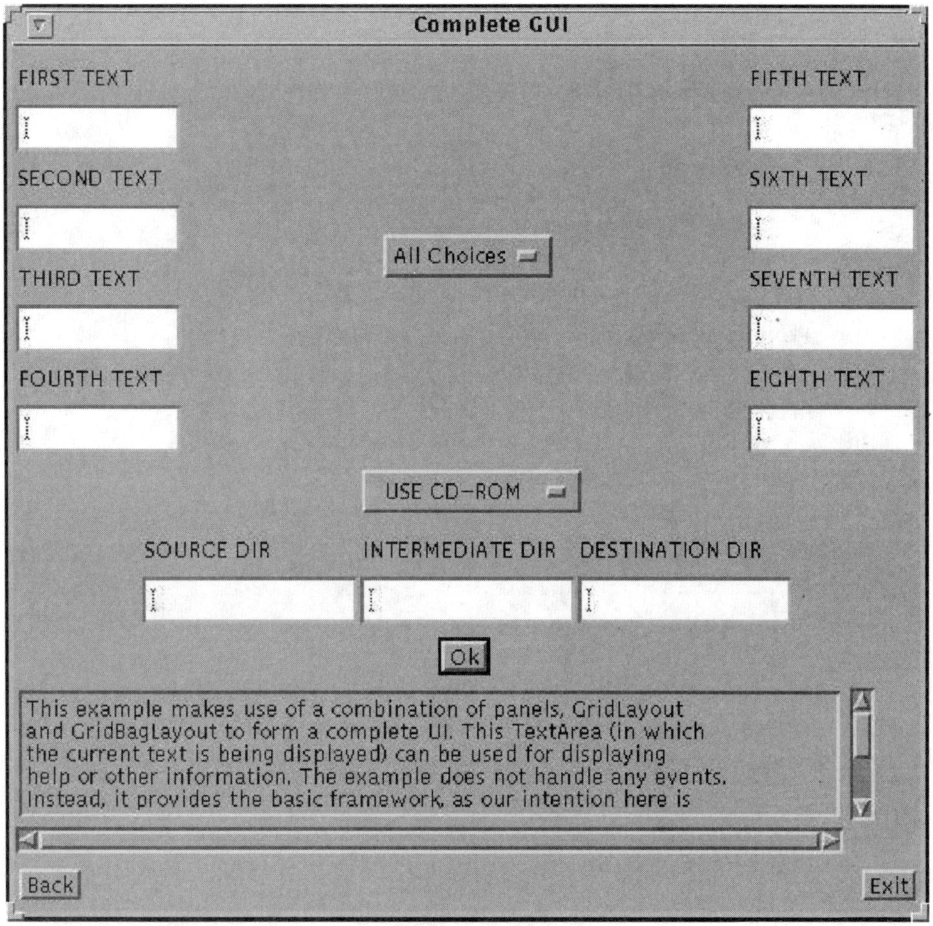

Figure 4-12

```
public class Ex6_Final
{

   public static void main(String[] args)
   {
      UI6_Final myUI = new UI6_Final();
      myUI.setSize(550,530);
      myUI.show();
   }
}
```

UI6_Final.java

```java
import java.io.*;
import java.awt.*;

public class UI6_Final extends Frame
{

  FourTextPanel f1;
  FourTextPanel f2;
  Button Back;
  Button Exit;
  Button Ok;
  ThreeTextPanel threeTxt;

  Choice NL;
  Choice InstallSrc;
  TextArea helpDisplay;
  char eolChar = '\n';
  UI6_Final()
  {
      this.setTitle("Complete GUI");

      /* Create text area which will display help */

      createHelpArea();

      /* Create two panels, each containing four text
         fields with labels above them. The last four
         arguments are the names of these labels */

      f1 = new FourTextPanel(this, "FIRST TEXT", "SECOND
          TEXT", "THIRD TEXT", "FOURTH TEXT");
      f2 = new FourTextPanel(this, "FIFTH TEXT", "SIXTH
          TEXT", "SEVENTH TEXT", "EIGHTH TEXT");

      GridBagLayout g = new GridBagLayout();
      setLayout(g);
      GridBagConstraints g1 = new GridBagConstraints();
```

```
/* Create the Choice near the middle of the screen
   */
createNLChoice();

/* Create another Choice list */
createInstallSrcChoice();

/* Creates a panel which will contain three text
   fields in the same row, one next to the other */

threeTxt = new ThreeTextPanel(this);

/* Add three buttons */

Back = new Button("Back");
Exit = new Button("Exit");
Ok = new Button("Ok");

g1.weightx = 1.0;
g1.weighty = 1.0;
g1.gridx = 0;
g1.gridy = 0;

/* Push f1 towards the WEST direction in its cell */
g1.anchor = GridBagConstraints.WEST;

g.setConstraints(f1, g1);

g1.gridy = 0;
g1.gridx = 1;
/* Push NL towards the CENTER of its cell */
g1.anchor = GridBagConstraints.CENTER;
g.setConstraints(NL, g1);

g1.gridy = 0;
g1.gridx = 2;
g1.anchor = GridBagConstraints.EAST;
g.setConstraints(f2, g1);

g1.gridy = 3;
```

```
g1.gridx = 1;
g1.anchor = GridBagConstraints.CENTER;
g.setConstraints(Ok, g1);

/* Create another instance of GridBagConstraints
   for the rest of the components. We could have
   used "g1", but all values set above that don't
   apply to the remaining components would have to
   be reset */

GridBagConstraints g2 = new GridBagConstraints();

g2.gridy = 1;
g2.gridx = 1;
g2.anchor = GridBagConstraints.CENTER;
g.setConstraints(InstallSrc, g2);

g2.weightx = 1.0;
g2.weighty = 1.0;
g2.gridy = 4;
g2.gridx = 0;
g2.anchor = GridBagConstraints.WEST;

/* helpDisplay should occupy 4 cells horizontally */
g2.gridwidth=4;

g.setConstraints(helpDisplay, g2);

g2.gridy = 5;
g2.gridx = 0;
g2.gridheight = 2;
g2.anchor = GridBagConstraints.WEST;
g.setConstraints(Back, g2);

g2.gridy = 5;
g2.gridx = 2;
g2.gridheight = 2;
g2.anchor = GridBagConstraints.EAST;
```

```
g.setConstraints(Exit, g2);

g2.gridheight = 1;
g2.gridy = 2;
g2.gridx = 0;
g2.anchor = GridBagConstraints.CENTER;
g.setConstraints(threeTxt, g2);

add(f1);
add(NL);
add(f2);
add(InstallSrc);
add(threeTxt);
add(Back);
add(Exit);
add(helpDisplay);
add(Ok);

/* Display the file HELP.doc which is present in
   the current directory in the help area */

displayFileInHelp("HELP.doc");

validate();
}


/* This method accepts the name and location of a
   file as input. It then displays contents of that
   file in the help area */

public void displayFileInHelp(String fileName)
{
   StringBuffer helpString = new StringBuffer();
   try
   {
      FileReader readFile = new FileReader(fileName);
      BufferedReader dataFile = new
      BufferedReader(readFile);
```

```
        String tempString;
        while((tempString = dataFile.readLine()) !=
        null)
        {
            helpString.append(tempString);
            helpString.append('\n');
        }
        }catch(IOException e)
        {
        System.err.println("Error in reading file " +
                        fileName);
        }
        helpDisplay.setText(new String(helpString));
}

public void createHelpArea()
{
    /* Create a text area with 5 rows and 60 columns */
    helpDisplay = new TextArea(5, 60);

    /* Make it impossible to edit the text area */
    helpDisplay.setEditable(false);
}
public void createNLChoice()
{
    NL = new Choice();
    NL.add("All Choices");
    NL.add("First");
    NL.add("Second");
    NL.add("Third");
    NL.add("Fourth");
    NL.add("Fifth");
}
public void createInstallSrcChoice()
{
    InstallSrc = new Choice();
    InstallSrc.addItem("USE CD-ROM");
    InstallSrc.addItem("USE TAPE");
    InstallSrc.addItem("USE NEW MEDIA");
```

```java
      }

}

   /* This class creates a panel containing three text
      fields with labels above them */

   class ThreeTextPanel extends Panel
   {
      TextField SourceDirTxt;
      TextField DestDirTxt;
      TextField IntermedDirTxt;
      Label SourceDirLbl;
      Label DestDirLbl;
      Label IntermedDirLbl;
      UI6_Final ParentOfPanel;

      ThreeTextPanel(UI6_Final Par)
      {
         this.ParentOfPanel = Par;
         createRemainingTxtFields();
      }
      public void createRemainingTxtFields()
      {
         setLayout(new GridLayout(2, 3));
         SourceDirTxt = new TextField(10);
         DestDirTxt = new TextField(10);
         IntermedDirTxt = new TextField(10);
         SourceDirLbl = new Label("SOURCE DIR");
         IntermedDirLbl = new Label("INTERMEDIATE DIR");
         DestDirLbl = new Label("DESTINATION DIR");
         add(SourceDirLbl);
         add(IntermedDirLbl);
         add(DestDirLbl);
         add(SourceDirTxt);
         add(DestDirTxt);
         add(IntermedDirTxt);
      }
   }
```

```
/* This class creates a panel containing four text
   fields with labels above them. The label names are
   passed to the constructor of this panel. */

class FourTextPanel extends Panel
{
  UI6_Final ParentOfPanel;
  TextField t1;
  TextField t2;
  TextField t3;
  TextField t4;
  Label l1;
  Label l2;
  Label l3;
  Label l4;

  FourTextPanel(UI6_Final Par, String FirstLabel, String
              SecondLabel, String ThirdLabel, String
              FourthLabel)
  {
    this.ParentOfPanel = Par;
    t1 = new TextField(10);
    t2 = new TextField(10);
    t3 = new TextField(10);
    t4 = new TextField(10);

    l1 = new Label(FirstLabel);
    l2 = new Label(SecondLabel);
    l3 = new Label(ThirdLabel);
    l4 = new Label(FourthLabel);

    /* The panel itself is making use of the GridLayout
       manager, dividing the panel's area into eight
       rows and one column */

    setLayout(new GridLayout(8, 1));
    add(l1);
    add(t1);
    add(l2);
```

```
        add(t2);
        add(l3);
        add(t3);
        add(l4);
        add(t4);
    }
}
```

Implementation

Since this is a wrap-up example (and a long one, too), we'll be giving only an overview. But we'll describe some of the new concepts in detail.

The screen has been split into several sections. We're making use of several panels. There's a FourTextPanel class. This class creates four text fields one below the other, each of them having a label above it. This class is being instantiated twice to form the two panels which contain four text fields each. These are the ones on the left and right edges of the screen. Between these two we've put a choice.

Below this there's another choice. Beneath this we're instantiating the ThreeTextPanel which creates three text fields in the same row. Then we have a button. Below this we have a text area. There are two more buttons below the text area.

At the top level we're using GridBagLayout. Using this, the two text panels are placed. The first one is in `gridx=0` and `gridy=0`, while the second one is in `gridx=2` and `gridy=0`. This is because we wish to place a choice box between the two panels and that will occupy `gridx=1`. We've set the weights equal to 1.0 so that the components don't clutter in the center.

Also, we're using the `anchor` constraint. This is being set to WEST for the first panel and to EAST for the second panel. Due to this, the panels are pushed toward the edges of the screen. It's set to CENTER for the choice box so that it moves as much to the center as possible.

The ok button is being added in `gridy` 3 and `gridx` 1 with a CENTER constraint so that it's below the two panels and is also centered. We're using a new instance of the GridBagConstraints for the remaining components.

The only important thing to be mentioned here is the `helpDisplay`, which is a text area. We're making this text area occupy four columns. This is why the text area appears so large.

So let's see how the text area is working. A text area is like a text field, but it can accommodate more than one line. As you can see, it has scroll bars on its sides so you can scroll the text.

We're declaring a variable to hold an instance of the text area:

```
TextArea helpDisplay;
```

The text area is being created in the method `createHelpArea()`:

```
helpDisplay = new TextArea(5, 60);
```

This text area will have 5 rows and 60 columns. Also, we want users to not be able to modify the text in this because we're using it to display help text:

```
helpDisplay.setEditable(false);
```

We're displaying text using the method `displayFileInHelp()`. This method takes the name of the file to be displayed as an argument. The file is read into a string, and then this string is displayed in the text area:

```
helpDisplay.setText(new String(helpString));
```

4.11 Java's Clipboard

In this last section of GUI we introduce you to a very new feature of Java: the clipboard. A clipboard allows transfer of data between applications (or within the same application). It is a space for holding data temporarily.

Normally a clipboard is used as follows. One application writes data to the clipboard. Then the same application or another application reads this data from the clipboard for its own consumption. This type of operation must be familiar to you; copy-paste is one of the most widely used techniques in computers (and one which often leads you into trouble — as one saying goes, "If you want to cover up a very stupid bug of yours, blame it on copy-paste").

Java allows you to create your own clipboard. It also allows you to use your system's clipboard. In our example, we'll show how you can use your system's clipboard to transfer data from one application to another.

Any kind of data that is to be transferred should be in the form of a transferable object. Transferable is an interface which is defined in `java.awt.data-transfer.Transferable`. If you wish to transfer a piece of data, the data must be stored in a class that implements this interface. This object will then be stored in the clipboard. Another application (or the same application) can then get this object from the clipboard. It will use the methods of this interface to get the actual data stored in this object.

The format in which the data is stored is known as a data flavor. A class that implements the transferable interface can store data in different formats (or flavors, using Java's terminology). When this data is extracted from the transferable object, the data flavor in which data should be returned needs to be specified.

The Java classes provide a number of basic data flavors. There is also a transferable class, StringSelection, which allows storage and retrieval of data in two flavors. We're going to make use of this class in our example. The class is defined in `java.awt.datatransfer.StringSelection`.

Let's look at the example now.

4.11.1 Example: Transferring Data Between Applications

Purpose of the Program
In this program we show how you can copy text written in one window to another through Java.

Concepts Covered in this Program
Here we show how you can use the system clipboard to transfer data between applications.

Source Code

From.java

```
/* This class creates a text area in which you can write
   some text. Then if you press the "Copy" button, the
   text you typed in will be stored in a buffer. Another
   application can request data from this buffer and use
   it. In our example, once you've pressed the copy button
   of this frame, you can press the "Paste" button of the
   class "To" — this will copy contents of "From" to the
   text area of "To". */

import java.awt.*;
import java.awt.event.*;
import java.awt.datatransfer.*;
public class From extends Frame implements ClipboardOwner,
```

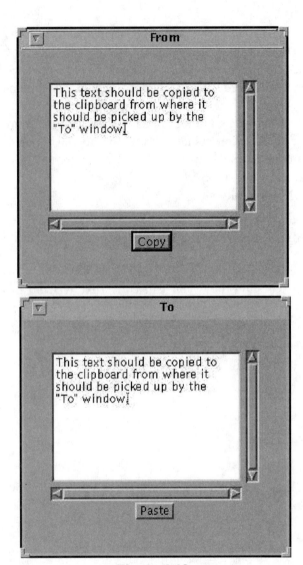

Figure 4-13

ActionListener

```
{
    /* Get a handle to the system clipboard. We'll be
       storing data in this. Other applications that need to
       retrieve the data can request it from the system
       clipboard. */
```

```
Clipboard sysBoard = getToolkit().getSystemClipboard();

TextArea txt;
Button copy;
String dataToCopy;
public static void main(String[] args)
{
   From myFrame = new From();
   myFrame.setSize(300,280);
   myFrame.setTitle("From");
   myFrame.show();
}
public From()
{
   GridBagLayout g = new GridBagLayout();
   GridBagConstraints c = new GridBagConstraints();
   setLayout(g);
   txt = new TextArea(10,25);
   copy = new Button("Copy");

   c.gridx = 0;
   c.gridy = 0;
   c.gridwidth = 3;
   g.setConstraints(txt, c);
   add(txt);

   c.gridx = 2;
   c.gridy = 1;
   c.gridwidth = 1;
   g.setConstraints(copy, c);
   add(copy);
   copy.addActionListener(this);

   validate();
}

/* This method is called when the "Copy" button is
   pressed */
```

```java
public void actionPerformed(ActionEvent e)
{
    Object source = e.getSource();
    if(source instanceof Button)
    {
        StringSelection transferData;

        /* Get the text that the user has entered in the
           text area */

        dataToCopy = txt.getText();

        if(dataToCopy != null)
        {
            /* Create a StringSelection object using this
               text */

            transferData = new StringSelection(dataToCopy);

            /* Put the StringSelection object in the system
               clipboard */

            sysBoard.setContents(transferData,this);
        }
    }
}
public void lostOwnership(Clipboard clipboard,
Transferable contents)
{
}
}
```

To.java

```java
/* This class creates a window with a text area and a
   "Paste" button. If you click the "Paste" button, any
   data stored in the system clipboard by a previous copy
   operation will be retrieved and written in the text
   area. */
```

```java
import java.awt.*;
import java.awt.event.*;
import java.awt.datatransfer.*;
public class To extends Frame implements ActionListener
{
   /* Get a handle to the system clipboard. This will be
      used for retrieving data written into the clipboard
      by another application */

   Clipboard sysBoard = getToolkit().getSystemClipboard();
   TextArea txt;
   Button paste;
   public static void main(String[] args)
   {
      To myFrame = new To();
      myFrame.setSize(300,280);
      myFrame.setTitle("To");
      myFrame.show();
   }
   public To()
   {
      GridBagLayout g = new GridBagLayout();
      GridBagConstraints c = new GridBagConstraints();
      setLayout(g);
      txt = new TextArea(10,25);
      paste = new Button("Paste");

      c.gridx = 0;
      c.gridy = 0;
      c.gridwidth = 3;
      g.setConstraints(txt, c);
      add(txt);

      c.gridx = 2;
      c.gridy = 1;
      c.gridwidth = 1;
      g.setConstraints(paste, c);
      add(paste);
      paste.addActionListener(this);
```

```
      validate();

}

/* This method will be invoked when the "Paste" button
   is clicked */

public void actionPerformed(ActionEvent e)
{
   String textCopied;
   Transferable transferData;
   Object source = e.getSource();
   if(source instanceof Button)
   {
      /* Retrieve the contents of the system clipboard in
         a Transferable object. */

      transferData = sysBoard.getContents(this);

      if(transferData != null)
      {
         try
         {
            /* Extract the contents of the Transferable
               object in String format*/

            textCopied =
            (String)transferData.getTransferData(DataFlav
            or.stringFlavor);
            txt.append(textCopied);
         } catch (Exception ex)
           {
            System.out.println("Error in getting contents
                        from clipboard");
           }
      }
   }
}
```

Implementation

The first class, From, creates a window containing a text area and a button called Copy. If you type some text in this and press the Copy button, the text is copied to the system's clipboard. The second class, To, creates a window containing a text area which is initially empty and a Paste button. If something has already been copied to the clipboard by the From class, this text is retrieved by To and is pasted in the text area when the Paste button is pressed.

A class that wishes to write to a clipboard must implement the Clipboard-Owner interface. This interface contains a method lostOwnership(). This method is called if another object gains the clipboard's ownership.

To write data to the clipboard, the method used is setContents(). This takes two arguments. The first is an object which implements the Transferable interface and the second is a handle to the object that is writing to the clipboard, i.e., the object that is the current owner of the clipboard.

Data is retrieved by using the method getContents(). This takes just one argument, the class requesting the data. It returns a Transferable object, the object put into the clipboard by the last setContents().

The From class is the one that is writing to the clipboard. So it must implement the ClipboardOwner interface. Also, copying to the clipboard is done when the user clicks the Copy button. This means that it needs to handle events. So we're implementing the ActionListener interface also in this:

```
public class From extends Frame implements ClipboardOwner,
ActionListener
```

We're making use of the system clipboard in our operation. For this we first get a handle to the system's clipboard:

```
Clipboard sysBoard = getToolkit().getSystemClipboard();
```

The main() method instantiates the frame, creating a text area and a button. When the button is clicked, we retrieve data from the text area:

```
dataToCopy = txt.getText();
```

But this data can't be directly written to the clipboard. As we saw above, the data that is to be written to the clipboard must be in a Transferable object. For this we're using a Transferable class that comes as part of the JDK: StringSelection. This class allows us to store string data.

The data which is written in the text area is first passed as an argument to the StringSelection class, which is defined in `java.awt.datatransfer.` `StringSelection.java`:

```
transferData = new StringSelection(dataToCopy);
```

This creates an instance of StringSelection. This class implements the Transferable interface. This means that we can store it in the clipboard using the `setContents()` method of Clipboard.

This transferable object is then written to the clipboard:

```
sysBoard.setContents(transferData,this);
```

Now look at `To.java` to see how this data is retrieved. Here we don't need to implement the ClipboardOwner interface as we'll just be reading from the clipboard. Once again here we're using the system clipboard, so we first get a handle to it:

```
Clipboard sysBoard = getToolkit().getSystemClipboard();
```

The screen with a Paste button and a text area is then created. When the button is pressed we first use the `getContents()` method to get the contents of the clipboard:

```
transferData = sysBoard.getContents(this);
```

This returns a Transferable object. This is the same object that was stored in the system clipboard when we pressed Copy in the first frame. Now we use the method `getTransferData()` to get the actual string we stored in this object. The method `getTransferData()` needs to know which format it should return the stored data in. For this we need to specify the flavor. It should be a flavor supported by the object. If you look at the Transferable interface you'll notice there are methods that tell you what flavors are supported by this object. For an implementation to see how this translates in an actual class, look at `StringSelection.java`.

Since we stored a string in the object and we want to retrieve it in the String format, we specify the corresponding data flavor, `stringFlavor`. This flavor is defined in `java.awt.datatransfer.DataFlavor.java`:

```
textCopied = (String)transferData.getTransferData(
        DataFlavor.stringFlavor);
```

The text thus returned is then written in the text area of the second frame:

```
txt.append(textCopied);
```

This wraps up our discussion of the clipboard. There's another feature of Java which is being developed on these lines, but is not expected to be released in Java 1.1: Drag 'n' Drop. This will allow items to be selected visually and dragged from one point to be dropped at another, pretty much like you drag and drop files/directories in a Windows interface.

Incidentally, this also wraps up the GUI chapter. By now you should be familiar with using several GUI components and should be able to write beautiful graphical interfaces. Though we wouldn't suggest putting the image of your dozing boss in the background — come on, we know you're not a millionaire!

CHART OF EVENT LISTENERS

Interface Name	Methods in Interface	Components which are handled by this Interface
ActionListener	actionPerformed(ActionEvent)	Button, List, MenuItem, TextField
AdjustmentListener	adjustmentValueChanged(AdjustmentEvent)	Scrollbar
ComponentListener	componentMoved(ComponentEvent) componentHidden(ComponentEvent) componentResized(ComponentEvent) componentShown(ComponentEvent)	Dialog, Frame
FocusListener	focusGained(FocusEvent) focusLost(FocusEvent)	Component
ItemListener	itemStateChanged(ItemEvent)	Checkbox, Choice, List, CheckboxMenuItem
KeyListener	keyPressed(KeyEvent) keyReleased(KeyEvent) keyTyped(KeyEvent)	Component
MouseListener	mousePressed(MouseEvent) mouseReleased(MouseEvent) mouseEntered(MouseEvent)	Canvas, Dialog, Frame, Panel, Window
MouseMotionListener	mouseDragged(MouseEvent) mouseMoved(MouseEvent)	Canvas, Dialog, Frame, Panel, Window
WindowListener	windowClosing(WindowEvent) windowOpened(WindowEvent) windowIconified(WindowEvent) windowDeiconified(WindowEvent) windowClosed(WindowEvent)	Dialog, Frame

CHAPTER 5

WORKING WITH STREAMS

If we had the luxury of discussing whatever we wanted, this chapter would surely have been dedicated to the art of river-rafting, both upstream and downstream. But then, in "Introduction to Java" we would have to discuss exotic coffees, and in "Threads" we would have to write about cotton, nylon, etc. So in the end we decided to come back to the shells to which software programmers are forever condemned and write something that was closer to reality — at least in our world.

5.1 Introduction to Streams

In this chapter we take you through a tour of streams. A stream can be considered an object used for manipulating a piece of data. For example, you can create a stream to read/write data from/to a file. Or you can create a stream to pass data between programs.

Our main focus in this chapter is on using streams to manipulate files. The last example shows a type of stream that can be used for communication between threads. The Networking chapter makes extensive use of streams for passing data from one program to another.

There are lots of streams offered by Java and you should take a look in `java.io` to see the various flavors that are available.

5.1.1 Example: Reading and Writing a File

Purpose of the Program
This program is invoked by passing the names of two files as arguments. It reads data from the first file and writes it to the other.

Concepts Covered in this Program
This program introduces you to file streams in Java and shows some of the methods used for reading and writing files.

To Run this Program

```
java ReadWrite1 firstFile secondFile
```

Here `firstFile` is a readable file that exists in the current directory and `secondFile` is the file to which output will be written.

Source Code

ReadWrite1.java

```
/* This program reads data from one file and writes it
   out to another */
import java.io.*;
public class ReadWrite1
{
  public static void main(String[] args)
  {
  /* Check the number of command-line arguments. The first
     one should be the name of the file to be copied, the
     second should be the name of the file to which it
     should be copied. */

    if(args.length !=2)
    {
      /* Incorrect number of arguments, so print error
         message and quit */
```

```
    System.out.println("You must specify two arguments:
                        the input file and the output
                        file");

    System.exit(1);
}
try
{
```

/* Create two File objects using the two command-line arguments. These will be used for creating input and output streams which we'll use for reading and writing to these files*/

```
File f1 = new File(args[0]);
File f2 = new File(args[1]);
```

/* Create the input and output streams using the File objects created above. We need to read from the first file so we're just creating an input stream around it. For the second one we only need to write so we're creating an output stream */

```
FileInputStream fis = new FileInputStream(f1);
FileOutputStream fos = new FileOutputStream(f2);
```

/* We'll be reading data from the first file one byte at a time into the byte buffer being created here */

```
byte[] buf = new byte[1];
```

/* Read data from the first stream one byte at a time into the buffer created above. When there is no more data the read method of the stream will return -1 */

```
while((fis.read(buf) != -1))
{
```

```
        /* Supply the buffer to the write method of the
           output stream so that this buffer gets
           written to the output file */

        fos.write(buf);
    }

/* Close the streams as we're done with them. */

    fis.close();
    fos.close();

} catch(FileNotFoundException e)
{
    System.err.println("File Not Found Error: " + e);
    System.exit(1);
}
catch(IOException e)
{

    System.err.println("I/O Exception");
    System.exit(1);
}
    }
}
```

Implementation

We first import the classes we will need. In this example we need classes from `java.io`:

```
import java.io.*;
```

In the `main()` method we check to make sure that the user has supplied exactly two arguments. If not, the program exits with an error message:

```
if(args.length !=2)
```

Here `args` is the parameter which has been passed to `main()`. Note that if you invoke a Java program with arguments, say, `java FirstArg SecondArg`

. . . ., these will be passed in an array of strings to the main() method and you can access them; arg[0] will be FirstArg, arg[1] will be SecondArg, and so on. We are using the length variable to determine the length of this array.

Once we have two arguments we can start the actual work. We begin by declaring two File objects:

```
File f1 = new File(args[0]);
File f2 = new File(args[1]);
```

The File class is present in java.io.File.java. This allows us to create an object which can be manipulated for reading and writing files. Now, f1 is associated with the first file, which we'll read, and f2 is associated with the second file to which we'll write the contents of f1.

But before we actually start reading and writing, we need to create other objects which contain methods for reading and writing. For the input file, we create a FileInputStream using f1:

```
FileInputStream fis = new FileInputStream(f1);
```

For the output file we create a FileOutputStream using f2:

```
FileOutputStream fos = new FileOutputStream(f2);
```

FileInputStream contains a method called read() which allows us to read an array of bytes from the file. FileOutputStream contains a method called write() which allows us to write an array of bytes to a file. So we first declare an array of bytes which will hold the data as it's read from the input file. This data will then be written to the output file. In our example, the size of this array is just 1 — you can modify it to a bigger size to get faster operations:

```
byte[] buf = new byte[1];
```

Then we use a while loop in which we read data from our FileInputStream fis into buf. The method read() returns -1 when all the data bytes have been read:

```
while((fis.read(buf) != -1))
```

Then we use the write() method of FileOutputStream to write these data bytes to the output file:

```
fos.write(buf);
```

Finally, we close the streams, as our work is done:

```
fis.close();
fos.close();
```

During this whole process, we can encounter errors, such as the input file doesn't exist or there is an error in reading or writing the files. For this, we're catching the corresponding exceptions that get raised: FileNotFoundException and IOException.

5.1.2 Example: More File I/O Streams

Purpose of the Program

This program shows how you can read/write a text file by reading and writing individual lines of text.

Concepts Covered in this Program

This program introduces you to the BufferedReader and PrintWriter streams which can be used for reading and writing strings to a file.

Source Code

ReadWrite2.java

```
/* This program reads and writes files one line at a time
   instead of one byte at a time as in the previous
   program */

import java.io.*;
public class ReadWrite2
{
  public static void main(String[] args)
  {
    if(args.length != 2)
    {
```

```
        System.out.println("You must specify two arguments:
                        the input file and the output
                        file");
        System.exit(1);
}
try
{
/* The BufferedReader class has methods for reading a
   stream one line at a time. It takes an object of
   the type Reader as its constructor argument, so we
   first create a FileReader using the name of the
   file and pass this as the command-line argument.
   Similarly, the PrintWriter has methods for writing
   output one line at a time */

    BufferedReader bis = new BufferedReader(new
                            FileReader(args[0]));
    PrintWriter pos = new PrintWriter(new
                            BufferedWriter(new
                            FileWriter(args[1])));
    String inpu;

/* The method readLine() reads one line from a
   stream. When it reaches the end of the stream it
   returns null */

    while((inpu = bis.readLine()) != null)
    {
        System.out.println(inpu);

        /* The method write() writes out a string to
           the stream */
        pos.write(inpu);

        /* The method println() prints out a newline
           character so that the next output begins on
           a new line */
        pos.println();
    }
```

```
        bis.close();
        pos.close();
    } catch(FileNotFoundException e)
      {
          System.err.println("File Not Found Error: " + e);
          System.exit(1);
      }
      catch(IOException e)
      {
          System.err.println("I/O Exception");
          System.exit(1);
      }
    }
}
```

Implementation

Here again we begin by importing `java.io.*` and by checking that two arguments have been supplied in the command line. Then we create the BufferedReader stream. If you look at the `BufferedReader()` constructor in `java.io.BufferedReader.java`, you'll notice that the constructor accepts a Reader object as an argument. Now look at `Reader.java` in `java.io`. This is an abstract class so we cannot create an instance of it to pass to `BufferedReader()`. But there are several classes that are of the Reader family, such as FileReader, and we can use those.

So, we create a FileReader object by passing the name of the input file as an argument. The resulting object is being passed to the constructor of the BufferedReader:

BufferedReader bis = new BufferedReader(new FileReader(args[0]));

A similar type of thing is done to create the PrintWriter. Here we're not using BufferedWriter as this doesn't have a method of writing out a string, so we create the PrintWriter stream on top of the BufferedWriter stream:

PrintWriter pos = new PrintWriter(new BufferedWriter(new FileWriter(args[1])));

As you can see, we can create one stream using another stream and we can keep doing so until we find a stream that implements the methods we require.

Next we use the `readLine()` method of BufferedReader to read the input file line by line:

```
while((inpu = bis.readLine()) != null)
```

The `while` loop will be terminated when the complete file has been read because at that stage `readLine()` will return a null.

We're printing the output on the screen:

```
System.out.println(inpu);
```

Also, we're writing the string to the output file:

```
pos.write(inpu);
```

The `write()` method doesn't put an end-of-line character. We're doing this with the `println()` method of the PrintWriter:

```
pos.println();
```

In the end, we're closing the streams.

5.1.3 Example: The skip() Method

Purpose of the Program
Read2 reads a data file line by line. It shows how a few characters can be skipped during the reading process.

Concepts Covered in this Program
This program shows you how to use the `skip()` method.

To Run this Program

java Read2 country.dat

```
Africa
Australia
Canada
```

Source Code

Read2.java

```
/* This program reads a file one line at a time. After
   reading two lines it skips one line and reads the
   fourth line instead */

import java.io.*;
public class Read2
{
  public static void main(String args[])
  {
    try
    {
      BufferedReader br = new BufferedReader(new
                              FileReader(args[0]));
      System.out.println(br.readLine());
      System.out.println(br.readLine());

     /* Using the skip() method you can skip a line from
        being read. This is the reason why the output
        shown above doesn't contain Brazil even though it
        is present in the data file country.dat */

      br.skip(7);

      System.out.println(br.readLine());
    } catch(FileNotFoundException e)
      {
        System.err.println("File Not Found Error: " + e);
        System.exit(1);
      }
      catch(IOException e)
      {
        System.err.println("I/O Exception");
        System.exit(1);
```

```
          }
       }
    }
```

DATA FILE *country.dat*

```
   Africa
   Australia
   Brazil
   Canada
```

Implementation

Here again we're creating a BufferedReader as we want to read the file line by line:

```
BufferedReader br = new BufferedReader(new
                          FileReader(args[0]));
```

Then we read two lines using the `readLine()` method and display them on the standard output. Next, we're skipping seven characters, using the `skip()` method. The result is that the file pointer moves forward by seven characters. In other words, when the next read is done, these seven characters are skipped. This is the reason why our output doesn't contain "Brazil" even though the file *country.dat* contains it:

```
br.skip(7);
System.out.println(br.readLine());
```

But wait a minute, the word "Brazil" contains six characters. So by skipping seven characters shouldn't the file pointer skip the "C" in Canada also? No, because the seventh character is an end-of-line character, which is present at the end of each line of the data file. You don't see this character if you view the file normally, but as far as the system is concerned, it does exist.

5.2 Data I/O Streams

Many times the need arises for reading and writing specific data types to a file arises. In the previous example we showed how strings can be read and written.

Here we will see how integers, doubles, characters, etc., can be written by making use of another set of streams.

5.2.1 Example: Using Data Streams

Purpose of the Program
We introduce you to DataInputStream and DataOutputStream through this example. The program Write1.java writes out certain data types to a file, while Read1.java reads that file.

Concepts Covered in this Program
DataInputStream and DataOutputStream are introduced, and we show how to use them for reading/writing.

To Run this Program
```
java Write1 <filename>
java Read1 <filename>
```

Source code

Write1.java

```
/* This program writes out primitive data types such as
   int and char to the output file. The program
   Read1.java, which is a counterpart of this, will read
   this file. */

import java.io.*;
public class Write1
{
  public static void main(String[] args)
  {
    if(args.length != 1)
    {
      System.err.println("Supply name of one file as an
                         argument");
      System.exit(1);
    }
```

```
    try
    {
        File f1 = new File(args[0]);

        /* The DataOutputStream contains methods for
        writing out primitive data types */

        DataOutputStream dos = new DataOutputStream(new
                                    FileOutputStream(f1));

        dos.writeInt(20);        // Write an int
        dos.writeChar('a');      // Write a char
        dos.writeDouble(5.11);   // Write a double
        dos.close();
    }catch(IOException e)
        {
        System.err.println("IO ERROR : " + e);
        System.exit(1);
        }
    }
}
```

Read1.java

```
/* This program reads the file written by Write1.java. It
    has to follow the same order in which data was written
    by Write1.java to get correct results. For example, the
    first thing that Write1.java wrote was an int, so the
    first thing that this should read is an int. If this
    order is not followed you'll get incorrect results. */

import java.io.*;
public class Read1
{
    public static void main(String[] args)
    {
        if(args.length != 1)
        {
```

```
      System.err.println("Supply name of one file as an
      argument");
      System.exit(1);
   }
   try
   {
      File f1 = new File(args[0]);
      FileInputStream f1is = new FileInputStream(f1);

      /* DataInputStream is the reader counterpart of
         DataOutputStream which we used above. This
         allows us to read primitive data types */
      DataInputStream dis = new DataInputStream(f1is);

      /* The available() method returns the size of the
         stream, i.e., number of available bytes */

      System.out.println("Size of the file is : " +
                         dis.available());

      System.out.println("Integer is : " +
      dis.readInt());                    // read int
      System.out.println("Character is : " +
      dis.readChar());                   // read char
      System.out.println("Double is : " +
      dis.readDouble());                 // read double
      dis.close();
   }
   catch(FileNotFoundException e)
   {
      System.err.println("Unable to locate file : " +
                         args[0]);
      System.exit(1);
   }
   catch(IOException e)
   {
      System.err.println("IO ERROR : " + e);
      System.exit(1);
   }
 }
}
```

Implementation

Let's first see how Write1 works. This program expects one argument, the name of the file to which data is to be written.

We create a File object using the first command-line argument, and then using this we create a DataOutputStream. The constructor requires an object of the type FileOutputStream, so we first create a FileOutputStream using the File object and pass it as an argument to the constructor of DataOutputStream:

```
File f1 = new File(args[0]);
DataOutputStream dos = new DataOutputStream(new
FileOutputStream(f1));
```

The reason we are creating a DataOutputStream is that it allows us to write specific data types such as integers, floats, characters, etc. There are methods available for writing these such as writeInt(), writeChar(), writeDouble(), etc. In our example, we're writing the following to the file: the integer 20, the character "a" and the double "5.11":

```
dos.writeInt(20);
dos.writeChar('a');
dos.writeDouble(5.11);
```

The DataOutputStream class which is present in java.io.DataOutputStream.java provides methods for lots of other data types such as Long, Float, Bytes, UTF, etc., and you can make use of them.

Finally we close the stream:

```
dos.close();
```

Note that writing can lead to an IOException, so we're catching it.

Now let's move our attention to Read1.java. This program has to read the data written out by Write1.java. Since there are specific data types which have been written by Write1.java, we need to read them in the same order in which they were written so as to get correct results. In other words, looking at the order in which writing was done in Write1.java, we need to read the data in the following sequence: read an integer, read a character, and then read a double.

This may seem cumbersome, but it works very well if you have a database with a uniformly repeated pattern. For instance, if we have a data file of a grocery store, we know that the data will be written in the following format:

```
<name_of_the_product (A String)> <price_of_the_product(a
                            Double)>.
```

In order to read the whole file, we can create a `while` loop which reads a string and a double alternately.

So, in our `Read1.java`, we first create a DataInputStream in the same way that we created the output stream:

```
DataInputStream dis = new DataInputStream(fis);
```

This program displays the size of the file by making use of the `available()` method:

```
System.out.println("Size of the file is : " +
                    dis.available());
```

Then we read an integer, a character and a double, and print them on the standard output:

```
System.out.println("Integer is : " + dis.readInt());
System.out.println("Character is : " + dis.readChar());
System.out.println("Double is : " + dis.readDouble());
```

After reading, we close the stream. We're also catching exceptions which might be raised: FileNotFoundException and IOException.

5.3 Pipe Streams

Pipe streams allow two programs to connect to each other and pass data between themselves. A pipe can be constructed between two threads so that they can communicate with one another. That is exactly what we're going to demonstrate in this example.

5.3.1 Example: Communication Between Threads Using Pipes

Purpose of the Program
This program shows how a connection can be established between two threads using pipes. The first thread writes data to this pipe, while the second one reads data from it.

Concepts Covered in this Program
Here we show how PipedReader and PipedWriter can be used for interthread communication.

To Run this Program
```
java Pipe1
```

```
Welco
me
```

Source Code

Pipe1.java

```
/* This program shows how two threads can communicate
   using a pipe stream. In the main method we create a
   read pipe and a write pipe and pass them to two
   threads. The write thread writes out a piece of data
   to the pipe, while the read thread reads this data
   five characters at a time and prints it out until
   there is no more data in the pipe. */

import java.io.*;
public class Pipe1
{
  public static void main(String[] args)
  {
    try
    {
      /* Create the PipedReader, which will be the
         reading end of the pipe. This will be passed to
         the reading thread so that it can read from the
         pipe */
```

```
        PipedReader pis = new PipedReader();

        /* Create the PipedWriter which will be the writing
           end of the pipe. This is created using the
           PipedReader object created above (pis). This is
           how a connection is established between the two
           ends of the pipe */
        PipedWriter pos = new PipedWriter(pis);

        /* Create the two threads and pass them the
           appropriate pipe object */
        ReadThread r = new ReadThread(pis);
        WriteThread w = new WriteThread(pos);

        r.start();
        w.start();
    }
    catch(IOException e)
    {
        System.err.println("Error in PrintWriter: " + e);
        System.exit(1);
    }
  }
}
class ReadThread extends Thread
{
    PipedReader bis;
    ReadThread(PipedReader pis)
    {
        /* Store the PipedReader as a local variable. This
           will be used for reading data written to the pipe
           by the WriteThread */

        bis = pis;
    }
    public void run()
    {
        String inpu;
        try
```

```
        {
            /* Create a char array of five characters into
               which we'll be reading data from the pipe */
            char cbuf[] = new char[5];

            /* Read data from the pipe, five characters at
               a time, until there is no more data in which
               case read() will return -1 */

            while((bis.read(cbuf, 0, 5)) != -1)
            {
                /* The method valueOf() constructs a String
                   from a char array */
                System.out.println(String.valueOf(cbuf));
                int i;
                for(i=0; i< 5; i++)
                    cbuf[i] = ` `;
            }
            bis.close();
        }
        catch(IOException e)
        {
            System.out.println("Error in reading stream");
            System.exit(1);
        }
    }
}
class WriteThread extends Thread
{
    PipedWriter bos;
    WriteThread(PipedWriter pos)
    {
        bos = pos;
    }
    public void run()
    {
        char valString[] = {`W','e','l','c','o','m','e'};
        int i = 0;
        try
```

```
{
    /* Write the first five characters of valString
       to the pipe */
    bos.write(valString, i, 5);

    i+=5;

    /* Write the remaining two characters to the
       pipe */
    bos.write(valString, i, 2);

    bos.close();
} catch(IOException e)
  {
  }
}
}
```

Implementation

First we create the PipedReader and PipedWriter:

```
PipedReader pis = new PipedReader();
PipedWriter pos = new PipedWriter(pis);
```

Note that while creating the PipedWriter we're passing as an argument the PipedReader that we created. This helps connect the two streams. Next, we create two threads, ReadThread and WriteThread, and pass the PipedReader and PipedWriter instantiated above as constructor arguments. The threads will use these for reading and writing data to the stream. Then the threads are started.

Now we take a look at the threads themselves to see exactly how they're making use of the pipe. First see the WriteThread. The PipedWriter which was passed to it as a constructor argument is stored as a local variable, bos:

```
WriteThread(PipedWriter pos)
{
  bos = pos;
```

In the run() qq method, we've defined a char array. Data from this will be written to the pipe and read by ReadThread. So we first use the `write()` method of the PipedWriter to write out the first five characters, i.e., "Welco":

```
char valString[] = {'W','e','l','c','o','m','e'};
...
bos.write(valString, i, 5);
```

The first argument to the `write()` method is the `char` array, the second is the offset from which characters should be written (in our case, 0, so it starts writing from the first character) and the number of characters to be written (in this example, five).

Then we write the remaining two characters by incrementing i by five:

```
i+=5;
bos.write(valString, i, 2);
```

But wait a minute, we're not doing anything to make sure that the ReadThread has read the data before we write the new one, so how can we be assured of data integrity? This is one place where the PipedReader and Piped-Writer help.

If you look at the `read()` and `write()` method implementations in `java.io.PipedReader.java` and `java.io.PipedWriter.java`, you'll notice that these methods are synchronized by a lock. Remember anything about synchronization? If you're saying, "Uh, what's he talking about?" we advise you to take a look at the section describing synchronization of multiple threads in the "Threads" chapter. Data integrity is ensured by this synchronization, and we don't need to put in a special mechanism for this.

The ReadThread also begins by saving a copy of the PipedReader:

```
PipedReader bis;
ReadThread(PipedReader pis)
{
   bis = pis;
```

It uses the `read()` method of the `PipedReader()` to read data into a `char` array. The `read()` method returns -1 when the end of the stream is reached:

```
char cbuf[] = new char[5];
```

```
while((bis.read(cbuf, 0, 5)) != -1)
{
```

We're using the `valueOf()` method of String to convert the read character array into a string, which is displayed on the system output:

```
System.out.println(String.valueOf(cbuf));
```

Just one more thing. Every time, we initialize the `char` array to blanks so that data from the previous read operation is cleared before the next read:

```
for(i=0; i< 5; i++)
  cbuf[i] = ' ';
```

In the end, we close the stream:

```
bis.close();
```

Now that you've diligently read this chapter and know what streams mean in "our" language, you deserve some rest. If you have a stream or river nearby, why don't you go ahead and take a swim or do some river-rafting? When you come back, you can modify the example programs to get a better understanding of the concept and start using streams more effectively.

Once again, we suggest that you browse through the `java.io` directory and take a look at the various streams that Java has to offer.

CHAPTER **6**

NETWORKING

If you were to choose one word in the field of programming that brings up alternating feelings of interest and fear, that word would be "networking". It is something that is of great interest to most people. Yet the complexity involved in writing a network-based program with traditional languages is so high that most programmers decide they'd rather break stones in a quarry.

6.1 Introduction to Java Networking

This is where Java comes in — it saves you from the quarry by providing an interface so easy to program that you'll love it. Writing a network program has now become as simple as programming any other application. (If you find the work of writing other applications also as tedious as working in a quarry, we advise you to use this book for fireplace fuel — at least you'll recover some of your investment!)

6.1.1 Example: Communication Between Two Computers

Purpose of the Program
Using this example, you can establish a connection between two computers and send a message from one to the other.

Concepts Covered in this Program

Here we introduce you to networking in Java. We show how new sockets can be created, how a server can wait for a client to connect to the socket, and also how a client can actually connect to a server.

Source Code

Server1.java

```
/* This is the server side of our network. It creates a
   new socket at port 2000 and waits for a client to
   request a connection on this computer at this port.
   Once the client has requested a connection, this
   program creates a client socket so that dedicated
   communication can occur. After establishment of this
   connection, the server reads data written by the client
   and prints it out on the standard output. It also
   writes data which can be read by the client. */

import java.io.*;
import java.net.*;
public class Server1
{
   public static void main(String args[])
   {
      ServerSocket serverSocket=null;
      Socket clientSocket;
      try
      {
         /* Create a socket at port 2000. The server will
            wait for clients to request a connection at this
            port */
         serverSocket = new ServerSocket(2000);
      }
      catch(BindException e)
      {
          System.out.println("Port 2000 seems to be in
                            use: Can't bind");
          System.exit(1);
```

```
}
catch(SocketException e)
{
    System.out.println("Socket Exception Error");
    System.exit(1);
}
catch(IOException e)
{
    System.out.println("I/O Exception at port
                    2000");
    System.exit(1);
}
System.out.println("Waiting for clients at port
                2000");
clientSocket = null;
try
{
    /* The accept() method makes the server wait
       until a client requests a connection. If all
       is ok, this method returns a ClientSocket
       which can be used for communication between
       the server and the client. */
    clientSocket = serverSocket.accept();
} catch(IOException e)
    {
    System.out.println("I/O Exception in
                    serverSocket.accept()");
    System.exit(1);
    }
try
{
    /* getInputStream() returns an input stream
       which can be used for reading data written
       by the client */
    BufferedReader is = new BufferedReader(new
                    InputStreamReader(
                    clientSocket.getInputStream
                    ())));
```

```
    /* getOutputStream() returns an output stream to
       which data can be written for the client to
       read */

PrintWriter os = new PrintWriter(
    new OutputStreamWriter(
        clientSocket.getOutputStream()));

String inpu;

    /* Read data written by the client one line at a
       time */
while((inpu = is.readLine()) != null)
{
    /* Print the data sent by the client */
    System.out.println("Received " + inpu);

    StringBuffer toSend = new StringBuffer();
    toSend.append("You sent the following message to
                   the server : ");
    toSend.append(inpu);

    /* Write data to the output stream. This can be
       read by the client. */
    os.println(new String(toSend));
    os.flush();
}
os.close();
is.close();
clientSocket.close();
serverSocket.close();
} catch(IOException e)
{
    System.err.println("I/O failed");
}
  }
}
```

ClientSide.java

```
/* This is the client side of our network. It tries to
   connect to the server on the ServerSide. While trying
   to establish this connection, the client tries to
   connect to port 2000 because the server is waiting at
   this port. Once this connection is established, it
   creates input and output streams so that data can be
   transferred between the two machines. */

import java.io.*;
import java.net.*;
public class ClientSide
{
  public static void main(String args[])
  {
    Socket clientSocket = null;
    PrintWriter os = null;
    BufferedReader is = null;

    /* Create a BufferedReader that reads line by line
       from the standard input. This line will be sent to
       the server. */

    BufferedReader stdIn = new BufferedReader(new
                   InputStreamReader(System.in));
    try
    {
      /* Establish connection with the server
         "myServer.abc.com" at which the server software
         is waiting for a client at port 2000 */
      clientSocket = new Socket("myServer.abc.com", 2000);

      /* Create input and output streams around the
         socket */
      os = new PrintWriter(new
         OutputStreamWriter
         (clientSocket.getOutputStream()));
```

```
    is = new BufferedReader(new
        InputStreamReader
        (clientSocket.getInputStream()));
}catch(UnknownHostException e)
{
        System.err.println("Don't know about host
        myServer.abc.com");
}
catch(ConnectException e)
{
        System.err.println("Failure in obtaining
        connection with server");

}
catch(IOException e)
{
        System.err.println("Couldn't get I/O for host
                            myServer.abc.com");
}

if(clientSocket != null && os != null && is != null)
{
   System.out.println("Established connection with
                       server");
   try
   {
       String inp;

       /* Read data from the standard input line by
          line. This data is sent to the server. */
       while((inp = stdIn.readLine()) != null)
       {
           /* Write data to the output stream so that
              it becomes available to the server */
           os.println(inp);

           os.flush();
           System.out.println("Sent to the server " +
                               inp);
```

```
            /* Read data from the input stream and write
               to the standard output. This is the data
               that has been written by the server. */
            System.out.println(is.readLine());
        }
        os.close();
        is.close();
        clientSocket.close();
    } catch(IOException e){
            System.err.println("I/O failed");
        }
    }
}
}
```

Operation of the Program

Server side:

java Server1
```
   Waiting for clients at port 2000
   Received Hello, How are you?
   Received I'm the client
```

Client side:

java ClientSide
```
   Established connection with server
   Hello, How are you?
   Sent to the server Hello, How are you?
   You sent the following message to the server: Hello, How
   are you?
   I'm the client
   Sent to the server I'm the client
   You sent the following message to the server: I'm the
   client
```

Implementation

This one needs a bit of theory before we delve into the actual program. Let us look at how the client/server model works. With all the buzz about networking and the more-complex-than-thou networking code (as written in other languages), naturally programmers get unnerved. However, with Java, you can do some of the commonly required networking stuff very easily, such as transferring files from one system to another, or sending messages from one machine to another.

A server is a machine that acts as a host for several guests (or clients) who try to connect to it. Once this connection is established, the actual data transfer begins. The server software can be written so that it allows multiple machines to connect to it. But the perplexing thing is: how can there be multiple server softwares running simultaneously on a single machine when there is only one physical wire going out of it? This is where ports and sockets come into the picture.

The application that implements the server (i.e., the software running on the server side which makes that machine act as a server) creates a socket on that machine using a specific port number. A socket is basically an endpoint for communication; both the client and the server need to create a socket, and the actual data transfer will take place between these sockets. The concept of port numbers is something more concrete as far as understanding the whole thing is concerned. By saying that a server has bound its socket with a port number, for example, 5000, we mean to say that any application on the client side that wants to connect with this server should create a socket which is bound to the server's machine at port number 5000.

In other words, the complete address which is required for a client to connect to a server consists of two parts: the Net address of the computer itself (such as *myServer.abc.com*) and a port number. The advantage of the port number is that it can be used for distinguishing different applications running on the same server that are expecting data coming over the Net. Each such port number can be used by only one application at a time. And how is this managed? Well, when the data is sent from the client, the port number goes along as part of the data. When this data reaches the server, the computer checks the port number and routes the data to the application that is using this port number.

Say, for example, there are two applications running on a server. The first one is expecting data from machine A, and the other one from machine B. The first application can create a socket using port number 5000, and the second one can use port number 5001. Correspondingly, when A is creating the client side of the socket, it must use port number 5000 and B must use 5001. Now, when A sends data, the number 5000 will be sent with it. Once it reaches the server, the underlying software of the machine will read the port number, and since the first application is using this port number, the data will be forwarded to it for consumption. Similarly, 5001 will be sent with B's data and it will be forwarded to the second application.

Note that there are some restrictions on the port numbers you can use. Numbers 0 through 1023 are reserved for applications such as http, ftp, etc., and cannot be used by normal applications. You can, however, use any number greater than 1023 and less than or equal to 65535.

There are two main methods of data transfer that are allowed in Java: UDP and TCP. We will be covering only TCP in this chapter. TCP is a protocol that ensures reliable transfer of data. UDP, on the other hand, doesn't guarantee that data sent from one machine will actually reach the other end, nor does it ensure that the packets sent arrive in the correct order (i.e., the order in which they were sent). So, does UDP sound totally useless? No. Because UDP doesn't do overhead jobs such as ensuring data integrity, it leads to a much faster service. In applications where this criteria is acceptable, UDP would be the preferred way.

Now we're in a position where we can start discussing our examples.

This example consists of two Java files: `Server1.java` and `ClientSide.java`. `Server1.java` implements the server side, while the other is the client. Server1 should be run on the system which is going to act as the server, and ClientSide should run on the client machine. This server creates a socket using port 2000 and allows just one client to connect to it. The client creates a socket using the server's name and port number 2000 so that data sent or received by it goes to the correct application, in this case Server1.

Server1.java begins by importing necessary Java classes:

```
import java.io.*;
import java.net.*;
```

Then it declares two types of sockets: ServerSocket and Socket:

```
ServerSocket serverSocket=null;
Socket clientSocket;
```

The `serverSocket` will be used for creation of the server's socket at port 2000. This is the place where the server will listen to any connections being attempted by a client. The `clientSocket` is a socket that will be established once the client connects to the server. This is the one that will be used for actual transfer of data between the client and the server.

So, first the server socket is created. For this, the ServerSocket class is instantiated:

```
serverSocket = new ServerSocket(2000);
```

Here, 2000 is the port number. In the above line of code we're binding a socket on the server at port number 2000. While trying to bind a socket, there can be several types of failures, such as binding error, I/O error, etc. All of these raise exceptions. That is why we have put the line of code within a try that catches these exceptions. Inside the catch of each of these we have put an error message which will be printed. For example, if there is a failure in binding the socket at this port (which could happen if there is another application using the same port), a BindException will be raised. And once this is raised, we would like to report the error to the users and exit:

```
catch(BindException e)
{
   System.out.println("Port 2000 seems to be in use: Can't
                      bind");
   System.exit(1);
}
```

Once this socket has been established, we make the server wait on the socket for a client to make a connection. This may seem familiar to those among you who have a servant whose job is to wait for the telephone to answer that His Majesty/Her Highness is taking a nap. On the other hand, if you do fall in the above category, why are you wasting time reading this book?

So, how do we make the server wait for clients? This is done through the accept() method of ServerSocket. This method blocks until a connection is made. In case there is some problem while it is waiting for the connection, it raises an IOException:

```
clientSocket = serverSocket.accept();
```

The accept() method returns a handle to the client socket — a socket which will be used for communication with this client. A new socket needs to be created for every client that connects to the server. You may view this as another level for routing the data. When the data first comes, it is sorted on the basis of the port number to determine which server it's meant for. Also, the client from which the data is coming should be known to the server so that it can transmit different data to different clients. This is achieved by instantiating a separate socket for each client. In this example, we can have only one client connect to the server, but in the next one we will show how multiple clients can connect to the server.

After this the operation is just like that on an ordinary stream. We first get the input stream for the client socket. This is done by using the getInput-Stream() method of the Socket class. Next we create an object of the type BufferedReader so that we have a Buffered Reader from which we can read data. Since BufferedReader requires an object of the type Reader in its constructor, we create an InputStreamReader from the client socket's input stream and use this new object as the argument to the constructor of the Buffered-Reader:

```
BufferedReader is =
  new BufferedReader(new
    InputStreamReader(clientSocket.getInputStream()));
```

To send the data back, we need to create a PrintWriter. This is achieved by getting the output stream of the client socket, using the getOutputStream() method. PrintWriter also requires an object of the Writer type for its constructor, so we create an object of the OutputStreamWriter type and pass this to the constructor:

```
PrintWriter os = new PrintWriter(
  new OutputStreamWriter(clientSocket.getOutputStream()));
```

After this, the server reads data from the socket line by line until the connection is broken:

```
while((inpu = is.readLine()) != null)
```

Here input is a String object in which the line data from the socket is stored. Using this, the return message is prepared. The return message consists of the message received from the client, preceded by the line: "You sent the following message to the server:"

We print the message received from the client on the server's standard output:

```
System.out.println("Received " + inpu);
```

The return message is then sent back to the client. To do this, the only thing that needs to be done is to write the message on the output stream. This is done by using the `println()` method of the OutputStreamWriter that we established above:

```
os.println(new String(toSend));
```

If any Input/Output error occurs during this period, an IOException is raised, which we're catching.

We close all the streams and sockets at the end:

```
os.close();
is.close();
clientSocket.close();
serverSocket.close();
```

Now let's look at the client side. This is implemented in the file `ClientSide.java`.

This one also begins by importing the required Java classes. Next we declare the client side socket:

```
Socket clientSocket = null;
```

Also, in this example (and the next) we'll take input from the standard input. For this, we create a BufferedReader stream using standard input (`System.in`):

```
BufferedReader stdIn = new BufferedReader(new
        InputStreamReader(System.in));
```

Note that `stdIn` is being used for reading data from the standard input only. For reading and writing data that is being transmitted to the host we'll need separate input and output streams connected to the socket connection that we establish with the server.

The client socket is then created. As we've explained in the theory above, there are two things we need to create this socket: the name of the server and the port number of the server application:

```
clientSocket = new Socket("myServer.abc.com", 2000);
```

Here `myServer.abc.com` is the name of your server machine. To use this program, replace this with the name of your server.

We also create the input and output streams on this client socket:

```
os = new PrintWriter(new OutputStreamWriter(
        clientSocket.getOutputStream()));
is = new BufferedReader(new InputStreamReader(
        clientSocket.getInputStream()));
```

Exceptions that can occur in this phase include failure in locating the server, or in creating the Connection or I/O exceptions.

Once the connection is established, it's just a matter of reading and writing from streams, as in the case of the server. We read from the standard input of the client:

```
while((inp = stdIn.readLine()) != null)
```

This data is then written to the output stream. It reads data that has been returned by the server by reading the input stream of the socket and prints it out:

```
System.out.println(is.readLine());
```

Once all the data transfer is over we explicitly close all the streams and the client socket as well:

```
os.close();
is.close();
clientSocket.close();
```

To run the program, run Server1 (`java Server1`) on your server and ClientSide on your client. Note that you can run both on the same machine, using different windows for the server and the client.

6.1.2 Example: Multiple Clients Communicating with a Server

Purpose of the Program

This program allows multiple clients to connect to the same server application.

Concepts Covered in this Program

In this program we show how threads can be used to lift the burden off the portion of the server listening for new clients, so that it can handle multiple clients.

Source code

Server2.java

```
/* This program is an extension of our earlier server
   program. This one can handle multiple clients. The main
   program waits for clients to connect at port 2000. Once
   a connection has been established with a client, a
   dedicated thread is created which will handle the
   communication between the client and the server. This
   frees up the main program to wait for more clients and
   create new threads. This server can handle a maximum of
   20 client connections. You can easily extend it to
   handle more clients. */

import java.io.*;
import java.net.*;
public class Server2
{
  public static ServerThread[] st = new ServerThread[20];
  static int currentThread = 0;
  public static void main(String args[])
  {
    ServerSocket serverSocket=null;
    Socket clientSocket;
    try
    {
      serverSocket = new ServerSocket(2000);
    }
    catch(BindException e)
    {
        System.out.println("Port 2000 seems to be in
                             use: Can't bind ");
    }
    catch(SocketException e)
```

```
{
    System.out.println("Socket Exception Error");
}
catch(IOException e)
{
    System.out.println("I/O Exception at port
                    2000");
    System.exit(1);
}

System.out.println("Waiting for connection at port
                2000");

/* This loop waits for clients to connect. Every time
   a client tries to establish a connection, a client
   socket is created and so is a thread which takes
   up the work of communicating with this socket
   (i.e., communication with the client for which
   this socket was created). */

while(true)
{
    try
    {
        clientSocket = serverSocket.accept();
        if(clientSocket != null)
        {

            /* clientSocket.toString() returns a string
               containing information about the client
               machine, such as its name. */
            System.out.println("Established connection
                        with client :" +
                        clientSocket.toString());

            /* Create a new thread and pass this socket
               to the thread so that the thread can
               communicate with the client */
```

```
                st[currentThread] = new ServerThread
                                        (clientSocket);
                st[currentThread].start();
                currentThread++;
                if(currentThread >= 20)
                        break;
            }
        } catch(IOException e)
          {
                System.out.println("Accept failed in
                                        Server");
                System.exit(1);
          }
    }
  }
}


/* This is the thread that will communicate with the
   client */
class ServerThread extends Thread
{
    static Socket clientSocket;
    static ServerSocket s;
    ServerThread(Socket clientSocket)
    {
       this.clientSocket = clientSocket;
    }
    public void run()
    {
       try
       {
          BufferedReader is = new BufferedReader(new
                  InputStreamReader(clientSocket.getInput
                  Stream()));
          PrintWriter os = new PrintWriter(
          new OutputStreamWriter
          (clientSocket.getOutputStream()));
          String inpu;
          while((inpu = is.readLine()) != null)
```

```
        {
            System.out.println("The server has received
                            " + inpu);
            StringBuffer toSend = new StringBuffer();
            toSend.append("You sent the following
                        message to the server: ");
            toSend.append(inpu);
            os.println(new String(toSend));
            os.flush();
        }
        is.close();
        os.close();
        clientSocket.close();
    } catch(IOException e)
    {
        System.err.println("I/O failed");
    }
  }
}
```

Operation of the Program

Server side:

```
java Server2
Waiting for connection at port 2000
Established connection with client
:Socket[addr=client1.abc.com/144.99.99.998,port=35832,
                                    localport=2000]
Established connection with client
:Socket[addr=client2.abc.com/144.99.99.999,port=35833,
                                    localport=2000]
The server has received Message from first client
The server has received Message from second client
```

Client 1:

```
java ClientSide
Established connection with server
Message from first client
```

```
Sent to the server Message from first client
You sent the following message to the server: Message from
                                                 first client
```

Client 2:

```
java ClientSide
Established connection with server
Message from second client
Sent to the server Message from second client
You sent the following message to the server: Message from
second client
```

Implementation

This program uses the same client side Java program that we used in the previous example. However, the server side implementation has changed. The server class being used here is Server2. This one bears a lot of similarity to Server1 because it uses the same mechanism for listening to a client, sending and receiving data.

In this case, we have split the functionality into two major areas. The first part simply waits for new connections to be made, while the second one does the actual data handling. The latter part is being handled by threads. For every new client that connects to the server, a new thread is started. This thread then handles all the data I/O operations for that particular client.

So right at the start of this class we are defining an array of ServerThread, a class that extends Thread and has been implemented in the same Java file, `Server2.java`:

```
public static ServerThread[] st = new ServerThread[20];
```

We are also maintaining a counter which will help us keep track of how many threads we have started so that if it exceeds 20 (the maximum number of threads that can be accommodated by this program), the server should stop listening for new clients:

```
static int currentThread = 0;
```

For listening to new connections, we have a `while` loop in which the `accept()` method of the ServerSocket is used:

```
while(true)
{
  try
  {
    clientSocket = serverSocket.accept();
```

Once a connection is established, we can get information about the client, such as its IP address, machine name, etc. For this purpose, Socket provides the toString() method. We're using that to print out information about the client that has just made the connection. This can be used for distinguishing one thread from the other:

```
System.out.println("Established connection with client :" +
        clientSocket.to\String());
```

We instantiate a ServerThread object. The current clientSocket is passed to ServerThread() as an argument in the constructor. This socket will be used by the thread for doing I/O:

```
st[currentThread] = new ServerThread(clientSocket);
```

The thread is started:

```
st[currentThread].start();
```

We now increment currentThread and check if it's equal to 20, the maximum allowed (as we have declared the st array to have 20 elements). If it is, we break out of the while loop:

```
currentThread++;
if(currentThread >= 20)
  break;
```

The thread object is created by extending the Thread class:

```
class ServerThread extends Thread
```

The constructor gets the client socket as an argument and we store it in the thread:

```
ServerThread(Socket clientSocket)
{
   this.clientSocket = clientSocket;
}
```

After this point the implementation is the same as in `Server1.java`. Data is written to and read from the socket by creating input and output streams on the client socket.

Next we show how you can use network programming in a more close-to-reality example.

6.2 File Transfer

In this section we show how you can transfer a file over the network. The example discussed here reads a file from the server and transports it to the client side.

6.2.1 Example: Transferring Files Between Machines

Purpose of the Program
This program show how a client can request that a file be transported to it from the server.

Concepts Covered in this Program
The example combines all that you've learned about file I/O with all that you've learned about networking to show you a real-life situation in which you need to transfer files over the network.

Source Code

```
/* GiveFile.java runs on the server. It reads a file and
      sends it to the clients that connect to it. */
```

GiveFile.java

```
import java.io.*;
import java.net.*;
public class GiveFile
```

```
{
  public static void main(String args[])
  {
    ServerSocket serverSocket=null;
    Socket clientSocket;
    try
    {
      serverSocket = new ServerSocket(2000);
    } catch(IOException e)
      {
         System.out.println("Couldn't listen to port
                            2000");
         System.exit(1);
      }
      System.out.println("Waiting for connection at port
                         2000");
    clientSocket = null;
    try
    {
      clientSocket = serverSocket.accept();
    } catch(IOException e)
      {
         System.out.println("I/O Exception in
                             serverSocket.accept()");
         System.exit(1);
      }
    try
      {
         File f = new File("myFile");
         FileInputStream fis = new FileInputStream(f);
         DataInputStream is = new DataInputStream(
           new BufferedInputStream
           (clientSocket.getInputStream()));
         OutputStream os = clientSocket.getOutputStream();
         DataOutputStream dos = new DataOutputStream(os);
         String inpu;
         int fSize = fis.available();
         System.out.println("Size is " + fSize);
```

```
/* First write the size of the file to the stream
   so that the client knows the number of bytes
   that will be transmitted to it */
dos.writeInt(fSize);
dos.flush();

/* Read a byte (which is written by the client). This
   "handshaking" is being done between the client and
   the server so that proper communication occurs. By
   waiting here the server knows for sure that the
   client has read the file size which was sent first
   before it sends the contents of the file "myFile".
   */

is.readByte();

byte[] buf = new byte[3000];

/* Read 3000 bytes at a time and send them to the
   client */
while((fis.read(buf)) != -1 )
{
    System.out.println("Sending");
    os.write(buf);
    os.flush();

    /* Wait for the client to confirm that it has
       received the bytes sent above */
    is.readByte();
}
fis.close();
os.close();
is.close();
} catch(IOException e)
{
        System.err.println("I/O Exception");
}
}
}
```

GetFile.java

```
/* This program runs on the client. It reads the file
   sent by the server and writes it to the file "myFile"
   on this machine */

import java.lang.*;
import java.io.*;
import java.net.*;

public class GetFile
{
  public static void main(String args[])
  {
    Socket echoSocket = null;
    DataOutputStream os = null;
    InputStream is = null;
    DataInputStream dis = null;
    try
    {
      echoSocket = new Socket("myServer.abc.com", 2000);
      os = new DataOutputStream
           (echoSocket.getOutputStream());
      is = echoSocket.getInputStream();
      dis = new DataInputStream
           (echoSocket.getInputStream());
    }catch(UnknownHostException e)
     {
       System.err.println("Don't know about host
                          myServer");
    }catch(IOException e)
     {
       System.err.println("Couldn't get I/O for host
                          myServer");
     }
    if(echoSocket != null && os != null && is != null)
    {
        System.out.println("Trying to receive data");
        try
```

```
{
    String inp;
    File outputFile = new File("myFile");
    FileOutputStream fos = new
    FileOutputStream(outputFile);
    byte[] buff = new byte[3000];
    int fSize;
    int sizeRead = 0;

    /* Read the size of the file sent by the
       server */
    fSize = dis.readInt();

    System.out.println("Size of file is " +
                    fSize);

    /* Send a byte to the server, as it is
       waiting for confirmation from the client */
    os.writeByte('\n');

    os.flush();

    /* Read data sent by the server, 3000 bytes
       at a time */
    while((is.read(buff)) != -1)
    {
        sizeRead+=3000;

        if(sizeRead < fSize)
           fos.write(buff);
        else
        {
        /* This part will be reached when the
           last set of bytes of the file has
           arrived. If the file size is not an
           exact multiple of 3000, the number of
           bytes read in this case will not be
           3000. Based on the number of bytes
```

read so far and the file size, we can
determine how many bytes in the
buffer are actual data bytes. We then
write these to another buffer which
we're writing to the output file. */

```java
            byte[] buff1 = new byte[fSize -
                        (sizeRead - 3000)];
            int i;
            for(i=0; i < (fSize - (sizeRead -
               3000)); i++)
               buff1[i] = buff[i];
            fos.write(buff1);
        }
        os.writeByte('\n');
        os.flush();
        System.out.println("Received");
      }
      os.close();
      is.close();
      fos.close();
      echoSocket.close();
    } catch(IOException e)
      {
      System.err.println("I/O failed");
      }
    }
  }
}
```

Operation of the Program

Server side:
```
  java GiveFile
  Waiting for connection at port 2000
  Size is 5364
  Sending
  Sending
```

Client side:
```
java GetFile
Trying to receive data
Size of file is 5364
Received
Received
```

Implementation

The server side of the implementation is present in the file GiveFile.java, while the client side is in GetFile.java. The names of the files should give you a fair idea of which file does what.

GiveFile creates a server socket and waits for clients to connect to it. Once the connection is made, it reads a file "myFile" and transports it across to the client.

The client, GetFile, connects to the server. As it receives these data bytes it stores them in "myFile" at the client's end.

Let's look at GiveFile. A ServerSocket is created at port 2000. Then it waits for a client to connect using the accept() method.

Once the connection is established, a File object is created using this file:

```
File f = new File("myFile");
```

Note that in this program we have hard-coded the names of the input as well as the output files; you can change them to whatever you want. Better still, you can extend this program so that it can accept any file names.

A FileInputStream is then created using this File object:

```
FileInputStream fis = new FileInputStream(f);
```

This will be used for reading the file.

As far as writing to the output stream is concerned, we need to write two types of data: an integer, which will be the size of the file, and an array of bytes, which will be the file data itself. So we create an OutputStream and a DataOutputStream for these two requirements:

```
OutputStream os = clientSocket.getOutputStream();
DataOutputStream dos = new DataOutputStream(os);
```

We'll also establish an input stream so that the client can inform the server that it has received a set of data bytes and is ready to receive more data:

```
DataInputStream is = new DataInputStream(
  new BufferedInputStream(clientSocket.getInputStream()));
```

The size of the file is determined by using the `available()` method of FileInputStream:

```
int fSize = fis.available();
```

This is then written to the DataOutputStream so that this integer gets transmitted over to the client's side:

```
dos.writeInt(fSize);
dos.flush();
```

We then wait for the client to respond that it has received the file size and that it is ready for the actual data:

```
is.readByte();
```

The data will be read into an array of bytes with 3000 elements:

```
byte[] buf = new byte[3000];
```

The server then starts reading the file:

```
while((fis.read(buf)) != -1 )
```

As each set of 3000 bytes is read it is written to the OutputStream, `os`:

```
os.write(buf);
os.flush();
```

Then it waits for confirmation from the client that it has received these bytes. This loop ends when the complete file has been read because "-1" will be returned by `read()`.

So how does the client handle the data? A socket is created here also which connects to the server using the server's name and the port number 2000.

An OutputStream is created which will be used for sending confirmation to the server that the client is ready to accept more data. An InputStream will be used for receiving data. A DataInputStream is created for receiving the file size which will be sent as an integer:

```
os = new DataOutputStream(echoSocket.getOutputStream());
is = echoSocket.getInputStream();
dis = new DataInputStream(echoSocket.getInputStream());
```

A File object is created using the name "myFile" — this will be the name of the output file:

```
File outputFile = new File("myFile");
```

A FileOutputStream is created for writing the data to this file:

```
FileOutputStream fos = new FileOutputStream(outputFile);
```

A byte array of 3000 bytes is created for receiving the data:

```
byte[] buff = new byte[3000];
```

Since we know that the size of the file is going to be first transmitted by the server as an integer, we read that from the socket using the readInt() method which reads an integer:

```
fSize = dis.readInt();
```

The client writes out a byte on the output stream so that the server knows that data has been received at the client's side:

```
os.writeByte('\n');
os.flush();
```

A while loop is implemented for reading data from the input stream:

```
while((is.read(buff)) != -1)
```

The data is written out to the output file by using the write() method of FileOutputStream:

```
fos.write(buff);
```

Here we're playing a small trick. We want to write only the actual number of bytes that have been received. So what happens if the file size is 500, i.e., less than 3000? Or if the file size is 3200 (i.e., not an exact multiple of 3000)? In these cases we shouldn't write the complete buffer, but only the relevant portion. To handle this, we maintain a counter `sizeRead` which keeps track of how many bytes have been read so far. Once this exceeds the file size we know that we've reached the condition where the number of bytes to be written out is less than 3000. In this case we create a new buffer, whose size is equal to the number of remaining bytes, and copy the bytes from the original buffer to this:

```
byte[] buff1 = new byte[fSize - (sizeRead - 3000)];
int i;
for(i=0; i < (fSize - (sizeRead - 3000)); i++)
    buff1[i] = buff[i];
```

Then we write out this buffer:

```
fos.write(buff1);
```

A good exercise for you would be to extend this program so that 1) multiple clients can connect to the server, and 2) the client can specify which file it needs. For 1), you can use the example in the previous section. For 2), you can first send the file name to the server as a string. The server should then check whether the file exists, and on the basis of this it should send a string telling the client whether it could locate the file. After this, if the file does exist, the actual file transfer should begin.

6.3 Reading a URL

The simple example in this section wraps up the chapter on networking by showing you how you can read a URL. For those among you who have spent life in the computer industry with eyes and ears closed and don't know what a URL is, the simplest example of a URL (Uniform Resource Locator) is a web page — you know, those weird characters that read like *http://abc.com/index.html*.

With Java, you don't need a browser to read a URL. Of course the downside is that you'll see it all as ASCII text — no pretty pictures, no formatting, etc.

— just as the file has been written, word for word, space for space.

Note that your URL must reside on a server that supports URL connections. For example, to read a web page using http, the machine you're trying to read from should be running an http server.

6.3.1 Example: Establishing and Reading URLs

ReadAURL.java

Purpose of the Program
This program shows you how you can read a URL.

Concepts Covered in this Program
Here we show you how to establish a URL connection and how to read from it.

Source Code

ReadAURL.java

```
/* This program reads index.html on the server
   myServer.abc.com. This file exists on that server in
   the directory /home/anu */

import java.net.*;
import java.io.*;
class ReadAURL
{
  public static void main(String[] args)
  {
    try
    {
      /* Create a URL object which we can use to read
         the file */
      URL myURL = new
          URL("http://myServer.abc.com/home/anu/index.ht
          ml");

      /* Open an input stream on this URL so that we can
         read the file */
      InputStreamReader inpStream = new
          InputStreamReader(myURL.openStream());
```

```
/* Create a BufferedReader using the input stream
   so that the file can be read line by line */
BufferedReader br = new BufferedReader(inpStream);

String inpLine;

while ((inpLine = br.readLine()) != null)
{
    System.out.println(inpLine);
}
br.close();
} catch (MalformedURLException ex1)
{
    System.out.println(" Received Exception
                        MalformedURLException:
                        " + ex1);
} catch (IOException ex2)
    {
    System.out.println(" Received Exception
                        IOException: " + ex2);
    }
    }
}
```

Implementation

We first establish a URL connection by using URL. The constructor can take different arguments. One constructor allows us to specify everything using a string. The information in the string should include the transfer protocol (in this case we're using http), name of the server and path of the file that we're interested in:

```
URL myURL = new
URL("http://myServer.abc.com/home/anu/HTML/index.html");
```

Here */home/anu* is the home directory of the user *anu, index.html* is the HTML file we're interested in reading that exists in */home/anu/HTML*, the transfer protocol is http, and the name of the server is *myServer.abc.com*.

Once this connection has been established, we simply create a stream to read from the URL by using the openStream() method of the URL:

```
InputStreamReader inpStream = new
                    InputStreamReader(myURL.openStream());
```

A BufferedReader is constructed using this InputStreamReader and we read from it, line by line:

```
BufferedReader br = new BufferedReader(inpStream);
String inpu;
while ((inpLine = br.readLine()) != null)
```

We are printing data as it is received on the system output:

```
System.out.println(inpLine);
```

Note that during the construction of the URL a MalformedURLException can arise. We are catching this:

```
catch (MalformedURLException ex1)
{
   System.out.println(" Received Exception
                    MalformedURLException:
                    " + ex1);
} catch (IOException ex2)
```

We hope that with these examples the ugly image of the world of networking that has been lingering in your nightmares has been dispelled. Now that you know how easy it is to write a networking software, why don't you go ahead and try out more exotic things? Or do you still think that the quarry is a better option?

## CHAPTER 7

NATIVE METHODS

In this chapter, we show how you can invoke programs written in languages other than Java from within your Java programs. The methods written in other programming languages are known as native methods.

7.1 Introduction to Native Methods

The one-line answer to why you need to know native method integration is: Java ain't God — at least, not yet! The need for using native methods arises at times when there is some functionality that can be implemented in another language, but is not available through Java. But Sunsoft definitely wants to make Java the right hand of God so that one day the need for other languages will be eliminated or reduced to a size visible only through an electron microscope. That's the reason why so many new libraries are coming up for use by Java programs.

In JDK 1.1, the integration with native methods is done through a programming interface known as the Java Native Interface (JNI). This interface allows code running within a Java Virtual Machine to interact with libraries containing methods written in other languages such as C, C++ and assembly.

The JNI provides a rich Application Programming Interface (API). This means that there are lots of functions available for programmers to be used in their native methods. These functions can be called by the native methods for doing various things like calling methods of Java programs, getting or setting variables defined in other classes, etc.

The steps involved in integrating native methods written in C/C++ with Java programs are as follows:

1. Create your Java file and declare any native method to be used with the "native" keyword.

    Also, use the `loadLibrary()` method to load a shared library which will contain an implementation of this method.

2. Compile the Java file using `javac`.

3. Invoke `javah` with the `-jni` argument on the generated class. This will create a `.h` file. This `.h` file will contain, among other things, a declaration of your native method.

    Create a `.c` file which will contain your native method. Include the generated `.h` file in this. Copy the declaration of the native method that is present in the generated `.h` file and write your code inside this.

5. Compile the native method code.

6. Generate a shared library/DLL using this code.

7. Set environment variables so that the library can be located.

8. Run your Java program in the normal way.

Do these steps look more intimidating than the tango? Don't worry. We'll explain all of them in the first example. In subsequent examples you should follow a similar approach.

7.1.1 Example: Calling a Native Method

Purpose of the Program
This program shows how a Java program can call a native method.

Concepts Covered in the Program
In this example we show how you can integrate native methods with your Java programs. Everything from writing code to generation of shared libraries is covered. We also show how a parameter can be passed to a native method.

Source Code

Main.java

```
public class Main
{
  /* Declaration of a native method is done using the
     keyword "native" */

  public native void natFunc(int i);

  /* Load the shared library that contains a definition of
     the native method. The Java Virtual Machine will
     refer to this when we try to invoke this method. */

  static
  {
    System.loadLibrary("Main");
  }

  public static void main(String args[])
  {
    Main m;
    m = new Main();

      /* Invoke the native method like a normal instance
         method */

      m.natFunc(20);
  }
}
```

Nat.c

```
/* Before Nat.c is written, we run javah on the class we
   created above. This will generate a .h file, "Main.h"
   which we have to include in the C file containing our
   native method. Also, the name of the native method that
   we have to use should be the same as the declaration
```

```
    which appears in "Main.h". In this case it is
    Java_Main_natFunc */
```

```
#include "Main.h"
JNIEXPORT void JNICALL Java_Main_natFunc
(JNIEnv *env, jobject obj, jint i)
{
    /* The Java Virtual Machine passes two other arguments
       when calling our native method besides the int
       argument that we passed to it: JNIEnv * and jobject.
       We will see the use of these in another example
       later */

    printf("\n The integer you passed to the native method
           is %d\n", i);
}
```

Operation of the Program

java Main
The integer you passed to the native method is 20.

Implementation
Our objective here is to invoke a method, natFunc(), which is written in the C language from within our Java program, Main.java. We also want to pass an argument to the native program, which should print this argument on the standard output.

Step 1:
First we create the Java file, Main.java. The native method to be invoked accepts an int argument, but doesn't return any value. Its declaration is similar to that of a normal Java method, except that the keyword "native" has been added before it to tell javac that this is a native method:

```
public native void natFunc(int i);
```

Once we've created our C file which will define this method, we will generate a shared library. This library needs to be loaded in the Java environment so that the method defined in the library can be used. The next few lines of code do exactly this:

```
static
{
    System.loadLibrary("Main");
}
```

On Solaris/MacOS, this tells the Java Virtual Machine to load libMain.so, while on Windows this translates to Main.dll. In other words, the shared library/DLL that we generate should have the name libMain.so/Main.dll.

After this the method natFunc() is treated like a normal Java method. In the main() we're creating an instance of the Main class and invoking nat-Func() by passing an int with value 20 to it:

```
m = new Main();
m.natFunc(20);
```

Step 2:
Now that we've written our Java program, we compile it in the normal way:

```
javac Main.java
```

This will create Main.class.

Step 3:
Now run javah.

```
javah -jni Main
```

This will create a file Main.h. This file looks like this:

```
/* DO NOT EDIT THIS FILE - it is machine generated */
#include <jni.h>
/* Header for class Main */

#ifndef _Included_Main
#define _Included_Main
#ifdef __cplusplus
extern "C" {
#endif
/*
```

```
 * Class: Main
 * Method: natFunc
 * Signature: (I)V
 */
JNIEXPORT void JNICALL Java_Main_natFunc
(JNIEnv *, jobject, jint);

#ifdef __cplusplus
}
#endif
#endif
```

This is a machine-generated file and you should not edit it. It contains a declaration of our native method. As you can see, Java has given its own name to this method. It is no longer just natFunc. Java_Main_ has been added before it. "Main" is the name of the class in which the native method is declared.

There are three arguments passed to this method. The values for the first two are supplied by the Java environment itself. After these come the arguments we wish to pass to the native method. In our case, we're passing an int argument. In native code this translates to jint.

The first argument is a pointer to JNIEnv, the Java Native Interface environment. We can use this pointer to invoke the methods that are made available by the JNI API for use by native programs. The second argument is a handle to the object that invoked the native method. In our case, this is an instance of the class Main. The third argument is the int that we passed to the native method.

This file also includes jni.h which contains a declaration of all the methods in the JNI API. This file exists in "¢¢¢the_directory_where_you_downloaded_JDK1.1>.jdk1.1.include".

In the next step we will use the native method declaration as determined by javah and then do coding within this.

Step 4:
Next we create our C file, Nat.c. Note that there are no restrictions on the naming of this file. First we include the generated header, "Main.h".

#include "Main.h"

Then we cut and paste the declaration of the native method and supply names to the arguments so that they can be used:

```
JNIEXPORT void JNICALL Java_Main_natFunc
       (JNIEnv *env, jobject obj, jint i)
```

We're using the `jint` argument as if it were an `int`. The primitive data types are defined in `jni.h` or `jni_md.h`, which contains platform specific data type definitions. For Solaris, `jint` is defined as a long in `jni_md.h`, so we can use it like an `int` for most purposes. Here we're printing the `int` passed to the native method:

```
printf("\n The integer you passed to the native method is
       %d\n", i);
```

Step 5:
After this, we need to compile the C/C++ program. We'll show how this is done on Solaris for compiling a C program. Using C++ is discussed at the end of the next section. For other platforms, a similar approach is followed:

```
cc -I/myMachine/myHome/JAVA1.1/java/include
-I/myMachine/myHome/JAVA1.1/java/include/solaris
-c Nat.c
```

This compiles `Nat.c` and produces `Nat.o` as an output. This object file will then be stuffed into a shared library/DLL.

Step 6:
The object file generated above is now put in a shared library/DLL. Follow the normal method for creating such libraries on your platform. Remember that the name of the library should include the name "Main", as we've used this in our `loadLibrary()` method above, and it should follow the naming convention standard for your platform. The library should include `Nat.o`. For Solaris you can use:

```
/usr/ccs/bin/ld -G -o libMain.so *.o
```

You can put as many native methods in the same shared library as you want. For platforms that don't support shared libraries you'll need to statically link everything with the libraries that provide functionality for the JNI API.

Step 7:
The library containing the native method is now ready. You should now set the

proper environment variables so that JVM knows where this library exists. For Solaris you need to set LD_LIBRARY_PATH. For example you could set it as follows (in the C-shell):

```
setenv LD_LIBRARY_PATH
<path_where_libMain.so_exists>:/usr/dt/lib
```

Step 8:
Run the Java program.

```
java Main
```

The method natFunc() will be invoked with the value 120 passed to it as an argument. Since the JVM knows that natFunc() is a native method (indicated to it by the "native" keyword in the method declaration), it will look up the function in the library which has been loaded by loadLibrary(). The method will then be executed.

The method receives 120 as an argument, so it prints it out, using printf().

You are now ready to graduate from the kindergarten of native methods. In the next few grades you'll learn how these native methods can themselves create new Java objects and call their methods or set their variables.

7.2 Invoking Static and Instance Methods

Before you begin this section or jump to the next sections, it would be a good idea to glance through jni.h, which contains declarations of all the methods in the JNI API that are available to you for use in your native programs. In the next few sections we'll be using these methods for such things as creating new objects within native programs, calling methods of Java classes, setting variables, etc.

7.2.1 Example: Native Method Calling Methods of Java Programs

Purpose of the Program
This program shows how a native method can invoke the methods of other Java programs.

Concepts Covered in this Program

Here we show how your native method can invoke instance and static methods which are defined in some Java classes.

Source Code

Main2.java

```java
class Main2
{
  public native void callOtherFuncs();

  static
  {
    System.loadLibrary ("Main2");
  }
  public static void main (String[] args)
  {
    Main2 m = new Main2();
    m.callOtherFuncs();
  }

  /* This instance method will be invoked by our native
     method */

  public void sayHello()

  {
    System.out.println("Hello from Main.java's sayHello()
                        method");
  }
}
```

New1.java

```java
public class New1
{
  /* This static method will also be invoked by our
     native method */
```

```
public static void printHello()
{
    System.out.println("Hello from New1.java's
    printHello() method");
}
}
```

Nat2.c

```
/* The first argument passed to the native method is a
   handle to the Java Native Interface (JNI) environment.
   Using this we can invoke methods of the JNI available
   for use in native programs. These methods are part of
   a rich API which allows several things like creating
   new instances from native programs (yes, instances of
   Java classes), calling their methods, setting
   variables, etc.

   The second argument is a handle to the instance that
   called this native method.

   This program invokes an instance method of the class
   Main2 which initially called this native method. It
   also invokes a static method of the class New1.
*/


#include "Main2.h"
JNIEXPORT void JNICALL Java_Main2_callOtherFuncs (JNIEnv
*env, jobject obj)
{
    jclass cls, cls1;
    jmethodID mid, mid1;
    cls = (*env)->FindClass(env, "Main2");

    /* Get the ID of the method we wish to invoke. This is
       a value which is unique for every method of a given
       class and is used for doing an operation on the
       method, such as invoking it. The last argument to
       this method is a type signature which is constructed
```

from the parameters that the method can accept and
its return value. This method has no parameters so
this part is represented by a pair of empty
parentheses. The return value is void and the
representation for this is "V". So, the type
signature of this method is "()V" */

```
mid = (*env)->GetMethodID(env, cls, "sayHello", "()V");
```

/* Using the JNI environment, call the instance method
   whose ID we obtained above */

```
(*env)->CallVoidMethod(env, obj, mid);

cls1 = (*env)->FindClass(env, "New1");
```

/* Get the ID of the static method printHello */

```
mid1 = (*env)->GetStaticMethodID(env, cls1, "printHello",
                                    "()V");
```

/* Invoke the static method */

```
(*env)->CallStaticVoidMethod(env, cls1,mid1);
}
```

Operation of the Program

```
java Main2
  Hello from Main.java's sayHello() method
  Hello from New1.java's printHello() method
```

Implementation

In this example we invoke the native method callOtherFuncs() from the
class Main2. This method calls two methods. It calls sayHello(), which is an
instance method defined in Main2, and it also calls printHello(), which is a
static method defined in another class, New2.

Main2.java is quite similar to our previous example Main.java. The
library it loads is Main2. However, you should understand that there is no

restriction that says this has to be Main2. It could very well be "Tommy" or "Nerdy" — the only requirement is that the same name should be used during generation of the shared library.

Main2.java also defines the instance method sayHello(), which will be invoked by callOtherFuncs().

New1.java contains a static method, printHello(), which will be invoked by callOtherFuncs().

Both these files are compiled with javac, but only Main2 will be used for javah as this is the only class which contains a declaration of a native method.

Now look at the heart of this program, the native method itself, which we've defined in Nat2.c.

We begin by including Main2.h, which is generated by running javah on Main2. This method is not getting any arguments from Main2, so it contains only two arguments of the type JNIEnv and jobject.

In order to call an instance method, we will use the CallMethod() set of functions provided by the JNI API. There are several methods that fall in this category, such as CallIntMethod(), CallVoidMethod(), etc., depending on the return value of the method. In this example, we're going to invoke sayHello() which has a void return value, so we'll use CallVoidMethod().

CallVoidMethod() requires three arguments: a handle to the JNI environment, a handle to the object in which the method is defined and a method ID which uniquely identifies the method that is to be invoked.

To get the method ID, which is a unique ID that JVM associates with every method, we use the GetMethodID() method. This requires, among other things, a handle to the class in which the method is defined. We're using FindClass() to get a handle to this class.

To get access to the methods of the JNI API we're using the pointer to the JNI environment which is passed to us by the JVM as the first argument.

We declare all the variables we'll require. We'll need two objects of the type jclass to hold handles of the two classes whose methods we're going to invoke:

```
jclass cls, cls1;
```

Similarly, we'll require placeholders for the method IDs of the two methods:

```
jmethodID mid, mid1;
```

Now we get a handle to the first class, Main2:

```
cls = (*env)->FindClass(env, "Main2");
```

The method ID of `callOtherFuncs()` which is defined in this class is obtained next:

```
mid = (*env)->GetMethodID(env, cls, "sayHello", "()V");
```

The first argument to this is the JNI Environment pointer passed to the native method. The second is a handle to the class in which the method is defined. This we obtained using `FindClass()`. The next argument is the name of the method whose ID we're trying to obtain. The final argument needs some explanation.

The final argument to `GetMethodID()` is a signature of the method. The signature is used for uniquely identifying a method. It's required because there can be more than one method with the same name in the same Java class.

The only way to distinguish among them is by looking at the arguments. The signature provides this very information.

To construct a signature you should use the chart given at the end of this chapter. The basic idea is that you supply the arguments being passed to the method within a pair of parentheses. Outside this, you write the type of return value. For example, if there is a method which accepts a string object as input and returns an `int` as the return value, according to our chart, its signature would be `(Ljava/lang/String;)I`. This is because, according to our chart, a Java class is represented by `Lfully_qualified_class;` and an `int` is represented by `I`.

In our example, the method `sayHello()` has no argument list, and it has a void return value, so its signature is `()V`.

Then we call the actual method using all this information we've gathered:

```
(*env)->CallVoidMethod(env, obj, mid);
```

This causes the first line of the output to be generated.

Next, we call the static method which is defined in New1. A similar approach is followed for static methods. But there is a different set of API functions for static methods. The method ID is obtained using `GetStaticMethodID()`:

```
mid1 = (*env)->GetStaticMethodID(env, cls1, "printHello",
                                 "()V");
```

The method is called by using `CallStaticVoidMethod()`. The second argument to this is a `jclass`, not a `jobject`. This is logical because static methods are associated with a class rather than with an instance of the class:

```
(*env)->CallStaticVoidMethod(env, cls1,mid1);
```

This invokes `printHello()` which prints out the second line of the output.

How to Write the Same Program in C++

If you're using C++, your life will be slightly easier, even though there isn't much difference between the method of integration of C++ programs and that of C programs.

At the top of the program you should put:

```
extern "C"
```

This specifies to the compiler that the C calling convention will be used. The place where your life becomes easier is in using env, the pointer to JNIEnv. Unlike in C where you have to access it using `(*env)`, you can directly use env in C++. So, if in C you wrote:

```
(*env)->CallVoidMethod(env, obj, mid);
```

In C++ you would write:

```
env->CallVoidMethod(env, obj, mid);
```

And that's about it.

7.3 Creating Instances/Setting Variables

At times you may feel the need to create a new instance within a native method and invoke methods of this instance. Java's quest for omnipotence doesn't fail you here. In this section we're going to show you how your native methods can create new instances.

7.3.1 Example: Native Method Creating a New Instance

Purpose of the Program
This example shows how a native method can create a new instance of a Java class.

Concepts Covered in this Program
The program shows the usage of `AllocObject()www` to create a new instance from a native method.

Source Code:

```
/* In this case the native method callOtherFuncs() will
   create a new instance of the class New3 and invoke one
   of its instance methods */
```

Main3.java

```
class Main3
{
  public native void callOtherFuncs();
  static
  {
    System.loadLibrary ("Main3");
  }
  public static void main (String[] args)
  {
    Main3 m = new Main3();
    m.callOtherFuncs();
  }
}
```

New3.java

```
class New3
{
  public void printHello()
  {
    System.out.println("Hello from New3's printHello()");
  }
}
```

Nat3.c

```
/* Allocating another Java object and calling its method
*/

#include "Main3.h"
JNIEXPORT void JNICALL Java_Main3_callOtherFuncs(JNIEnv
*env, jobject obj)
{
  jclass cls;
  jmethodID mid;

  cls = (*env)->FindClass(env, "New3");

  /* Create an instance of the class New3 */
  obj = (*env)->AllocObject(env, cls);

  /* Get the ID of an instance method of the instance
     created above and invoke that method */

  mid = (*env)->GetMethodID(env, cls, "printHello",
                            "()V");
  (*env)->CallVoidMethod(env, obj, mid);
}
```

Operation of the Program

```
java Main3
  Hello from New3's printHello()
```

Implementation

In this example Main3 invokes the native method `callOtherFuncs()`, which creates an instance of the class New3 and invokes the instance method `printHello`.

It's very easy to create an instance of a Java class from a native method. The two main methods that the JNI API provides for this are `AllocObject()` and `NewObject()`. The difference between these two is that `AllocObject()` doesn't call the constructor method while creating the instance, whereas in `NewObject()` you can specify which constructor should be called.

`AllocObject()` takes two arguments: the `JNIEnv` argument and a handle to the class whose instance we want to create. So we first get the handle to the class:

```
cls = (*env)->FindClass(env, "New3");
```

The instance is then created:

```
obj = (*env)->AllocObject(env, cls);
```

Now we can use this like any other instance (such as the one passed to the native method as the second argument, `obj`). We're calling the method `print-Hello()` of this instance just like we did in the previous example:

```
mid = (*env)->GetMethodID(env, cls, "printHello", "()V");
(*env)->CallVoidMethod(env, obj, mid);
```

This instance method prints the text which we're getting as output.

The next thing you may want to learn is how a native method can set values of static and instance variables of Java classes.

7.3.2 Example: Native Method Setting Static and Instance Variables

Purpose of the Program
This program shows how a native method can set the static and instance variables of Java classes.

Concepts Covered in the Program
In this program we show how the `SetField()` and `SetStaticField()` family of methods can be used.

Source Code

```
/* The native method of this program creates an instance
   of the class New4. It then sets one instance variable
   and one static variable of that class */
```

Main4.java

```
class Main4
{
  public native void callOtherFuncs();
  static
  {
    System.loadLibrary ("Main4");
  }
  public static void main (String[] args)
  {
    Main4 m = new Main4();
    m.callOtherFuncs();
  }
}
```

New4.java

```
class New4
{
  public static int value = 0;
  public int new2Val = 0;

  public void printValue()
  {
    System.out.println("The variable 'value' is " +
                          value);
    System.out.println("The variable 'new2Val' is " +
                          new2Val);
  }
}
```

Nat4.c

```
#include "Main4.h"
JNIEXPORT void JNICALL Java_Main4_callOtherFuncs(JNIEnv
*env, jobject obj1)
{
```

```
jclass cls;
jmethodID mid;
jobject obj;
jfieldID fid, fid2;

cls = (*env)->FindClass(env, "New4");

/* Create an instance of New4 */

obj = (*env)->AllocObject(env, cls);

/* Print value of variable before setting */

mid = (*env)->GetMethodID(env, cls, "printValue",
"()V");
(*env)->CallVoidMethod(env, obj, mid);

/* Every field of a class has a unique ID which can be
   used for accessing that field. This line gets the ID
   of the field new2Val so that it can be manipulated.
   */

fid = (*env)->GetFieldID(env, cls, "new2Val", "I");

/* Set the instance variable's value as 900 */

(*env)->SetIntField(env, obj, fid, 900);

/* Print value of variable after setting */

(*env)->CallVoidMethod(env, obj, mid);

/* Similarly, get the ID of the static variable "value"
   of the class New4 */

fid2 = (*env)->GetStaticFieldID(env, cls, "value", "I");

/* Set the value of this static variable as 500 */
```

```
    (*env)->SetStaticIntField(env, obj, fid2, 500);

    (*env)->CallVoidMethod(env, obj, mid);
}
```

Operation of the Program

```
java Main4
  The variable "value" is 0
  The variable "new2Val" is 0
  The variable "value" is 0
  The variable "new2Val" is 900
  The variable "value" is 500
  The variable "new2Val" is 900
```

Implementation

In this example, the native method callOtherFuncs() is invoked from Main4. This method in turn sets the field "new2Val", which is an instance variable defined in another class, New4. It also sets the variable "value", which is a static field defined in New4.

To explicitly show this, the native method calls printValue(), a method defined in New4, just before it sets a variable and just after. The method prints out the values of the two variables "new2Val" and "value".

We're first creating an instance of the class New4:

```
obj = (*env)->AllocObject(env, cls);
```

The method ID of printValue() is then obtained and is used for calling the method. This prints out the initial two values of "value" and "new2Val", both of which are 0.

Then it sets the field "new2Val". To do this, it first needs to obtain the ID of this field. This is similar to a method ID. For instance variables, the JNI API method used is GetFieldID():

```
fid = (*env)->GetFieldID(env, cls, "new2Val", "I");
```

The last argument once again is the signature of the field. Since new2Val is an int, its signature is "I".

The field is set by using the `SetField()` family of API routines. Since this field is an `int`, we're using the method `SetIntField()`:

```
(*env)->SetIntField(env, obj, fid, 900);
```

The third argument is the field ID we obtained above. The last one is the value to which we wish to set the variable. Now "new2Val" is set to 900, but "value" is still 0. When we invoke `printValue()` now it displays these two values.

After this we set the static variable "value", using the `SetStaticField()` family:

```
fid2 = (*env)->GetStaticFieldID(env, cls, "value", "I");
(*env)->SetStaticIntField(env, obj, fid2, 500);
```

Now that the static field has also been set, a call to `printValue()` shows that "new2Val" is now 900 and "value" is 500.

7.4 Passing Objects as Parameters

Until now we've used a large number of methods of the JNI API so you should feel pretty comfortable exploring other methods that the API offers. To wrap up, let's look at one more example of variable setting. In the previous examples we've just been dealing with the primitive data types. In this example we show how you can pass around a Java object, specifically, a string.

7.4.1 Example: Passing a String and Setting a String Object

Purpose of the Program
This program shows how a native method can accept a string object as an input. It also shows how the native method can set the string variable which is defined in a Java class.

Concepts Covered in the Program
This example extends some of the concepts we've learned so far. In previous examples these were applied on primitive data types; here we show how they can be extended to accommodate Java objects.

Source Code

```
/* In this program we're passing a string object to the
   native method which prints it on the standard output.
   The native method also sets the value of a string
   variable declared in Main5. */
```

Main5.java

```java
public class Main5
{
  public native void natFunc(String s);
  public String instString;
  static
  {
    System.loadLibrary("Main5");
  }
  public static void main(String args[])
  {
    Main5 m;
    m = new Main5();
    String s = new String("My String");

    /* Initialize the value of the instance variable
       instString */

    m.instString = new String("Initial String");

    /* Call the native method and pass a string object to
       it as a parameter */

    m.natFunc(s);
  }

  /* This method will be invoked by the native method to
     print the current value of instString */

  public void printVal()
  {
```

```
        System.out.println("'instString' is " + instString);
    }
}
```

Nat5.c

```c
#include "Main5.h"
JNIEXPORT void JNICALL Java_Main5_natFunc (JNIEnv *env,
jobject obj, jstring s)
{
    const char *theString;
    const char *newStringBytes = "The New String";
    jstring newString;
    jboolean *isCopy = 0;
    jclass cls;
    jmethodID mid;
    jfieldID fid;

    /* The method GetStringUTFChars() is being used to
       convert the string object to an array of characters so
       that our C program can handle it like a C string */

    theString = (*env)->GetStringUTFChars(env, s, isCopy);

    /* Now that we've done the conversion we can use this
       string as a normal array of characters */

    printf("\n The string passed to native method is %s\n",
    theString);

    cls = (*env)->FindClass(env, "Main5");

    mid = (*env)->GetMethodID(env, cls, "printVal", "()V");

    /* Call the method printVal() of Main5 so that the
       initial value of instString is displayed */

    (*env)->CallVoidMethod(env, obj, mid);
```

/* Get the ID of instString as we want to modify it. To see how the type signature of this is obtained, refer to the chart given at the end of the chapter. */

```
fid = (*env)->GetFieldID(env, cls, "instString",
"Ljava/lang/String;");
```

/* Convert the array of char newStringBytes to a jstring so that we can set the string object instString of the class Main5 */

```
newString = (*env)->NewStringUTF(env, newStringBytes);
```

/* Set the field instString */

```
(*env)->SetObjectField(env, obj, fid, newString);
```

/* Invoke printVal() again to print the newly set value of instString */

```
(*env)->CallVoidMethod(env, obj, mid);
}
```

Operation of the Program

```
java Main5
    The string passed to native method is My String
    instString is Initial String
    instString is The New String
```

Implementation

Main5 calls the native method natFunc() defined in Nat5.c. It passes a string as an argument to this function. natFunc() prints this string by first converting it to an array of characters and then using printf(). natFunc() then creates a new string object and sets a string variable defined in Main5 to this value. It invokes the method printVal() which displays the value of the variable before and after its value is set by natFunc().

Main5.java declares natFunc() as a native method. It also declares the string instString. An instance of the class is created in the main() method. instString is then set to "Initial String":

```
m.instString = new String("Initial String");
```

The string object s is created and passed as an argument to natFunc(). The method printVal() is a public method which, when invoked, prints out the value of instString.

Take a look at Nat5.c now. The string goes as a jstring argument to the native method. We need to convert it to a form that can be used in a C function. The API provides methods for this. We're making use of GetStringUT-FChars() which returns pointer to an array of characters:

```
const char *theString;
.....
theString = (*env)->GetStringUTFChars(env, s, isCopy);
```

So now we have theString which is a pointer to char. This means that we can use it like a normal C string. In fact, we're using it in printf() to print out the string:

```
printf("\n The string passed to native method is %s\n",
        theString);
```

Then we invoke the printVal() method to show that the value of inst-String is "Initial String".

After this we create a new string object and set the value of instString equal to this. The new string is created by using NewStringUTF():

```
newString = (*env)->NewStringUTF(env, newStringBytes);
```

Here newStringBytes is a pointer to char which we declared above and initialized to "The New String":

```
const char *newStringBytes = "The New String";
```

To set the field, we need to get its ID:

```
fid = (*env)->GetFieldID(env, cls, "instString",
                         "Ljava/lang/String;");
```

Here the signature is "Ljava/lang/String;" in accordance with what we learned in our discussion on signatures.

Then we use `SetObjectField()`, another method of the `SetField()` family, to set the value of `instString`:

```
(*env)->SetObjectField(env, obj, fid, newString);
```

The method `printVal()` is again invoked to show the new value of `instString` which has now been set to "`The New String`".

Now, you know very well that if Dad won't give you money, you can get it by conning the guy next door into buying your worst-seller "How to Become a Billionaire"—i.e., if Java doesn't offer you something, you can achieve the same results by integrating native methods that offer the capability.

Chart of Type Signatures
The signature of a method looks as follows:

```
(argument-types) return-type
```

The `argument-types` and `return-type` can be derived from the following chart:

Java Representation	Signature Representation
boolean	Z
byte	B
char	C
short	S
int	I
long	J
float	F
double	D
fully-qualified-class	L fully-qualified-class;
type[]	[type

An example of a representation
A representation of:

```
short myMethod(char c, String s, float[] f)
```

would be:

```
(CLjava/lang/String;[F)S
```

CHAPTER 8

OBJECT SERIALIZATION

In the chapter on streams we saw how different data types such as int, char and String can be stored in a file or passed around in streams. JDK 1.1 goes one step further — it also allows Java objects to be stored and retrieved from streams. This is the focus of discussion in the lone example of this brief but important chapter.

8.1 Introduction to Object Serialization

An object must either implement the Serializable interface or the Externalizable interface for it to be storable in a stream. In this chapter we'll be looking at Serializable objects.

An instance of a class which implements the java.io.Serializable interface can be stored in a stream and later retrieved from it. The retrieved instance will be exactly like the stored instance, and values of the variables which were set before the class was stored will be available. Moreover, you can even declare certain fields to be such that their values are not retrievable. These are typically fields which contain some private, confidential data.

8.1.1 Example: Storing and Retrieving an Object in a File

Purpose of the Program
This program shows how an object can be stored in a file and how it can be retrieved from the file.

Concepts Covered in the Program
The example shows how the Serializable interface can be used for storing and retrieving objects just as if they were ordinary data types.

Source Code

```
/* In this program we're creating a class SerObj which is
   serializable. This means that the class can be written
   to a stream and later retrieved from it just like a
   primitive data type.

   The class WriteObj will create an instance of this
   class and store it in a file.

   The class ReadObj will then read that file to retrieve
   the instance. */
```

SerObj.java

```
import java.io.*;
public class SerObj implements java.io.Serializable
{
  int value;
  static int statVal;
  SerObj2 s;
  private transient int transVal;
  SerObj()
  {
    value=45;
    s = new SerObj2();
    s.obj2Val = 55;
    transVal = 65; // This value cannot be retrieved as
    its private transient
    statVal = 75; // This value will be reset to 0 as
    static values are not stored
  }
```

```
   }
class SerObj2 implements java.io.Serializable
{
   int obj2Val;
}
```

WriteObj.java

```
import java.io.*;
class WriteObj
{
   public static void main(String[] args)
   {
      SerObj s1 = new SerObj();
      try
      {
        FileOutputStream f1 = new
        FileOutputStream("SrlFile");

        /* Create an ObjectOutputStream around the output
           stream of this file. This allows us to write
           out objects in a serial fashion via its
           writeObject() method. */

        ObjectOutputStream os = new ObjectOutputStream(f1);

        /* Write the object s1 to the file SrlFile. This
           can be later retrieved by a readObject() in the
           same class or by another class. */

        os.writeObject(s1);

        os.flush();
        os.close();
      }catch(IOException e){}
   }
}
```

ReadObj.java

```
import java.io.*;
class ReadObj
```

```java
{
  public static void main(String[] args)
  {
    SerObj s2;
    try
    {
      FileInputStream f2 = new FileInputStream("SrlFile");

      /* Create an ObjectInputStream around the input
         stream of this file. This allows us to read
         objects in a serial fashion via its readObject()
         method. */

      ObjectInputStream is = new ObjectInputStream(f2);
      try
      {

        /* Read the object stored by WriteObj. We're
           type casting it to SerObj because we know
           that the object stored by WriteObj was an
           instance of this class. */

        s2 = (SerObj)is.readObject();

        /* Print out the values of the variables
           defined in the object just retrieved. Their
           values should be the same as they were when
           WriteObj wrote the object. */

            System.out.println("Value of 'value' is " +
                                  s2.value);
            System.out.println("Value of 'statVal' is "
                                  + s2.statVal);
            System.out.println("Value of 'obj2Val' is "
                                  + s2.s.obj2Val);

      }catch(ClassNotFoundException c)
            {c.printStackTrace();}
      is.close();
    }catch(IOException e){}
  }
}
```

To Compile and Run

```
javac WriteObj.java ReadObj.java SerObj.java

java WriteObj
java ReadObj
```

Output of the Program

When you run ReadObj, the output is:

```
Value of 'value' is 45
Value of 'statVal' is 0
Value of 'obj2Val' is 55
```

Implementation

A serializable object is one which can be stored in a stream. This means that by making an object serializable you can pass the object around between programs that are connected to the same stream. It also means that the object can be written to a file (which is nothing but another stream-based operation).

An instance of a class which implements the Serializable interface is a serializable object. When such an object is stored in a stream, sufficient information is stored in the stream so that the fields of the object can be retrieved when the object is being read from the stream. As we'll see, you can specify that particular fields be nonretrievable.

In our example, we have a class SerObj whose instance we want to store in a file. The class is defined in SerObj.java, and its instance is created in WriteObj.java and is stored into the file SrlFile. ReadObj.java retrieves the object from SrlFile.

Now, down to the actual code.

The class SerObj which exists in SerObj.java implements the Serializable interface. This means that we can store an instance of this class in a stream and later retrieve it. There are four variables defined in this class—value, statVal, s and transVal:

```
int value;
static int statVal;
SerObj2 s;
private transient int transVal;
```

value is an int, statVal is a static int, s is an object of the class SerObj2, and transVal is another int defined with two more modifiers before it.

The constructor SerObj() sets value equal to 45, sets statVal equal to 75, and creates a new instance of the class SerObj2 and sets one of its variables to 55. It also sets the variable transVal to 65.

The class SerObj2 which also implements Serializable is also defined in this Java file. As you saw above, this class is being instantiated by SerObj() which also sets its variable obj2Val.

Now we see how this serializable object is stored in a file. The implementation of this is in WriteObj.java.

First, an instance of the class SerObj is created:

```
SerObj s1 = new SerObj();
```

The class WriteObj creates a new file, "SrlFile", to which the object will be written. To write an object we make use of another stream, ObjectOutput-Stream. An ObjectOutputStream is created by using an output stream. In this case we're using FileOutputStream to create our ObjectOutputStream:

```
FileOutputStream f1 = new FileOutputStream("SrlFile");
ObjectOutputStream os = new ObjectOutputStream(f1);
```

ObjectOutputStream implements the method writeObject() for writing objects to a stream. We're using this method to write the object s1 to SrlFile:

```
os.writeObject(s1);
```

And that's it. The object has been stored in SrlFile and can be retrieved by another program (or the same program). Note that we're not explicitly storing the object SerObj2. This is because when an object is stored, all serializable objects that it refers to are stored as well.

writeObject() serializes the specified object (in this case, s1), and it also traverses other objects it references and serializes them as well. All this serialized information is then written to the stream. This information includes stuff which will help to restore the respective objects when the readObject() method is invoked.

The code for retrieval has been written in ReadObj.java. In this we create an ObjectInputStream on the file SrlFile. An ObjectOutputStream is being created because this stream allows us to read objects via the `readObject()` method:

```
FileInputStream f2 = new FileInputStream("SrlFile");
ObjectInputStream is = new ObjectInputStream(f2);
```

The object is read by using the method `readObject()`:

```
s2 = (SerObj)is.readObject();
```

We're then printing the values of the variables `value`, `statVal` and `obj2Val`:

```
System.out.println("Value of 'value' is " + s2.value);
System.out.println("Value of 'statVal' is " + s2.statVal);
System.out.println("Value of 'obj2Val' is " +
                 s2.s.obj2Val);
```

Even though the instance `s` of SerObj2 was never explicitly stored in `WriteObj.java`, it is available, which is why we're printing the value of the variable `obj2Val`.

But we're not even attempting to print the variable `transVal` defined in SerObj. And the reason is not that we were too lazy to write that piece of code. If you look at `SerObj.java`, you'll see that `transVal` is defined as:

```
private transient int transVal;
```

The private transient modifier indicates that this variable is confidential material and should not be stored when the object is being written to SrlFile. In fact, if you try to reference this in `ReadObj.java`, `javac` will give you an error.

Similarly, the value of static variables is also not stored in the serial output file. However, the compiler doesn't give an error if you try to access static variables. However, to be safe, it is advised that you don't put confidential data in serializable objects.

CHAPTER 9

REMOTE
METHOD
INVOCATION

The remote control — perhaps the most widely used gadget today. A TV without a remote doesn't sell anymore. The power that this small device gives us couch potatoes is so enormous that many a mini-Waterloo in households has stemmed from the obsessive desire to gain control of it.

And with programming going from structured to object-oriented, with a goal of pushing software as close to reality as possible, how far behind can the concept of remote control remain?

9.1 Introduction to RMI

In the chapter on networking we saw how two applications can communicate over the network. But this communication was limited to data transfer from one to the other. However, the complexity of programs being churned out today requires us to go many steps further — applications should be able to remotely invoke each other's methods. The age of distributed applications has come.

Version 1.1 of Java makes this possible through Remote Method Invocation (RMI). Using this, you can create applications running on different (or the same) host(s) which can invoke one another's methods.

The overall idea is surprisingly simple. There can be one or more servers running Java applications. Other Java applications can invoke the methods of these remote objects.

Every remote object needs to be registered. This registration can be done through RMI classes with a bootstrap naming service. This bootstrap naming service is provided to us by Java. Remote objects can register themselves with it. A client can then check this service in the desired host to locate the object whose method it wishes to invoke (remotely). Once this object has been located, a reference to it is obtained and this reference is then used for invoking its methods.

For every remote object there is a local surrogate object (also known as a stub) that resides on the client that wishes to invoke methods of the remote object. This stub contains information about the methods of the remote object that can be invoked and serves as the interface used by the client.

The client communicates only with the stub, not with the actual remote object.

Stubs are generated by using the `rmic` compiler.

RMI makes use of object serialization (which we've already discussed) for passing around parameters between these methods. A parameter or a return value can be any Java type that is serializable. This means that you can pass around all Java primitive types, remote objects and other objects that implement the Serializable interface.

There are a number of interfaces and classes that make RMI available. These are defined in the packages `java.rmi` and `java.rmi.server`.

9.1.1 Example: Application Invoking a Remote Object's Methods

Purpose of the Program

This program shows how an application running on one machine can invoke the methods of another application running on another machine.

Concepts Covered in this Program

This example introduces you to RMI and shows how one application can call another, pass parameters to it and receive return values.

Source Code

```
/* In this program we have an object, FileServerImpl,
   which is running on the server. There is an object,
   ClientSide, running on the client, which tries to
   invoke  methods of this server-side object. */
```

Server side:

FileServer.java

```
/* For an object to allow itself to be available for
   Remote Method Invocation, it should implement the
   Remote interface or an interface extended from that.
   We're declaring the FileServer interface here in which
   we're declaring all the methods of our object that can
   be remotely invoked. */

public interface FileServer extends java.rmi.Remote
{
   String readFromServer() throws java.rmi.RemoteException;
   void writeToServer(String a) throws
   java.rmi.RemoteException;
}
```

FileServerImpl.java

```
/* This is the class whose instance will be running on
   the server. It implements the interface we created
   above so it can allow remote method invocation. */

import java.rmi.*;
import java.rmi.server.UnicastRemoteObject;
public class FileServerImpl
   extends UnicastRemoteObject
   implements FileServer
{
   public FileServerImpl() throws java.rmi.RemoteException
   {
      /* By invoking the constructor of UnicastRemoteObject,
         this object is exported so that it can listen for
         incoming calls from clients trying to invoke its
         methods. */

      super();
   }
```

```
public static void main(String args[])
{
  // Create and install the security manager
  System.setSecurityManager(new RMISecurityManager());

  try
  {
    /* Create an instance of our object */

    FileServerImpl obj = new FileServerImpl();

    /* This object is bound in the registry service of
       this machine with the name "FileServer". Any
       client which needs to access this object's
       methods will first have to request a handle from
       the registry naming service, which maintains a
       table associating objects with names to which
       they're bound. */

    Naming.rebind("FileServer", obj);

    System.out.println("Name FileServer bound to
                        registry");

  } catch (Exception e)
    {
    System.out.println("Exception occurred in
                        FileServerImpl: ");
    e.printStackTrace();
    }
  }

/* This is a method which can be remotely invoked by a
   client. It accepts a string passed as a parameter by
   the client and prints it on the standard output of the
   server. */
}
public void writeToServer(String message) throws
RemoteException
{
```

```
      System.out.println("This message is from the client: " +
                          message);
   }


   /* This is another method which can be remotely invoked by
      a client. It returns a string to the client. The client
      will print this string on its standard output. */

   public String readFromServer() throws RemoteException
   {
      String toReturn = new String("Server says hello");
      return toReturn;
   }


}
```

Client side:

```
   /* This object runs on the client machine. It invokes
      methods of the remote object running on the server
      "myServer.abc.com", bound to the name "FileServer". */
```

ClientSide.java

```
   import java.rmi.*;

   public class ClientSide
   {
      public static void main(String args[])
      {
         String message = "";
         try
         {

            String n = "//myServer.abc.com/FileServer";

            /* Look up the naming registry service of the
               machine myServer.abc.com for an object which is
               bound to the name "FileServer". */
```

```
    FileServer obj = (FileServer) Naming.lookup(n);

    /* Invoke methods of the remote object */

    message = obj.readFromServer();
    obj.writeToServer("Hello from client");

    /* Print the String returned by the method
       readFromServer() */

    System.out.println("Message from server: " +
                          message);
} catch (Exception e)
    {
        System.out.println("Exception in ");
        e.printStackTrace();
    }
}
}
```

Compiling and Running

On the server:

1. Move `java` files to a directory, say, `/myDir/HTML`.

2. Compile `java` files:

    `javac *.java`

3. Set CLASSPATH (e.g., on Solaris: `setenv CLASSPATH /myDir/HTML`).

4. Run RMI compiler:

    `rmic FileServerImpl`

5. Start `rmiregistry`:

    On Solaris: "`rmiregistry &`"

    On Windows: "`start rmiregistry`" or "`javaw rmiregistry`"

6. Transfer following files to the client (e.g., using ftp):

```
FileServer.class FileServerImpl_Stub.class
```

7. Execute `FileServerImpl` using `java`:

    ```
    java -Djava.rmi.server.codebase=
    ```
    http://myServer.abc.com/myDir/HTML/

    FileServerImpl

On the client:

1. Move ClientSide.java to directory where files were put in step 6 above.

2. javac ClientSide.java

3. java ClientSide

Output of the Program

On the server:

```
This message is from the client: Hello from client
```

On the client:

```
Message from server: Server says hello
```

Implementation

On the server side, we first create an interface in `FileServer.java` which contains all the methods of the object on the server that can be remotely invoked. The object is then created in `FileServerImpl.java`, which implements this interface. The methods which are declared in the interface are defined in this `java` file.

These two files are compiled. Then we set our CLASSPATH to include the directory in which these files exist and run the RMI stub compiler, `rmic`, which will generate two more `.class` files: `FileServerImpl_Skel.class` and `FileServerImpl_Stub.class`. These are the skeleton and stub files that contain information about the remote object.

The skeleton remains on the server side. It contains a method that dispatches calls to the actual remote method implementation. The stub, on the other hand, resides on the client. If a remote method is called, the stub sends it to the server on which the actual implementation is present. So the client never directly calls a remote method — it just talks to the stub which actually forwards the method invocation.

Next we run `rmiregistry` on the server. This starts up the remote object registry which maintains information about the remote objects available on a particular port. A remote object needs to bind itself to the `rmiregistry` for it to become available to other clients. Once it is registered, a client can look it up and make remote method invocations.

You can specify the port number on which to run `rmiregistry` by using the optional port parameter (e.g., rmigistry port 2001). By default (i.e., if you omit the port parameter), port 1099 is used.

Then we transfer the files `FileServer.class` and `FileServerImpl_Stub.class` to the client. These are required by the client to make the remote method invocation. As we discussed above, the client doesn't directly do the invocation — it uses the stub file for this.

The remote object is then started using `java`. In the code, we're binding this remote object to the name "FileServer" with the RMI registry naming service.

The code in `ClientSide.java` locates a reference to this object by using the Naming class, which checks the naming service of the specified server for a remote object with a particular name (in this case, "FileServer").

Once this reference has been obtained, the remote methods can be called just like normal methods of another object. Now, to the code.

We first create the interface file that will define an interface to be used by our implementation. The interface is defined in `FileServer.java`, and its implementation is in `FileServerImpl.java`.

This interface extends the Remote interface, which is an interface used to identify all remote objects. Only the methods defined in this interface will be available for remote invocation:

```
public interface FileServer extends java.rmi.Remote
```

We wish to provide two methods for remote invocation: `readFromServer()` and `writeToServer()`. The first one returns a string object, while the second one accepts a string object and writes the value to the standard output.

In the case of remote methods, several types of errors can occur. For this, each remote method is required to throw an exception, RemoteException. So our methods are declared as follows in the interface:

```
String readFromServer() throws java.rmi.RemoteException;
void writeToServer(String a) throws
java.rmi.RemoteException;
```

The actual implementation is provided in `FileServerImpl.java`. Let's look at this file now.

We're first importing the `java.rmi` package, as we'll need some classes from this:

```
import java.rmi.*;
```

Remote objects must extend the RemoteObject class. Typically, they should extend the class UnicastRemoteObject, which is defined in `java.rmi.server`. So we're importing this:

```
import java.rmi.server.UnicastRemoteObject;
```

Our implementation has to extend this class, and it also needs to implement the interface we created above. Here's what the declaration looks like:

```
public class FileServerImpl extends UnicastRemoteObject
implements
FileServer
```

In the constructor, we're calling the `super()` method so that initialization of the remote object is done. This invokes a constructor of UnicastRemoteObject. This exports the remote object by listening for incoming calls to the remote object:

```
public FileServerImpl() throws java.rmi.RemoteException
{
   super();
}
```

In the `main()` method, we first set the security manager. We're creating a new instance of RMISecurityManager for the purpose. The security manager is required to prevent unwanted operations:

```
System.setSecurityManager(new RMISecurityManager());
```

Next, we create an instance of FileServerImpl. The `rebind()` method of the class Naming is then used to bind this object to the registry naming service with the name "FileServer". This means that when a client asks for "FileServer", a reference to this object will be returned to it. This allows communication to occur:

```
Naming.rebind("FileServer", obj);
```

The method `writeToServer()` accepts a string object. As we explained in the interface, it needs to throw the RemoteException. This method receives a string object from the client and prints it on the standard output of the server:

```
System.out.println("This message is from the client: " +
                    message);
```

FileServerImpl also defines another method, `readFromServer()`, which returns a string object to the client:

```
String toReturn = new String("Server says hello");
return toReturn;
```

Now our object is all set to accept calls from the client. So let's see how the client does the remote method invocation. This functionality is implemented in `ClientSide.java`. First the `java.rmi` package is imported in this.

In the `main()` method we declare an object of the type String. This will be used to store the value returned by the remote method `readFromServer()`.

In order to locate a reference to the remote object we need to make use of the `lookup()` method of the Naming class. The argument supplied to it is in a URL form. It contains the name of the server whose registry naming service has to be looked up. It also contains the name to which the object has been bound in the naming service on that server. We're defining this URL in a string, n:

```
String n = "//myServer.abc.com/FileServer";
```

A reference to the object is then obtained using this URL:

```
FileServer obj = (FileServer) Naming.lookup(n);
```

Now we can use this object like any other local object. First we're invoking the method readFromServer(). If you look at FileServerImpl.java, you'll see that this method returns a string. We're storing this string in the variable message that we defined above. We'll be printing this later:

```
message = obj.readFromServer();
```

Similarly, the method writeToServer() is also invoked. We're passing a string to this method, which will be displayed on the server:

```
obj.writeToServer("Hello from client");
```

Next we simply print the message we stored above on the standard output of the client:

```
System.out.println("Message from server: " + message);
```

There are several exceptions which can occur. For example, if the name File-Server has not been bound on the server, a NotBoundException will be thrown. If the registry cannot be contacted a RemoteException will be thrown, and if the server host is unknown to this system an UnknownHostException will be thrown. We're catching all these exceptions with the generic "Exception":

```
catch (Exception e)
```

More information about the exact exception can be obtained from the stack trace of the exception we're printing:

```
e.printStackTrace();
```

This finishes our discussion about how one application can use RMI to invoke methods of another. But this idea is not limited to applications. As we'll see in the next example, an applet can also invoke methods of an application.

The same concept can be applied for remote method invocation from an applet to an application. That's what we're covering in this final example on RMI.

9.1.2 Example: An Applet Invoking Remote Methods of an Application

Purpose of the Program
This program shows how an applet can invoke methods of a remote application.

Concepts Covered in this Program
This example simply extends the concepts covered in the previous example to show how they can be applied to applets.

Source Code

On the server:

FileServer.java and FileServerImpl.java—same as in the previous example

On the client:

```
/* This applet invokes methods of the object
   FileServerImpl that's running on the server */
```

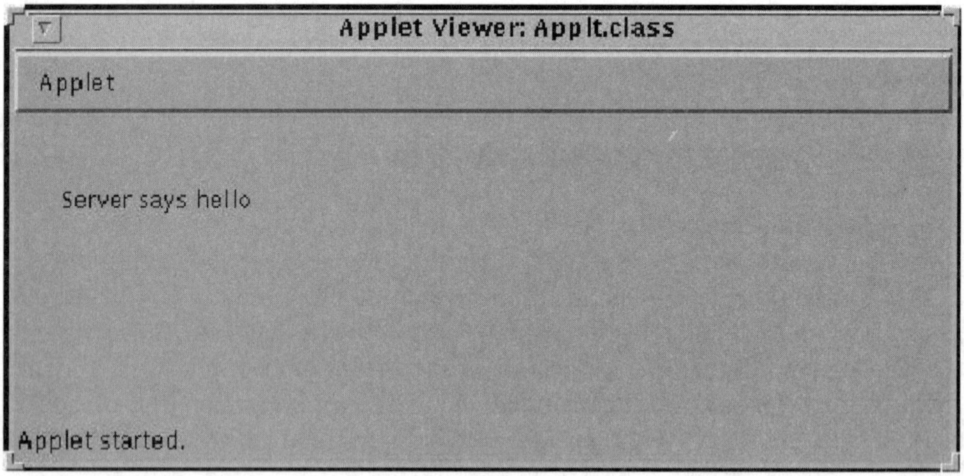

Figure 9-1

Applt.java

```java
import java.rmi.*;
import java.awt.*;
import java.applet.*;

public class Applt extends Applet
{
    String message = "";
    public void init()
    {
      try
      {
        String n = "//myServer.abc.com/FileServer";

        /* Locate the object on "myServer.abc.com" that
           is bound to the name "FileServer" in the
           registry naming service of that machine */

        FileServer obj = (FileServer) Naming.lookup(n);

        /* Invoke methods of this remote object */

        message = obj.readFromServer();
        obj.writeToServer("Hello from the applet
                          Applt");
      } catch (Exception e)
      {
      System.out.println("Applt: an exception occurred in ");
      e.printStackTrace();
      }
    }
    public void paint(Graphics g)
    {
      g.drawString(message, 25, 50);
    }
}
```

myApp.html

```
<HTML>
<HEAD>
<BODY>
<applet
codebase="http://serverOnWhichAppletIsPresent.abc.com"
code=Applt.class height=160 width=500>
</applet>
</BODY>
</HTML>
```

Compiling and Running

On the server:
Same steps as in previous example.

On the client:

1. Copy `Applt.java` and `myApp.html` to the directory into which the stub file has been transferred.

2. `javac Applt.java`

3. Set the CLASSPATH to include this directory.

4. `appletviewer myApp.html`

Output of the Program

On the server:
This message is from the client: Hello from the applet Applt

On the client:
The applet looks as shown above.

Implementation
If you read the implementation details of the previous example, this one doesn't need any explanation. The only reason this example is included is to show you that the concept of Remote Method Invocation can be extended to applets.

Here we have an HTTP server `serverOnWhichAppletIsPresent` on which we're running the applet `Applt`. This applet invokes methods of the remote object FileServerImpl which is running on the server `myServer`.

Now you know how to create a distributed application. For example, you can have one or more servers doing a specific job. There can be clients doing their own jobs. Whenever these clients need some data from the server or need to invoke some of the server's methods, they can do so using RMI. This way, a truly distributed system can be created.

CHAPTER 10

JAR FILES

Before JDK 1.1, all the individual components of an applet had to be downloaded by the browser separately. So, if an applet referred to a number of images and classes, each of these was downloaded separately, which meant a lot of wasted time.

This problem has been solved in 1.1 through the use of JAR files. A JAR file is an archive that contains all related files in one giant file. So if an applet refers to some classes and images/sound files or any other piece of data, all these files can be put in one JAR file. The browser will then download this complete file in one stroke, greatly improving the speed of downloading.

In addition, when a JAR file is created, its contents are compressed. This further improves the downloading time. (The JAR file is based on the ZIP file format.) As an added advantage, JAR files can be signed, which allows the receiver to verify that the data is coming from the right source. This feature is discussed in great detail in the chapter on security.

10.1 Using the JAR Tool

Java provides us with a tool to create JAR files and to extract data out of them.

For those of you familiar with the **tar** utility, which is available on most systems, the Java archiving tool **jar** has a similar command-line interface.

10.1.1 Example: Creating a JAR File

```
jar cf TrstApp.jar TrstApp.class ws.html
```

To create a JAR file, you can use the `jar` tool and supply arguments `cf` to it, followed by the name of the output JAR file, followed by a list of classes/sound files/images that you wish to archive in this file. In this example, we're creating a JAR file called `TrstApp.jar`. The archive will consist of one class, `TrstApp.class`, and one HTML file, `ws.html`.

10.1.2 Example: Extracting the Contents of a JAR File

```
jar xf TrstApp.jar
```

The `xf` parameter extracts the contents of the JAR file; i.e., the class `TrstApp.class` and the HTML file `ws.html` will be extracted from the JAR file `TrstApp.jar` with the above command.

10.1.3 Example: Informing the Browser of the JAR File

We have now created and extracted a JAR file. But how do we tell our browser that our applet and all its required files exist in a JAR file (instead of individual files)?

To do this, a new tag, `archive`, is added to the HTML file.

```
<HTML>
<BODY>
<applet codebase=http://myServer/HTML code=TrstApp.class
archive="jarFile/TrstApp.jar" width=500 height=200
</applet>
</BODY>
</HTML>
```

Here, the browser is being informed that it should download the JAR file `TrstApp.jar` which exists on `myServer` in the directory `HTML/jarFile`. The archive tag is being used for this purpose. Note that we still need to supply the code tag. This is because an archive can contain multiple class files, so the browser needs to know which one it should execute first.

10.1.4 Example: Specifying Multiple JAR Files

You can use the archives tag to specify multiple JAR files to be downloaded. Each of these files must be separated by a comma.

```
<HTML>
<BODY>
<applet codebase=http://myServer/HTML code=TrstApp.class
archives="jarFile1/a.jar, jarFile2/b.jar, jarFile3/c.jar"
          width=500
height=200
</applet>
</BODY>
</HTML>
```

10.1.5 Example: Seeing the Contents of Your JAR File

```
jar tf TrstApp.jar
```

You can use the tf option to view the contents of the JAR file. The output of this command would look like this:

```
META-INF/MANIFEST.MF
TrstApp.class
ws.html
```

Wait a minute! You never added the directory META-INF or the file MANI-FEST.MF. So why do they suddenly appear in this JAR file? In fact, even when you extract (using jar xf), these will appear. META-INF is a directory that contains meta data associated with the JAR file. When jar is used, this directory is created. A manifest file called MANIFEST.MF is also created in this directory. The manifest file contains a list of files present in the archive.

As you'll see in the chapter on security, the signature file will also be stored in this directory.

CHAPTER 11

SECURITY

With the advent of Internet programming, one major concern emerged: what if someone connects to your machine over the Internet and wipes out your hard disk? Or finds out personal information and cleans out your bank account? The risks involved in sending confidential data over the Net have concerned many people. The best brains in the industry are working on these problems, and they're coming up with solutions, which at this time seem to be growing at a faster rate than the brilliant but insidious hacking algorithms.

In this chapter, we'll discuss some issues related to data security. We'll also provide Java's answer to these problems. The three examples that follow make use of the Java security framework. But first, you may want to learn a bit about security issues in general and ways to solve security problems.

11.1 Elements of Data Security

There are two major issues involved in data security:

1.   The receiver must be able to verify that data was indeed sent by the correct person.

2. The sender must be able to encrypt the data, and the receiver must be the only one able to decrypt this data.

There are several data security mechanisms available to solve these problems. Java has provided a layer above some of the data security mechanisms. This layer is, like the rest of Java, a platform-independent layer. Java provides you with a set of classes and methods you can use to request usage of a particular security algorithm, without having to bother about the actual implementation. The implementation of the algorithm is provided by a third party (or you can provide your own implementation). In fact, even if the implementation is changed, your Java code should not be affected. These third parties are known as providers. Java includes one default provider, called SUN.

There are different types of classes associated with different security features. Your programs can get an instance of the desired class and use its methods to apply that security feature.

So what are these security features? Well, all these features revolve around solving the two security-related issues we mentioned above. One of the most important features is a set of keys: a public key and a private key.

11.1.1 Key Pairs

You may think of these keys as a set of unique numbers. The public key and the private key come in tightly coupled pairs. For every public key, there is one, and only one, private key, and vice versa.

Let's solve a typical problem using keys. A person receiving data needs to be sure that data is coming from the right person. This is required because you don't want somebody else to intercept the data being sent to you and replace it with malicious or incorrect data.

For this, the sender generates a pair of public and private keys. The public key is then sent to the receiver, while the private key is retained by the sender.

The public key, as the name suggests, is not a very secret thing. Even if it gets into the wrong hands, it can't do any harm. This is because the public key in this case is just being used for verification at the receiver's end that the data came from the correct sender. Even if the data is intercepted, the only thing the public key can do is check whether the data came from the intended sender. The private key, on the other hand, should not be transmitted under normal conditions.

The sender "signs" the code using the private key, which resides only with the sender. In other words, using the private key, the sender creates a unique value which is sent to you (the receiver) along with the actual data that is being transmitted.

Once you receive this unique value, you can use the public key (which was earlier made available to you by the sender) to verify the data. The verification test will pass only if the data was signed using the private key that is associated with the public key you have.

So, if the verification test passes, you can be sure that the data was signed by a person who has the private key. This solves our first security problem. Now look at the next one. The sender needs to be sure that the data sent can be read only by intended readers. The simplest way to do this would be to have a connection for data transmission to which nobody else has access. But this is not the case with the Internet. Your data may be intercepted on the way by another person. Certainly you wouldn't want this data to be read by a crook, especially if it contains confidential information such as your Social Security number, credit card numbers, etc.

The next-best solution is to encode this data in such a manner that only a person who has the correct decoding key can decode the data and read its actual contents. This is exactly the model being followed.

A person who wants to *receive* an encrypted piece of data must generate a public-private key pair, then send the public key to the sender. The sender will encrypt the data using this public key and send the encrypted data to the receiver. This data can then be decrypted only by the receiver, as he is the only one who has the private key.

So a combination of the two solutions we've discussed above can be used for more secure transmission of confidential data. This complete solution, as you have seen, requires two pairs of public-private keys (unless both the sender and the receiver share the same key pair, which is not a very good idea, as a private key is meant to be known only to one party).

One question remains. How do the sender and receiver exchange their public keys? This can be done through email, ftp, floppies, or some other such mechanism. One common method is through the use of certificates.

A certificate can be thought of as a piece of data that contains an entity's public key and other information about that entity, such as the entity's name. The certificate is normally created by a Certificate Authority (CA), which is a business trusted to create certificates for others. So, if you want to send your public key to someone, you'll first get a certificate made by a CA (although you can make a certificate yourself, they are not normally acceptable by receivers). You need to supply your public key to the CA so that the certificate can be prepared. You can then send this certificate to your receivers.

Next, we get down to being more Java-specific.

11.2 Data Security in Java

As of version 1.1, Java's classes don't provide mechanisms for exchanging keys or data encryption, mainly because these mechanisms are not exportable out of the U.S. right now. Java also doesn't support certificate parsing, etc. These features will be provided in later releases.

Enough of what's *not* there. Let's look at what is already present. Java provides classes for creating key pairs as well as for signing and verifying data.

The class KeyPairGenerator can be used for generation of a pair of keys. The Signature class can be used for signing and verifying data. In order to manage keys, a database needs to be created. The Identity class is the basic key management class. An identity represents an actual object such as a person or a company. Each identity has a name and a public key.

Another class, called IdentityScope, is a subclass of Identity and is used for determining the scope of an Identity object. A good example for distinguishing between Identity and IdentityScope is email ID. Let's say there's a person (identity) with the name "abcd" who is part of a company (identity scope) called "xyz". The email ID of the person, following the standards of the company, would be "abcd@xyz.com" The email ID of the person is uniquely identified by using both the identity and the identity scope in which this identity is defined. The advantage of this is that it doesn't preclude another person with the same name in another company from getting an email ID containing that person's name. So there can be a different email ID called "abcd@rst.com".

But if another person whose name is "abcd" comes to "xyz", that person's email ID will have to be different — probably "abcd_1@xyz.com". In other words, within the same identity scope, every identity has a unique name and public key.

On every machine, a database is maintained which contains information about all the identities present on the system. The public key of each such identity is also stored in this database. If the identity has signing powers, it will also have a private key associated with it. This private key is stored in the database.

An entity that can sign data uses the Signature class to sign. As you may recall from above, in order to sign, this entity must have the private key. Moreover, this entity must be of the type Signer, which is a subclass of Identity (i.e., a special type of identity). In order to sign data, an instance of Signature is created. The Signer is obtained from the IdentityScope within which it is defined. The private key associated with this Signer is extracted from the database. This key is then supplied to the Signature object, which creates the signature.

To wrap up, the overall picture looks like this:

For person X to sign a piece of data, the following general steps need to be followed:

1. X must first create an identity and add it to the security database being maintained on X's system. If there is no database, it will be created the first time an identity is added.

2. X must then generate a pair of public and private keys. The public key will be sent to the receiver, and the private key will be used for signing the data.

3. X must generate a certificate (or get it generated from a CA) and send it to the receiver. The certificate must be generated using the public key of X. (X may very well not use certificates and instead use some other mechanism to send the public key to the receiver).

4. X must read the data to be signed, sign it using its own private key, and send the signature as well as the data file to the receiver.

For a person Y to verify that a piece of data came from X, these steps need to be followed:

1. Y must create an identity X in its security database and tell the security manager that this entity is trusted, i.e., it is okay to give some privileges to this entity.

2. Y must then add the public key received from X to the database. If the key has been sent in the form of a certificate, this certificate needs to be imported into the database.

3. Y must read the data file as well as the signature file and supply them to the verifier, which will verify whether the private key used to generate the signature matches with the public key that is present in the database for identity X.

11.2.1 Example: A Trusted Applet

Purpose of the Program

This program shows how an applet can be allowed to read/write files on your system.

Concepts Covered in this Program

This example explains what a trusted applet is and how "trust" can be used to override some of the security restrictions placed on applets. The program also shows how you can use a tool called `javakey`.

Source Code

TrstApp.java

```java
import java.awt.*;
import java.io.*;
import java.applet.*;

public class TrstApp extends Applet
{

   public void paint(Graphics g)

   {
     try
     {
       /* Try to create a file "tmpFile" on the client's
          machine and write a string in the file */
       PrintWriter pos = new PrintWriter(new
                           BufferedWriter(new
                           FileWriter("tmpFile")));
       String toWrite = new String("See, this applet can
                           write to a file
                           on your system - of course if you
                           allow it do so!");
       pos.write(toWrite);
       pos.close();
     } catch(IOException e){ e.printStackTrace();}
   }
}
```

ws.html

```html
<HTML>
<BODY>
```

```
<H1>WRITING TO A FILE</H1>
<applet codebase=http://myServer/home/vsharma/HTML
code=TrstApp.class
archive="TrstApp.jar"
width=500 height=50>
</applet>
</BODY></HTML>
```

Certificate directives:

cert_sh


```
# This is a sample certificate directive file.

# the ID of the signer
issuer.name=Sharma

# the cert to use for the signing
issuer.cert=1

# the ID of the subject
subject.name=Sharma

# the components of the X500 name for the subject
subject.real.name=Sharma
subject.org.unit=Sharma
subject.org=Sharma
subject.country=US

# Period of certificate validity
start.date=1 Jan 1997
end.date=31 Dec 1997

# Serial number of certificate
serial.number=1001

# Name of certificate file to be generated
out.file=Sharma.x509
```

sign_sh

```
# Signing directive. This is the directive file used by
# javakey to sign a jar file.

# Which signer to use. This must be in the system's
# database.
signer=Sharma

# Cert number to use for this signer. This determines which
# certificate will be included in the PKCS7 block. This is
# mandatory and is 1 based.
cert=1

# Cert chain depth of a chain of certificate to include.
# This is currently not supported.
chain=0

# The name to give to the signature file
signature.file=TrstApp
```

To Compile and Run

On the server where the applet is suppose to reside:

1. Compile the applet:

    ```
    java TrstApp.java
    ```

2. Create a trusted identity called Sharma with signing power:

    ```
    javakey -cs Sharma true
    ```

3. Generate 512 bit keys for Sharma using the DSA algorithm:

    ```
    javakey -gk Sharma DSA 512
    ```

4. Generate a certificate containing the public key of Sharma:

    ```
    javakey -gc cert_sh
    ```

5. Create a JAR file containing the applet and its HTML file:

   jar cf TrstApp.jar TrstApp.class ws.html

6. Sign the JAR file:

   javakey -gs sign_sh TrstApp.jar

7. Rename the generated signed file:

   On Solaris:

   ```
   mv TrstApp.jar.sig TrstApp.jar
   ```

   On Windows:

   ```
   rename TrstApp.jar.sig TrstApp.jar
   ```

   On the client side where the applet is to be run:

1. Transfer `certificate Sharma.x509` from the server to the client machine.

2. Create a trusted Identity called Sharma with no signing power:

   javakey -c Sharma true

3. Import a certificate of `Sharma` so that the public key of `Sharma` is stored in the database of `Sharma` on this machine:

   javakey -ic Sharma Sharma.x509

Execute the applet by opening the web page appletviewer:

```
http://myServer/home/vsharma/HTML/ws.html
```

Output of the Program
The file `tmpFile` will be created in the directory from which appletviewer was run by the client (so long as the person running appletviewer has write permissions in the directory).

Implementation
So what is a trusted applet? In the chapter on applets we said that an applet cannot read/write files on a client's machine. We don't need to belabor the

importance of this security restriction. But then, if you're sure that the applet belongs to a nonmalicious person, you may want to remove these restrictions. And with the new Java security features, you can do so.

A trusted applet is one which is given more privileges by the client. For an applet to be "trusted" it must be in a JAR file signed by a trusted person, and you should have a certificate for that person so that you can verify the signature on the file.

Look at the applet `TrstApp.java`. The applet is trying to write to the file `tmpFile` in the current directory. Under normal circumstances this will not be allowed because of security restrictions. Let's see how these restrictions can be lifted.

There are two tools we'll be using to remove the security restrictions: `javakey` and `jar`. `javakey` is used to create an identity both on the client and the server. It's also used to generate key pairs and a certificate which will contain the server's public key. `jar` is used to create a JAR file — a collection of all the files that need to be transmitted for the applet to execute (i.e., all files/images that the applet refers to will be sent in one stroke rather than being sent independently as is the normal case). `javakey` is then used by the server to sign this file.

In order to create a certificate and sign a file, `javakey` needs some parameters, such as the name of the person or organization performing these actions, the country to which it belongs, the validity period of the certificate, the name of the output certificate/signature file, etc. These are supplied in the form of parameter directive files. We're using `cert_sh` (for certificate generation) and `sign_sh` (for signature generation) directive files in our example.

Let's look at the overall picture.

On the server side, the trusted identity is created (if it's not already present) and given the power to sign other files. A pair of keys is generated; the private key will be used on the server side to sign the files. Using the public key, a certificate is generated. This certificate is transmitted to the client.

The client also creates a trusted identity with the same name as the identity created on the server. It imports the certificate sent by the server into this identity's database so that the database knows the public key of the identity. Once this is done, "trusted" communication can occur from the client to the server.

For this, the server simply needs to create a JAR file which contains all the files required by the applet. The server also needs to sign this JAR file and indicate in the HTML file that the transmission that will occur will contain a JAR file instead of individual files being sent separately.

Now, when the client tries to browse the HTML page of the server, the applet will be downloaded as a JAR file. The security manager on the client side will verify the signature (which will be contained within the JAR file) to make sure it was signed by the correct server. If it passes the verification, the applet will be given the required privileges on the client side.

Keeping these things in mind, it should be easy for you to understand the steps we've taken above. Nevertheless, here's an explanation:

Server Side

1. `java TrstApp.java`

   If you don't understand this step, maybe you're reading this book in the wrong direction.

2. `javakey -cs Sharma true`

   The `javakey -c` option is used to add an identity to the security database maintained by it. With `-c`, however, the identity doesn't have a signing authority. For this, you use `-cs`. This is followed by the name of the identity. The next argument is optional and specifies whether the signer is "trusted" or not. So the above line adds a trusted identity by the name of "Sharma" to the database. This identity has the power to sign files.

3. `javakey -gk Sharma DSA 512`

   An identity that needs to sign a document must have a pair of public and private keys associated with it. The above command is generating a pair of keys for "Sharma". Out of these, the public key will be sent in the form of a certificate to the client, and the private key will be retained and used for signing the JAR file, which will be generated in step 5. The `-gk` option generates keys. DSA is the name of the algorithm being used for key generation, and 512 is the size of the keys in bits.

4. `javakey -gc cert_sh`

   The public key has to be transported to the client. Instead of going through a CA, we're generating our own certificate. Directives are given to `javakey` using the directive file `cert_sh`. Let's look at some of the major fields of this file:

   `issuer.name=Sharma`

This is the name of the issuer of the certificate. It could be the name of a CA. This is different from **subject.name**, which tells you the name of the person who requested this certificate (the owner of the server).

start.date and **end.date** tell the validity period of the certificate. The signature verifier looks at these values before checking the validity of the signature to make sure the certificate has not expired.

out.file is the name of the file to which the certificate will be written. You can use cert_sh as a template to generate your own certificates.

In our example, upon running javakey -gc cert_sh, a certificate containing the public key of Sharma will be generated in the file Sharma.x509. This certificate will copied by the client for signature verification.

5. **jar cf TrstApp.jar TrstApp.class ws.html**

The JAR file is being created in this step. TrstApp.jar is the name of the output JAR file. The arguments following this are the files that will go into this JAR file. Since our applet needs two files to run, ws.html and TrstApp.class, we're putting both of them in the JAR file.

6. **javakey -gs sign_sh TrstApp.jar**

The JAR file now needs to be signed so that the client can verify the signature. Again, javakey is used for this. The -gs option generates the signature. sign_sh is the directive file which gives some information about signing to javakey. TrstApp.jar is the file that needs to be signed. This will create the signature file and put some meta data into the JAR file. The output file will be TrstApp.jar.sig, which needs to be renamed.

In sign_sh, signer is the name of the identity creating the signature. signature.file is the name of the file to which the signature should be written.

7. **mv TrstApp.jar.sig TrstApp.jar**

For non-Unix people, the mv command is being used to rename the TrstApp.jar.sig file TrstApp.jar. Use the corresponding command on your system for this purpose.

This renaming is required because in our HTML file we're indicating that the archive is TrstApp.jar:

codebase=http://myServer/home/vsharma/HTML code=TrstApp.class
archive="TrstApp.jar"

The appletviewer will try to look for `TrstApp.jar` in `/home/vsharma/` `HTML` on the server `myServer` and download it. Since a JAR file can contain more than one class file, the `code` parameter is required to indicate which is the first file of the applet that is to be executed.

Client Side

1. Transfer the certificate `Sharma.x509` from the server to the client machine. Until we have the certificate on the client machine, no signature verification can be done. So we transfer the file `Sharma.x509`, which was generated on the server in step 4 above, to the client machine.

2. **`javakey -c Sharma true`**

   An identity having the same name as the identity whose certificate was transported in step 1 needs to be added to the database on the client side. But this one is not going to have signing power, so we use the `-c` option instead of `-cs`. And yes, it needs to be "trusted", so the last parameter is `true`.

3. **`javakey -ic Sharma Sharma.x509`**

   We want the database to associate the identity `Sharma` with its public key which is present in the certificate `Sharma.x509`. We import this certificate using the `-ic` option in the database associated with the identity `Sharma`.

   Now we're all set to download a trusted applet from the server and allow it to wreak havoc on our system.

4. **`appletviewer http://myServer/home/vsharma/HTML/ws.html`**

   Does this need an explanation?

11.3 Security in Applications

You've seen how an applet can be given more powers, and have gotten an introduction to the basic security mechanism, including signing of files and creation of identities and certificates. Now let's look at how the same concepts can be applied to applications. In this example and the next we'll use a combination of `javakey` and some of the security-related classes that come as part of the JDK (as opposed to relying on just `javakey` as in the previous example).

11.3.1 Example: Code Signing and Verification in Applications

Purpose of the Program
This program shows how data can be signed on the server and how the signature can be verified by another application running on the client.

Concepts Covered in this Program
Here we show the usage of Java classes, such as Signer, Signature, Identity, etc., for the purpose of signing and verification of data. A mix and match of javakey and the Java classes is being used in this example.

Source Code

Server side:

SignFile.java

```java
import java.security.*;
import java.io.*;
class SignFile
{
  public static void main(String[] args)
  {
    /* Get the system scope of this Java Virtual Machine */
    IdentityScope s = IdentityScope.getSystemScope();

    /* Get the signer identity "Vivek". This signer
       identity should have been created earlier using
       javakey or some other method.

       Once we have a handle to this we can retrieve the
       private key of this signer (which again should
       have been generated earlier) */

    Signer s1 = (Signer)s.getIdentity("Vivek");

    try
    {
      /* toSign.dat is the file to be signed */
```

```
File f1 = new File("toSign.dat");
FileInputStream fis = new FileInputStream(f1);
DataInputStream dis = new DataInputStream(fis);

/* The signature will be produced using the private
   key and the contents of toSign.dat. The
   signature itself will be an array of bytes which
   we're storing in theSign.dat which will be sent
   along with toSign.dat to the clients so that
   they can verify the signature */
File f2 = new File("theSign.dat");

FileOutputStream fos = new FileOutputStream(f2);

int size = dis.available();

/* Allocate a byte array whose size is equal to
   the size of toSign.dat */
byte buf[] = new byte[size];

/* Read contents of toSign.dat */
fis.read(buf);

try
{
    /* Create an instance of a Signature object
       which will create the signature using the
       DSA algorithm */
    Signature sig = Signature.getInstance("DSA");
    /* Get private key of identity Vivek (s1) */
    PrivateKey p = s1.getPrivateKey();
    try
    {
        /* Initialize the Signature object so it
           knows it has to sign data using the
           private key of Vivek which we retrieved
           above in "p" */
        sig.initSign(p);
```

```
/* Supply bytes of toSign.dat. The Signature
   object will use these and the private key
   to create the signature */
sig.update(buf);

/* Since all the data bytes of the input
   file have been supplied to the Signature
   object using "update", we can now create
   the signature using the sign() method */
byte[] theSignature = sig.sign();

/* Write the signature generated above to
   the file theSign.dat */
fos.write(theSignature);


     }catch(InvalidKeyException ik1){}
      catch(SignatureException se2){}
   }catch(NoSuchAlgorithmException ns1){}

   dis.close();
   fis.close();
   fos.close();
 }catch(FileNotFoundException e){}
 catch(IOException e)
 { System.out.println("File read error");
 }
  }
}
```

toSign.dat

This is the file being signed. We're signing all the data present within this file.

Certificate file - cert_viv

```
issuer.name=Vivek
issuer.cert=1
subject.name=Vivek
subject.real.name=Vivek
```

```
subject.org.unit=Vivek
subject.org=Vivek
subject.country=US
start.date=1 Jan 1997
end.date=31 Dec 1997
serial.number=1002
out.file=Vivek.x509
```

Client side:

VerFile.java

```java
/* This class verifies the signature generated by
   SignFile */

import java.security.*;
import java.io.*;
class VerFile
{
  public static void main(String[] args)
  {
    IdentityScope s = IdentityScope.getSystemScope();
    Identity s1 = (Identity)s.getIdentity("Vivek");
    try
    {
      File f1 = new File("toSign.dat");
      FileInputStream fis1 = new FileInputStream(f1);
      DataInputStream dis1 = new DataInputStream(fis1);
      int size1 = dis1.available();

      File f2 = new File("theSign.dat");
      FileInputStream fis2 = new FileInputStream(f2);
      DataInputStream dis2 = new DataInputStream(fis2);
      int size2 = dis2.available();

      byte[] b1 = new byte[size1];
      byte[] b2 = new byte[size2];

      /* Read the files toSign.dat and theSign.dat. Data
         from both of them will be used for verification.
         */
```

```
fis1.read(b1);
fis2.read(b2);

try
{
    Signature sig = Signature.getInstance("DSA");

    /* Get the public key of Vivek */
    PublicKey p = s1.getPublicKey();

    /* Tell the Signature object that it is going
       to be used for verification of a signature
       using the public key of Vivek */
    sig.initVerify(p);

     /* Supply data bytes of the original file
        toSign.dat */
    sig.update(b1);

    /* Verify the signature's bytes as stored in
       theSign.dat */
    boolean ver = sig.verify(b2);

    if(ver)
        System.out.println("Signature verifies
                            correctly");
    else
        System.out.println("Invalid Signature");

}
catch(InvalidKeyException ik1){System.out.println
                            ("INVALID KEY
                            EXCEPTION");}
catch(SignatureException se2){System.out.println
                ("SIGNATURE EXCEPTION");
                se2.printStackTrace();}
catch(NoSuchAlgorithmException  ns1)
                            {System.out.println("NO
                            SUCH ALGORITHM ");}
```

```
        fis1.close();
        dis1.close();
        fis2.close();
        dis2.close();
    }catch(FileNotFoundException e)
      {System.out.println("FILE NOT FOUND");}
    catch(IOException e){ System.out.println("FILE I/O
                                    ERROR"); }

    }
  }
```

To Compile and Run

On the server:

1. `javakey -cs Vivek true`

2. `javakey -gk Vivek DSA 512`

3. `javakey -gc cert_viv`

4. `javac SignFile.java`

5. `java SignFile`

On the client:

1. Transferred `Vivek.x509` from server to client.

2. `javakey -c Vivek true`

3. `javakey -ic Vivek Vivek.x509`

4. `javac VerFile.java`

5. Transferred files `toSign.dat` and `theSign.dat` from server to client.

6. `java VerFile`

Output of the Program

On the server, the file `theSign.dat` is created when `SignFile` is executed. This contains the signature created by `SignFile`. The signature in `theSign.dat` is verified, and if it verifies correctly, a success message is displayed.

Implementation

As in our previous program, we're first creating a trusted, signable identity on the server using `javakey`. Keys and a certificate are generated for this, also using `javakey`. The actual signing, however, is not done with `javakey`. For this, we're using some of the classes in `java.security`. This is done in `Sign-File.java`.

The signature thus produced is written to a file called `theSign.dat`. The file being signed is `toSign.dat`.

For the client to be able to verify this signature, it needs to have its house in order. In other words, it needs to create a trusted identity with the name "Vivek" in its security database. This is done using `javakey`. It also needs to get the certificate from the server, and the certificate needs to be imported in Vivek's database on the client. Certificate importing is also done using `javakey`.

Both the signature file (`theSign.dat`) and the data file (`toSign.dat`) need to be transported to the client for it to be able to verify the signature. The verification is done using Java security classes in the file `VerFile.java`.

You should refer to the `java` files in `java.security` (the source documentation) as we go through the implementation of the two `java` files.

On the server side we have `SignFile.java`, which uses certain `java` classes to sign the file `toSign.dat`. It assumes that a trusted entity with signing authority has already been created and that keys have been generated for this entity (we've already done this in steps 1 and 2 on the server).

This file begins by importing the security package:

```
import java.security.*;
```

It will also need to do file I/O so the IO package is also imported. Then it needs to get hold of the identity Vivek. Every identity is an object of the Identity class. If you look at the source documentation, you'll see that an identity can be a simple Identity or one of its subclasses, such as Signer or IdentityScope.

The Signer and IdentityScope classes are simply extensions of Identity. An entity can be either of these depending on how it was created.

IdentityScope is an entity that determines the scope of other identities that can exist in it. So, if there is an IdentityScope "A", it can contain any number of other identities in it, such as "Sharma", "Rajiv" and "Vivek".

Some of these will be plain identities with no signing power. These entities will be objects of the type Identity. Others which have a signing authority will be represented by Signer.

You can look upon IdentityScope as your means of accessing the security database. You don't read the database file directly. Instead, you get a handle to the identity scope you're interested in, and from that you get hold of the identity you want (contained in that scope).

Every Java Virtual Machine has a default identity scope associated with it. When we create an identity using `javakey`, the identity is added to this scope. So, to retrieve that identity and perform operations on it, we first need to get a handle to the scope. This scope can be retrieved using the method `getSystem-Scope()`, which is a static method in IdentityScope:

```
IdentityScope s = IdentityScope.getSystemScope();
```

Since we created the identity Vivek using the `-cs` option of `javakey`, Vivek is an identity with signing power and will be an object of the type Signer. We're using the `getIdentity()` method of IdentityScope to get hold of this Signer:

```
Signer s1 = (Signer)s.getIdentity("Vivek");
```

Now let's see how the actual signing is done. First, the file which is to be signed is read in. An instance of the Signature class is retrieved, and the data bytes are supplied to it. The Signature object needs the private key to sign data. This is retrieved by using the Signer object `s1` which we got from the database.

So we first open `toSign.dat`, which contains the data to be signed. We also open another file, `theSign.dat`, for output. We will be storing the signature in this file. The signature in this file will be verified by the client.

The bytes of `toSign.dat` are read into an array of bytes called `buf`:

```
byte buf[] = new byte[size];
fis.read(buf);
```

The Signature class is an abstract class. So we can't create an instance of this class in the normal way (such as `new Signature()`). Instead, we use a static method in this class, `getInstance()`. The `getInstance()` that we're using takes one parameter: the name of the algorithm which is to be used for signing the object. You can use any algorithm available through your provider. Common ones are DSA and RSA with MD5. In our example, we're using DSA:

```
Signature sig = Signature.getInstance("DSA");
```

The private key associated with the identity Vivek is obtained by using the `getPrivateKey()` method of the Signer class:

```
PrivateKey p = s1.getPrivateKey();
```

Before a Signature object can be used, we need to specify which state it's in. For example, we may be using it to sign an object, or we may be using it to verify a signature created earlier. In our case, we're going to sign an object. This is specified by calling the `initSign()` method of Signature, which takes a private key as an argument:

```
sig.initSign(p);
```

The data to be signed is supplied to the Signature object before actual signing. This is done by using the `update()` method of Signature:

```
sig.update(buf);
```

Here we've given all the data bytes of the file to be signed to `update()`. Note that if you're using a different mechanism to read data bytes (i.e., instead of reading the complete file in one stroke into `buf` you're reading smaller chunks), all the bytes need to be supplied to `update()`. Successive calls to this append the data bytes to the buffer which the Signature object is going to sign. Finally the `sign()` method is called, which produces the signature in the form of a byte array:

```
byte[] theSignature = sig.sign();
```

We're writing this signature to the file `theSign.dat` so that the signature can be sent to the client along with the original data file for verification:

```
fos.write(theSignature);
```

As you may have noticed, a large number of exceptions can occur, such as an error in creating the signature, a wrong algorithm being specified during the instantiation of a Signature object, or a wrong private key being used. All these exceptions need to be caught.

Next, we turn our attention to the client to see how the signature created above is verified. This is being handled by the class VerFile, which is in Ver-

`File.java`. The approach followed in this is more or less similar to that followed in SignFile. It expects that an identity Vivek would have been created earlier and that the public key associated with the identity would be available in the database for this identity.

These requirements are met in steps 1, 2 and 3 on the client side. We get the certificate from the server, create the trusted identity Vivek (with no signing powers), and import the certificate (thus making Vivek's public key available to the database).

VerFile also imports `java.security` as those classes will be used. It gets a handle to the system scope. A handle to the identity Vivek is then obtained from this scope. Note that, unlike in `SignFile.java`, this identity has no signing power, so it's represented by an Identity object and not a Signer object:

```
Identity s1 = (Identity)s.getIdentity("Vivek");
```

In order to verify the signature, once again the Signature object will be used. The process of verification requires both the signature and the data file. So we're first reading the data and the signature bytes into two byte arrays, b1 and b2:

```
fis1.read(b1);
fis2.read(b2);
```

An instance of Signature is created just like it was done in `SignFile.java` using the DSA algorithm.

Signature verification requires the public key corresponding to the private key which was used for signing the data. We've already made this key available to the database by importing the certificate. The key can be retrieved by using the `getPublicKey()` method of Identity:

```
PublicKey p = s1.getPublicKey();
```

The signature object's state needs to be set correctly so that it knows it's supposed to verify a signature:

```
sig.initVerify(p);
```

To verify the signature, first the data file needs to be supplied to the Signature object using `update()`:

```
sig.update(b1);
```

The actual verification is done using the `verify()` method which takes a byte array as an argument. This argument should be the signature that needs to be verified. We've already read this signature from the signature file `the-Sign.dat` above into the byte array `b2`:

```
boolean ver = sig.verify(b2);
```

The method will return `true` if the signature verifies correctly, otherwise it will return `false`. We're printing the result to the standard output. Once again, exceptions such as invalid key, signature exception and no such algorithm need to be caught.

Just to convince yourself that all this works, you can modify `VerFile.java` and replace "Vivek" with "Sharma", the identity we created in the previous example. You should get an invalid signature message because the signature was created by the identity Vivek and not by Sharma, which means that it won't pass verification using Sharma's public key.

11.4 Message Digests

The next example simply extends the previous example to introduce a new concept: message digests. We'll be showing what message digests are and how you can use them in the Java security model.

A message digest is a hash value generated from some piece of data. In other words, it's a unique value which has been derived using the data supplied for its generation. There are several algorithms available which you can use to compute the message digest for a given piece of data. Every time you use the same algorithm on the same piece of data you'll get the same hash value.

The algorithm also guarantees that if any other piece of data is used it will generate a different hash value, i.e., the algorithm will not generate the same message digest for two or more different pieces of data.

Signatures are normally created using message digests instead of the actual data. This is because a message digest can be computed much faster than a signature, and since it is small compared to a large file, the whole process of signing can be done much faster by computing a digest and signing it rather than the data file.

11.4.1 Example: Using Message Digests for Signing Data

Purpose of the Program
This program shows how message digests can be used.

Concepts Covered in this Program
In this program, we introduce you to the concept of message digests.

Source Code

Server side:

SignF12.java

```java
import java.security.*;
import java.io.*;
class SignF12
{
  public static void main(String[] args)
  {
    IdentityScope s = IdentityScope.getSystemScope();

    /* Get the signer. Will be used for getting the
       private key. */
    Signer s1 = (Signer)s.getIdentity("Vivek");

    try
    {
      File f1 = new File("toSign.dat");
      FileInputStream fis = new FileInputStream(f1);
      DataInputStream dis = new DataInputStream(fis);
      File f2 = new File("theSign.dat");
      FileOutputStream fos = new FileOutputStream(f2);

      /* This time, in addition to toSign.dat and
         theSign.dat, the server will also need to send
         the message digest file for the client to be
         able to verify the signature. */
      File f3 = new File("msgDgst.dat");
```

```
FileOutputStream fos3 = new FileOutputStream(f3);

int size = dis.available();
byte buf[] = new byte[size];
fis.read(buf);

try
{

    /* Create an instance of a MessageDigest which
       will use the MD5 algorithm for computing the
       digest */
    MessageDigest md =
    MessageDigest.getInstance("MD5");

    /* Create a signature object which will use the
       DSA algorithm for signing */
    Signature sig = Signature.getInstance("DSA");

    /* Supply data bytes of toSign.dat to the
       message digest */

    md.update(buf);

    /* Compute the hash value */
    byte[] hashVal = md.digest();

    PrivateKey p = s1.getPrivateKey();
    try
    {
        sig.initSign(p);

        /* Supply the hash value (message digest)
           computed above rather than bytes of
           toSign.dat to the Signature object for
           signing */
        sig.update(hashVal);

        byte[] theSignature = sig.sign();
        fos.write(theSignature);
```

```
            /* Write the message digest we computed
               above to msgDgst.dat which will be sent
               along with toSign.dat and theSign.dat to
               the client for signature verification */
            fos3.write(hashVal);

        }catch(InvalidKeyException
               ik1){ik1.printStackTrace();}
        catch(SignatureException
               se2){se2.printStackTrace();}
        }catch(NoSuchAlgorithmException
               ns1){ns1.printStackTrace();}

        dis.close();
        fis.close();
        fos.close();
        fos3.close();
    }catch(FileNotFoundException e){}
    catch(IOException e){ System.out.println("File read
                                              error"); }
    }
  }
```

Client side:
Here we use VerFile.java as in the previous example with a slight modification. Instead of reading toSign.dat and supplying it to update(), we read msgDgst.dat and supply this to update().

To Compile and Run
Follow the same steps as in the previous example except that one more file needs to be transported from the server to the client: msgDgst.dat. Note that if you've already created the identity Vivek on both the client and the server and have imported the certificate, you don't need to repeat the process.

Output of the Program
On the server, in addition to the signature file, the message digest file msgDgst.dat is created. On the client, the result of the signature verification is displayed.

Implementation

The implementation of this is the same for the most part as that of Sign-File.java. The difference is that instead of supplying the contents of toSign.dat to the Signature object, we're supplying them to another object, MessageDigest.

So what is a message digest? A message digest is an object that reads a piece of data and produces a hash value as an output. This hash value is guaranteed to be unique for a given piece of data. So, for example, if File A's contents are being used to produce a hash value using a message digest, there can be no other file whose contents will produce the same hash value using the same message digest (unless the contents of the two files are exactly identical, of course).

So where is a message digest used? The hash value returned by a message digest is generally the piece of data which is actually signed (instead of the data itself, as was the case in our previous example). The reason a message digest is used for signing is that creation of a message digest and signing it takes less time than signing the data itself (typically, a hash is computed faster than a signature). So, if the data is very large, it's better to compute the message digest, which is much smaller, and sign this instead of the data.

Java facilitates message digests through the class MessageDigest. You can get an instance of this just like you get an instance of the Signature class by supplying the algorithm you want to use (such as MD5 or SHA):

```
MessageDigest md = MessageDigest.getInstance("MD5");
```

The data from the data file is supplied to this message digest via the update() method in a byte array:

```
md.update(buf);
```

The hash value is computed using the digest() method of MessageDigest:

```
byte[] hashVal = md.digest();
```

After this, the procedure is the same as that in SignFile.java. Instead of supplying the file's data to the update() method of the Signature object, we supply the hash value computed above. This hash value is stored in a file called msgDgst.dat, which will also need to be transmitted to the client side for signature verification.

On the client side, instead of reading `toSign.dat` and `theSign.dat`, we're reading `msgDgst.dat` and `theSign.dat`. The signature is verified using these two.

That completes our explanation of how message digests are used. We've covered the major security features in this chapter. Just before leaving, though, we'd like to answer one question which might have come to your mind while reading the trusted applet example: where exactly is the signature file and how does the appletviewer extract it?

To dig up the answer, extract the contents of the JAR file and see for yourself. If you invoke `jar xf TrstApp.jar`, you'll see that the HTML file and the class we JARred are extracted. Besides, the directory `META-INF` is created. Within this directory you'll see three files, one of which (with the extension `.SF`) contains the signature. There's the file `MANIFEST.MF` also within that directory containing information about the files belonging to this JAR file and the algorithms used for signing. Since `META-INF` and `MANIFEST.MF` are reserved names, the appletviewer knows exactly where to look for the signature file.

COMPLETE EXAMPLE

Here we present a complete example which integrates a number of features that have been taught in the previous chapters. This multifile Java program is a ready-to-use installer, which can be used for software installation. One of the features of this installer is that it allows software to be installed over a network.

12.1 How to Use the Installer

The installer presents you with an information-gathering screen in which you specify various things such as the machine on which the software resides and the directory in which you wish to install it. The source software could be lying on the same machine (for example, in the CD-ROM directory) or it could be lying on another machine in this network. So, the first thing that you specify is whether the source software is lying on this machine or on another.

If it's on another machine, you'll have to specify the name of the remote machine as well as the port number at which the server is running on that machine.

Next, you'll be prompted for the directory in which the source software exists and the destination directory in which you wish to install the software.

All during these procedures, there is a help screen at the bottom of the window which will display the appropriate help file.

For the installer to work, you should have a file called **files.1st**, which should exist in your source software directory. This file should contain a list of all the files that need to be installed. The format of this file is:

```
<total size of all the files>
"<source file>" "<destination file>"
"<source file>" "<destination file>"
.....
```

The first line of this file is the total size of all the files that belong to the software being installed. This will be used in advancing the progress bar which shows what percentage of the installation is over.

The subsequent lines contain two entries per line: 1) the name and location of the source file, relative to the source directory the user will be specifying in the information-gathering screen, and 2) the name and location to which this file should be copied, relative to the destination directory.

A sample files.1st looks like this:

```
14659
"bin/a.out" "bin/a.out"
"HTML/ProgressBarFrame.java" "HTML/ProgressBarFrame.java"
"helpme" "MESG/helpme"
```

To begin, type: **java Main**.

This will bring up the information-gathering screen. First you need to select whether you wish to install software from this machine or another machine and click the OK button. Note that you need to create a files.1st in the source directory to make the program work, unless it's already present in the source area. It's expected that the software package which is to be installed will contain this file in addition to the other files that belong to the package.

Then, depending on your choice, you may have to type in the name of the remote server and the port to which you should connect in order to get the software. For a network-based installation, you should execute GiveFile (java GiveFile) on the remote server (java GiveFile) before running the installer. In our example, the port being used is 2000.

You'll be prompted for the source directory in which the software resides. Give the full path of the source directory. In case of remote installations, also give the full path where the software resides on the remote machine, just like you're specifying it for the local machine.

Then you'll have to type in the destination directory, which should be a writeable directory in the current machine. The directory need not exist, but you must have permissions to create the directory.

After that, you can click the Install button. A progress bar will come up displaying the percentage of software installed. Once the installation is over, the program will exit.

12.1.1 Implementation

Unlike previous examples, in this one we're going to give you only the overall picture in this section. The code has been lavishly commented, and you should try to understand from there. With the amount of Java knowledge that has been drilled into you, we don't think you need to be led by the hand any longer to understand what's going on.

The entire code has been implemented in the following Java files: `Main.java`, `ActionL.java`, `ProgressBarFrame.java`, `GiveFile.java`, `MainInst.java`, and `UI.java`. `Main.java` is the top level file with the main method. Its only purpose is to instantiate the class that creates the GUI window in which we are asking questions from the user.

The GUI window is being created in `UI.java`. The class UI is making use of Panels, TextFields, Buttons, a TextArea, and a List. It makes use of both the GridBagLayout and GridLayout in order to achieve the desired component layout. Initially all components are disabled except for the List. Once a selection is made here, the appropriate component is enabled. For example, if you select "...this machine", the Source text field will be enabled, as we don't require the name of a remote machine. On the other hand, if you select "...another machine", the Remote M/C text field will be enabled. (See Figure 12-1.)

We have separated the Event listening stuff from the GUI creation. This is being handled by `ActionL.java`.

`MainInst.java` controls the actual installation. Depending upon whether it's a local or a remote installation, it calls the appropriate methods for installation. It contains methods that do the actual file copying.

`ProgressBarFrame.java` controls the progress bar which shows how much progress has been made in the installation.

`GiveFile.java` is the server software that runs on the server on which the software package resides. This creates a server socket and waits for clients to connect. When this connection is made, it transfers the files requested by the client.

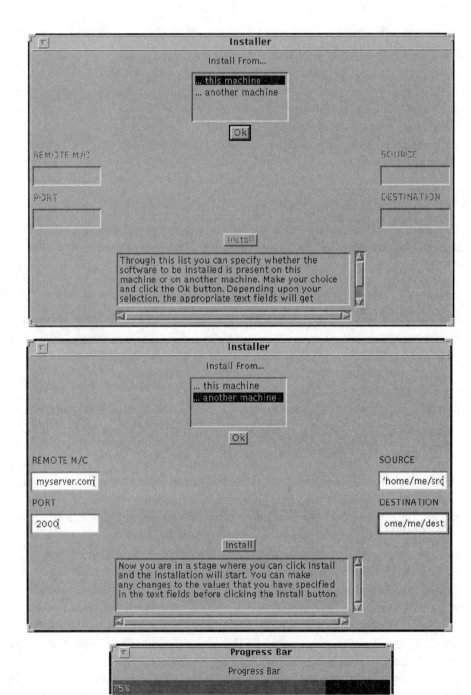

Figure 12-1

Flow of Control

Client side:

```
Main.java==>UI.java==>ActionL.java==>(MainInst.java and
ProgressBarFrame.java).
```

Server side:

```
GiveFile.java
```

Source Code

Main.java

```
/* This is the top level routine of the installer. It
   creates the GUI which gathers information that is
   required by the installer. */

import java.awt.*;
public class Main
{
  public static void main(String[] args)
  {
    UI myUI = new UI();
    myUI.setSize(600,400);
    myUI.show();
  }
}
```

UI.java

```
/* This class draws the GUI components which will be used
   for gathering information for this install session.
   However, it doesn't handle any events. The event
   handling is being done in ActionL.java. */

import java.awt.*;
```

```java
import java.io.*;
public class UI extends Frame
{

/* These variables will be set based upon the user's
   response to various questions being asked by the GUI
   window. The setting of these is being done in
   ActionL.java. */

   public String Source;
   public String Dest;
   public int Port;
   public String Remote;
   public int TypeOfInstall;

/* These are the GUI components that form part of the
   window. */

   public List l1;
   public TwoTextPanel p1, p2;
   public Button Inst;
   public Label l;
   public TextArea helpArea;
   public Button Ok;

/* This is a handle to the event listener. */

   public ActionL aListener;

/* These variables will be used by the progress bar which
shows what percentage of the installation is over. */

   public int totalSizeInstalledSoFar;
   public int totalSize;
   public boolean installComplete;
   UI()
   {
     installComplete = false;
     totalSizeInstalledSoFar = -1;
     totalSize = 0;
```

```
aListener = new ActionL(this);
this.setTitle("Installer");
GridBagLayout g = new GridBagLayout();
setLayout(g);
GridBagConstraints g1 = new GridBagConstraints();

createList();
createTwoTextPanels();
```

/* **The OK button, Install button and helpArea are being created. The buttons are being added to the event listener. */**
```
Inst = new Button("Install");
Inst.setEnabled(false);
Inst.addActionListener(aListener);
Ok = new Button("Ok");
Ok.addActionListener(aListener);
helpArea = new TextArea(5, 40);
helpArea.setEditable(false);
displayFileInHelp("insFrm.hlp");
```

/* **Lay out the components in the window */**

```
g1.weightx = 1.0;
g1.weighty = 1.0;

g1.gridx = 1;
g1.gridy = 0;
g1.anchor = GridBagConstraints.CENTER;
g.setConstraints(l, g1);
add(l);

g1.gridx = 1;
g1.gridy = 1;
g1.anchor = GridBagConstraints.CENTER;
g.setConstraints(l1, g1);
add(l1);
```

```
        g1.gridx = 1;
        g1.gridy = 2;
        g1.anchor = GridBagConstraints.CENTER;
        g.setConstraints(Ok, g1);
        add(Ok);

        g1.gridx = 0;
        g1.gridy = 3;
        g1.anchor = GridBagConstraints.WEST;
        g.setConstraints(p1, g1);
        add(p1);

        g1.gridx = 2;
        g1.gridy = 3;
        g1.anchor = GridBagConstraints.EAST;
        g.setConstraints(p2, g1);
        add(p2);

        g1.gridx = 1;
        g1.gridy = 4;
        g1.anchor = GridBagConstraints.CENTER;
        g.setConstraints(Inst, g1);
        add(Inst);

        g1.gridx = 1;
        g1.gridy = 5;
        g.setConstraints(helpArea, g1);
        add(helpArea);
        validate();
    }

/* Method for creating the list that asks whether it's a
remote install. It also places a label over the list. */

    public void createList()
    {
        l = new Label("Install From...");
        l1 = new List(4, false);
        l1.add("... this machine");
```

```
    l1.add("... another machine");
    l1.select(0);
}


/* Method for creating two panels, each containing a pair
of text fields. */

  public void createTwoTextPanels()
  {
    p1 = new TwoTextPanel(this, "REMOTE M/C", "PORT");
    p2 = new TwoTextPanel(this, "SOURCE", "DESTINATION");
  }


/* This method displays the help file in the text area.
   The name of the help file to be displayed is passed as
   an argument to this method. */

  public void displayFileInHelp(String fileName)
  {
    StringBuffer helpString;
    helpString = new StringBuffer();
    try
    {
      BufferedReader dataFile = new BufferedReader(new
                                    FileReader(fileName));
      String tempString;
      while((tempString = dataFile.readLine()) != null)
      {
        helpString.append(tempString);
        helpString.append('\n');
      }
    }catch(IOException e)
     {
      System.err.println("Error in reading file " +
                        fileName);
     }
    helpArea.setText(new String(helpString));
  }
}
```

```
/* This class is being used for a panel that will contain
two text fields, one above the other. */

class TwoTextPanel extends Panel
{
  String lab1, lab2;
  TextField t1, t2;
  Label l1, l2;
  UI parent;
  TwoTextPanel(UI par, String label1, String label2)
  {
    parent = par;
    lab1 = new String(label1);
    lab2 = new String(label2);
    makeThePanel();
  }
  void makeThePanel()
  {
    l1 = new Label(lab1);
    l2 = new Label(lab2);
    t1 = new TextField(10);
    t2 = new TextField(10);
    setLayout(new GridLayout(4, 1));
    add(l1);
    add(t1);
    add(l2);
    add(t2);

    /* All elements are being disabled initially. */
    l1.setEnabled(false);
    l2.setEnabled(false);
    t1.setEditable(false);
    t2.setEditable(false);
    /* The text fields are being added to the event
       listener. */
    t1.addActionListener(parent.aListener);
    t2.addActionListener(parent.aListener);
  }
}
```

ActionL.java

/* This is the event listener. We are making use of the
   actionPerformed method which is invoked if a button is
   clicked or a return is pressed in the text field.
   Based on the kind of event, we enable another component
   or start the installation. For instance, when return is
   pressed in the SOURCE text field, the DESTINATION text
   field is enabled and so is the label which is
   associated with it. When the Install button is pressed,
   we instantiate MainInst, which does the rest of the
   operation.

   There are specific methods for handling activity in
   each of the components, e.g., handleOkButton() takes
   care of the work to be done when the OK button is
   pressed. */

```java
import java.awt.event.*;
import java.awt.*;
public class ActionL implements ActionListener
{
  UI myUI;
  ActionL(UI myUI)
  {
    this.myUI = myUI;
  }
  public void actionPerformed(ActionEvent e)
  {
    Object source = e.getSource();
    if(source instanceof Button)
    {
      /* If a button has been clicked we check which
         button it was and call the appropriate method.
      */
      Button b = (Button)source;
      if(b == myUI.Ok)
      {
        handleOkButton();
      }
```

```
      else
      if(b == myUI.Inst)
      {
         handleInstButton();
      }
   }
   if(source instanceof TextField)
   {
   /* If return was pressed in a text field, we check
      which text field it was and call the appropriate
      method. */
      TextField t = (TextField)source;
      if(t == myUI.p1.t1)
         handleRemoteMc();
      else
      if(t == myUI.p1.t2)
         handlePort();
      else
      if(t == myUI.p2.t1)
         handleSource();
      else
      if(t == myUI.p2.t2)
         handleDest();
   }
}


/* This method handles activity when the OK button is
   pressed. It first checks which element was selected
   from the list. The value is stored in the TypeOfInstall
   field of UI. Then based upon the selection, it
   activates the appropriate text field, e.g., if the user
   selected "...from this machine", it activates the
   SOURCE text field which is the text field t1 in the
   second panel, p2, as well as the corresponding label,
   p2.11.
*/
   void handleOkButton()
   {
      if(myUI.11.getSelectedIndex() == 0)
```

```
      {
        myUI.TypeOfInstall = 0;
        myUI.p2.t1.setEditable(true);
        myUI.p2.l1.setEnabled(true);
        myUI.displayFileInHelp("src.hlp");
      }
      else
      {
        myUI.TypeOfInstall = 1;
        myUI.p1.t1.setEditable(true);
        myUI.p1.l1.setEnabled(true);
        myUI.displayFileInHelp("remote.hlp");
      }
  }
```

```
/* When the Install button is pressed, control goes out of
   this class as we instantiate MainInst(), which does the
   rest of the job. At this stage, we have gathered all
   the data that is required.
*/
```

```
  void handleInstButton()
  {
    MainInst m = new MainInst(myUI);
  }
```

```
/* This method is called when return is pressed in the
SOURCE text field. We're storing the value entered by the
user in the corresponding String variable in UI. Then the
DEST label and text field are enabled and their help is
displayed.
*/
```

```
  void handleSource()
  {
    myUI.Source = new String(myUI.p2.t1.getText());
    myUI.p2.t2.setEditable(true);
    myUI.p2.l2.setEnabled(true);
    myUI.displayFileInHelp("dest.hlp");
  }
```

/* This method is called when return is pressed in the
   DEST text field. We're storing the value entered by the
   user in the corresponding String variable in UI. Then
   the Install button is enabled and its help is
   displayed. Also, we create the Progress Dialog box by
   instantiating its class, ProgressBarFrame.
*/

```
void handleDest()
{
  myUI.Dest = new String(myUI.p2.t2.getText());
  myUI.Inst.setEnabled(true);
  myUI.displayFileInHelp("inst.hlp");
  ProgressBarFrame p = new ProgressBarFrame(myUI);
}
```

/* This method is called when return is pressed and
   "...another machine" is selected from the "Install
   From...." List. We're storing the value entered by the
   user in the corresponding String variable in UI. Then
   the PORT label and text field are enabled and their
   help is displayed.
*/

```
void handleRemoteMc()
{
  myUI.Remote = new String(myUI.p1.t1.getText());
  myUI.p1.t2.setEditable(true);
  myUI.p1.l2.setEnabled(true);
  myUI.displayFileInHelp("port.hlp");
}
```

/* This method is called when return is pressed in the
   REMOTE M/C text field. We're storing the value entered
   by the user in the corresponding String variable in UI.
   Then the SOURCE label and text field are enabled and
   their help is displayed.
*/

```
void handlePort()
```

```
{
    String portNo = new String(myUI.p1.t2.getText());
    myUI.Port = (Integer.valueOf(portNo).intValue());
    myUI.p2.t1.setEditable(true);
    myUI.p2.l1.setEnabled(true);
    myUI.displayFileInHelp("src.hlp");
    }
}
```

MainInst.java

```
/* This class controls the actual installation. It is
instantiated by ActionL.java after all the user inputs
have been received and the Install button has been
clicked.

It first creates the destination directory. Then,
depending upon whether it's a local or a remote
install, the appropriate methods are called.

For local installs, it first copies the file
"files.1st" from the source directory to the
destination directory. Then it reads the file line by
line and copies each file mentioned in it from the
source directory to the destination directory. The
first line in "files.1st", the total size of all the
files in the install package, is stored in the variable
totalSize. This is used by the progress bar to
determine the extent of installation that's over. As
each file from "files.1st" is copied, its size is added
to the variable totalSizeInstalledSoFar. It is this
variable in conjunction with totalSize that tells the
Progress Bar how much progress has been made. In the
case of remote installs, you should first run GiveFile
on the server. Then MainInst() establishes a connection
with the server. First the "files.1st" file is copied
over to the destination directory. Then this file is
read line by line and all the files mentioned in it
```

are copied from the remote machine's source directory
to the destination directory in the current machine.
Here again totalSize and totalSizeInstalledSoFar are
updated to keep the progress bar updated.
*/

```java
import java.net.*;
import java.io.*;
public class MainInst
{
  UI theUI;
  String lstFile;
```

/* Streams that will be used for getting data from the
remote machine.
*/

```java
  Socket echoSocket = null;
  DataOutputStream os = null;
  InputStream is = null;
  DataInputStream dis = null;
  PrintWriter pos;
  OutputStream os1;

  MainInst(UI theUI)
  {
    this.theUI = theUI;
    mainControl();
  }
```

/* Here we first create the destination directory. Then
depending upon the kind of install the user wants, the
method for remote or local install is called.

After this activity is over, a boolean
"installComplete" is set to true. This will indicate to
the progress bar that the install activity is over.
*/

```java
  void mainControl()
  {
```

```
    createDir(theUI.Dest);
    if(theUI.TypeOfInstall == 0)
      thisMachineInstall();
    else
      networkInstall();
    theUI.installComplete = true;
  }
```

/* This is the controlling method for local installs. */

```
  void thisMachineInstall()
  {
    copyFileListing(); /* Copy "files.lst" to destination */
    startCopying(); /* Start the actual copying of files */
  }
```

/* This is the controlling method for network installs. */

```
  void networkInstall()
  {
    establishConnection(); /* Create the socket and
                              streams */
    netCopyFileListing(); /* Copy "files.lst from remote
                             machine to destination dir in
                             local machine */
    netStartCopying(); /* Start actual copying of files
                          from remote machine to local
                          machine. */
  }
```

/* Creates a directory. Takes the name of the directory as
   an argument. */

```
  void createDir(String dirName)
  {
    File dir = new File(dirName);
    try
    {
```

```
        if(!dir.exists())
        {
            if(!dir.mkdirs())
            {
                System.out.println("ERROR IN CREATING
                                    DESTINATION DIR");
                System.exit(1);
            }
        }
    }catch(NullPointerException e){}
}
void copyFileListing()
{
    /* Copy the listing file, "files.lst", which contains
       a list of all the files that need to be moved
       from source to destination. The file "files.lst"
       is picked up from the source directory and is
       copied over to the destination directory as that
       is where the actual file copy function will read
       it from.
    */
    try
    {
        StringBuffer s1 = new StringBuffer();
        s1.append(theUI.Source);
        s1.append("/files.lst");
        StringBuffer s2 = new StringBuffer();
        s2.append(theUI.Dest);
        s2.append("/files.lst");
        File f1 = new File(new String(s1));
        File f2 = new File(new String(s2));
        FileInputStream fis = new FileInputStream(f1);
        FileOutputStream fos = new FileOutputStream(f2);
        byte[] buf = new byte[1];
        lstFile = new String(new String(s2));
        while((fis.read(buf) != -1))
        {
            fos.write(buf);
        }
```

```
            fis.close();
            fos.close();
    } catch(FileNotFoundException e)
        {
            System.err.println("File Not Found Error: " + e);
            System.exit(1);
        }
        catch(IOException e)
        {
            System.err.println("I/O Exception: " + e);
            System.exit(1);
        }
}
```

```
/* This method controls the copying of files. It reads
   "files.lst" and calls the appropriate method which does
   the actual copy.
*/
void startCopying()
{
    try
    {
        BufferedReader bis = new BufferedReader(
                new FileReader(lstFile));
        String inpu, sourceFile, destFile;
        inpu = bis.readLine();
```

```
    /* The first entry in "files.lst" is the size of all
       the files in this software package.
    */
        theUI.totalSize =
        (Integer.valueOf(inpu)).intValue();
```

```
        /* Read "files.lst"(lstFile) line by line and call
           copyFile() which will do the actual copying. */
```

```
        while((inpu = bis.readLine()) != null)
```

```
        {
            sourceFile = getSourceFile(inpu);
            destFile = getDestFile(inpu);
            copyFile(sourceFile, destFile);
        }
    } catch(FileNotFoundException e)
        {
            System.err.println("File Not Found Error: "
                                + e);
            System.exit(1);
        }
        catch(IOException e)
        {
            System.err.println("I/O Exception");
            System.exit(1);
        }
    }
```

/* **This method takes as input one line from "files.1st"
and parses it to retrieve the relative name and path
of the source file. The value of Source, as specified
by the user in the information-gathering screen is
added to the beginning of this and the resulting String
is returned. This will be the full path name of the
source file.**
*/

```
    String getSourceFile(String inpLine)
    {
        int length = inpLine.length();
        int i,j;

        for(i=0; i<length; i++)
        {
            if(inpLine.charAt(i) == '\"')
                break;
        }
        StringBuffer temp = new StringBuffer();
        temp.append(theUI.Source);
```

```
        temp.append("/");
        for(j=i+1; j<length; j++)
        {
            if(inpLine.charAt(j) == '\"')
                break;
            temp.append(inpLine.charAt(j));
        }
        String toReturn = new String(temp);
        return(toReturn); /* This is the complete name
                             of the source file. */

    }
```

/* **This method takes as input one line from "files.1st"
and parses it to retrieve the relative name and path
of the destination file. The value of Dest, as
specified by the user in the information-gathering
screen, is added to the beginning of this and the
resulting String is returned. This will be the full
path name of the destination file.**
*/

```
    String getDestFile(String inpLine)
    {
        int numQuotes = 0;
        int length = inpLine.length();
        int i,j;

        for(i=0; i<length; i++)
        {
            if(numQuotes == 3)
                break;
            if(inpLine.charAt(i) == '\"')
                numQuotes++;
        }
        StringBuffer temp = new StringBuffer();
        temp.append(theUI.Dest);
        temp.append("/");
        for(j=i; j<length; j++)
```

```
    {
        if(inpLine.charAt(j) == '\"')
            break;
        temp.append(inpLine.charAt(j));
    }
    String toReturn = new String(temp);
    return(toReturn); /* This is the complete name
                         of the source file */

}
```

/* **This method reads the source file and copies it over
   to the destination mentioned in "files.1st". Before
   copying the file it creates the destination directory.**
*/

```
    void copyFile(String sourceFile, String destFile)
    {
```

/* **The destination directory is derived from "destFile"
   and created.** */

```
    String destDir = getDestDir(destFile);
    createDir(destDir);

    try
    {

        FileInputStream fis = new
                        FileInputStream(new
                        File(sourceFile));
        FileOutputStream fos = new
                        FileOutputStream(new
                        File(destFile));
        theUI.totalSizeInstalledSoFar +=
                    fis.available();
        byte [] buf = new byte[1];
        while((fis.read(buf) != -1))
        {
            fos.write(buf);
        }
```

```
        fis.close();
        fos.close();
} catch(FileNotFoundException e)
    {
        System.err.println("File Not Found Error:
                        " + e);
        System.exit(1);
    }
    catch(IOException e)
    {
        System.err.println("I/O Exception");
        System.exit(1);
    }
}
```

/* **The destination directory is derived from "destFile".**
For this the string is parsed from its last character
backwards until the first "/" is encountered.
*/

```
        String getDestDir(String destFile)
        {
            int length = destFile.length();
            int i;
            String toReturn;
            for(i=(length - 1); i>=0; i—)
            {
                if(destFile.charAt(i) == '/')
                break;
            }
            if(i != 0)
                toReturn = destFile.substring(0,i);
            else
                toReturn = new String("/");
            return(toReturn);
        }
```

/* **This is the first method called for network installs.**
It establishes a connection with the server. The

server's name has been specified by the user in the information-gathering screen. So has the port number.

If the connection is established, the appropriate streams are created.
*/

```java
void establishConnection()
{
    try
    {
        echoSocket = new Socket(theUI.Remote,
                                theUI.Port);
        os1 = echoSocket.getOutputStream();
        os = new DataOutputStream(os1);
        is = echoSocket.getInputStream();
        dis = new DataInputStream
                    (echoSocket.getInputStream());
        pos = new PrintWriter( new
                    OutputStreamWriter(os));
    } catch(UnknownHostException e)
      {
        System.err.println("Don't know about host
                            " + theUI.Remote);
    } catch(IOException e)
      {
        System.err.println("Couldn't get I/O for
                            host " +
                            theUI.Remote);
      }
}
```

/* This method copies "files.1st" from the remote machine to the local machine's destination directory. The communication between the local machine and the server works as follows:

The local machine writes to the stream the name of the

file it wants transferred over. The server reads this and first returns the size of the file. Then it starts transferring the actual data bytes through a byte array. As the local machine receives each array of bytes it sends back an acknowledgement by writing a byte on the stream. When the server receives this it knows that the previous byte array has been consumed, so it sends the next one.

The local machine keeps track of the number of bytes that have been received. Once this becomes equal to or greater than the size of the file, it breaks out of the loop that is reading bytes.

Then it waits until it receives an integer from the server. This integer is not being used anywhere. It is being used just for ensuring that the server and client are in sync with each other.
*/

```
void netCopyFileListing()
{
    try
    {
        StringBuffer temp1 = new StringBuffer();
        temp1.append(theUI.Source);
        temp1.append("/files.lst");

        StringBuffer temp2 = new StringBuffer();
        temp2.append(theUI.Dest);
        temp2.append("/files.lst");
        FileOutputStream fos = new
                        FileOutputStream(new
                        String(temp2));
```

/* The name of the file to be transferred, in this case "files.lst", is written on the stream for the server to read. The server will read this and then open the file

and send its data bytes over.
`*/`

```
                os.writeUTF(new String(temp1));
                os.flush();
                int fSize = dis.readInt(); /* size of
                        the file */

                byte[] buff = new byte[3000];
                int sizeRead = 0;
                os.writeByte('\n');
                os.flush();

                while((is.read(buff)) != -1)
                {
                    sizeRead+=3000;
                    if(sizeRead < fSize)
                        fos.write(buff);
                    else
                    {
                        byte[] buff1 = new byte[fSize -
                                    (sizeRead - 3000)];
                        int i;
                        for(i=0; i < (fSize - (sizeRead -
                                    3000)); i++)
                                    buff1[i] = buff[i];
                        fos.write(buff1);
                        os.writeByte('\n');
                        os.flush();
```

`/* Once the complete file has been sent over, we break`
`   out of the while loop.`
`*/`

```
                        break;
                    }
                    os.writeByte('\n');
                    os.flush();
                }
```

```
/* The local machine waits for an integer. This integer is
   not being used anywhere. It is there just to maintain
   the client and the server in sync with each other.
*/

                dis.readInt();

                fos.close();
            }catch(IOException e)
            {
                System.err.println("I/O failed");
            }
        }
```

```
/* This is the controlling method which reads "files.1st"
   line by line and invokes the method for copying files
   from the remote server to the destination directory of
   the local machine.
*/

            void netStartCopying()
            {
                try
                {
                    StringBuffer temp2 = new StringBuffer();
                    temp2.append(theUI.Dest);
                    temp2.append("/files.1st");
                    BufferedReader bis = new
                            BufferedReader(new FileReader(new
                            String(temp2)));
                    String inpu,sourceFile, destFile;
                    inpu = bis.readLine();
```

```
/* The total size of all files in the software package is
   read and stored in totalSize.
*/

                theUI.totalSize =
                        (Integer.valueOf(inpu)).intValue();
```

/* **"files.1st" is read line by line. The complete path of
the source file is written to the stream and the
method netCopyFile() is invoked, which copies the file
to the destination directory.**
*/

```
            while((inpu = bis.readLine()) != null)
            /* Read the files.1st line by line and
               copy all files */
            {
                sourceFile = getSourceFile(inpu);
                destFile = getDestFile(inpu);
                os.writeUTF(sourceFile);
                os.flush();
                netCopyFile(destFile);
                dis.readInt();
            }
```

/* **Once all the files mentioned in "files.1st" are copied
over, all the streams are closed.**
*/

```
            pos.close();
            bis.close();
            is.close();
            dis.close();
            os.close();
        }catch(FileNotFoundException e)
        {
            System.err.println("File Not Found Error:
                                " + e);
            System.exit(1);
        }
        catch(IOException e)
        {
            System.err.println("I/O Exception");
            System.exit(1);
        }
    }
```

```
/* This method follows an approach similar to
   netCopyFileListing(). It first creates the destination
   directory and then copies the file from the remote
   machine to the destination directory of the local
   machine.
*/
```

```java
            void netCopyFile(String destFile)
            {
                String destDir = getDestDir(destFile);
                createDir(destDir);
                try
                {
                    int fSize = dis.readInt();
                    os.writeByte('\n');
                    os.flush();
                    theUI.totalSizeInstalledSoFar += fSize;
                    byte[] buff = new byte[3000];
                    int sizeRead = 0;
                    FileOutputStream fos = new
                                FileOutputStream(destFile);

                    while((is.read(buff)) != -1)
                    {
                        sizeRead+=3000;
                        if(sizeRead < fSize)
                            fos.write(buff);
                        else
                        {
                            byte[] buff1 = new byte[fSize -
                                        (sizeRead - 3000)];
                            int i;
                            for(i=0; i < (fSize - (sizeRead -
                                        3000)); i++)
                                        buff1[i] = buff[i];
                            fos.write(buff1);
                            os.writeByte('\n');
                            os.flush();
                            break;
                        }
                }
```

```
                        os.writeByte('\n');
                        os.flush();
                 }
                 fos.close();
            }catch(IOException e)
            {
                 System.err.println("I/O Exception in
                                     netCopyFile");
                 System.exit(1);
            }
        }
    }
```

ProgressBarFrame.java

```
/* This class implements the progress bar which informs
   the user how much of the installation is over.

   It creates a canvas on which the bar is drawn. A
   thread is started which polls the variables "totalSize"
   and "totalSizeInstalledSoFar" to determine the length
   of the bar and the percentage number that should be
   displayed.
*/

import java.awt.*;
import java.io.*;
public class ProgressBarFrame extends Frame implements
Runnable
{
  public UI theUI;
  public static ProgressBarCan progBar;
  public static int LENGTH_OF_PROGRESS_BAR = 400;
  public static int HEIGHT_OF_PROGRESS_BAR = 20;
  public Graphics gr;
  public Thread t1;
  int t;
  ProgressBarFrame(UI theUI)
  {
      this.theUI = theUI;
```

/* A canvas is created for displaying the progress bar. */

```
    progBar = new ProgressBarCan();
    this.setTitle("Progress Bar");
    setLayout(new GridLayout(2,1));
    add(new Label(" Progress Bar"));
    add(progBar);
    progBar.setSize(LENGTH_OF_PROGRESS_BAR,
                    HEIGHT_OF_PROGRESS_BAR);
    setSize(400, 80);
    progBar.setVisible(true);
    show();
```

/* The thread determines the length of the progress bar. */

```
    t1 = new Thread(this);
    t1.start();
  }
  public void run()
  {
    while(true)
    {
```

/* We give the thread maximum priority so that it can
   give us the up-to-date information about the progress
   made in the installation.
*/

```
      t1.setPriority(Thread.MAX_PRIORITY);
      float p1, p2, p3, p4;
      int x1, x;
      int x2;
      if(theUI.totalSize == 0)
      {
```

/* totalSize will be 0 when the installation has not
   started. At that time we want to display a 0 length
   progress.
*/

```
        x = 0;
        x2 = 0;
    }
    else
    {
```

/* **The length of the progress bar is determined as
follows: (total size installed/total size to be
installed)*(Total length of progress bar). totalSize is
set in MainInst() when "files.1st" is first read.
totalSizeInstalledSoFar is updated in MainInst() as
each file is copied over.**
*/

```
            p1 = (float)theUI.totalSizeInstalledSoFar;
            p2 = (float)theUI.totalSize;
            p3 = p1/p2;
            p4 = p3*ProgressBarFrame.LENGTH_OF_PROGRESS_BAR;
            x = Math.round(p4);
            x2=x;
    }
    float a,b,c,d;
    a = (float)x2;
    c = (float)ProgressBarFrame.LENGTH_OF_PROGRESS_BAR;
    b = a/c;
    d = b*100;
    t = Math.round(d);
    if(t > 99 )
    {
```

/* **This piece of code ensures that the progress bar
doesn't reach 100% if total installation has not yet
been done. Note that this could happen if the total
size written in "files.1st" is incorrect.**
*/

```
            if(!theUI.installComplete)
            {
```

```
                  t=99;
              }
          }
```

/* **We are capturing the Graphics Context of the canvas so
   that we can draw on it.**
*/

```
      gr = progBar.getGraphics();
      if(gr != null)
      {
          StringBuffer temp1 = new StringBuffer();
          temp1.append(String.valueOf(t));
          temp1.append("%");
          gr.setColor(new Color(255, 0, 0));
```

/* **The red bar is being drawn.** */

```
          gr.fillRect(
                  0,0,x,ProgressBarFrame.HEIGHT_OF_PROG
                  RESS_BAR);
          gr.setColor(new Color(255, 255, 255));
```

/* **The numeric value of percentage of installation is
   being written.** */

```
          gr.drawString(new String(temp1),0,15);
      }
      if(theUI.installComplete)
      {
```

/* **This piece of code ensures that the progress bar
   reaches 100% if total installation has been done. Note
   that 100% may not be reached if the total size written
   in "files.1st" is incorrect.**
*/

```
          if(gr == null)
              gr = progBar.getGraphics();
```

```
        if(gr != null)
        {
```

/* Since the installation is over, we're drawing the full-
   length Progress Bar and displaying 100%.
*/

```
            gr.setColor(new Color(255, 0, 0));
            gr.fillRect(0,0,
                ProgressBarFrame.LENGTH_OF_PROGRESS_BAR,
                ProgressBarFrame.HEIGHT_OF_PROGRESS_BAR);
            gr.setColor(new Color(255, 255, 255));
            gr.drawString("100%",0,15);
        }
    break;
}
try
{
```

/* The thread sleeps for 50 milliseconds before waking up
to redraw the progress bar.
*/

```
    t1.sleep(50);
} catch(InterruptedException e)
    {
    }
}
System.out.println("Installation successfully
                completed");
try
{
```

/* We make the system sleep for two seconds so
   that the user can see from the progress bar
   that the installation is over. Then we exit.
*/

```
    t1.sleep(2000);
} catch(InterruptedException e){}
```

```
        System.exit(1);
    }
  }
```

/* The canvas which will be used for drawing the progress
   bar is being created in this class.
*/

```
  class ProgressBarCan extends Canvas
  {
    public void update(Graphics g)
    {
      paint(g);
    }
    public void paint(Graphics g)
    {
```

/* A black bar is drawn here. The actual progress
   bar, which is red, will be drawn over it.
*/

```
      g.setColor(new Color(0,0,0));

      g.fillRect(0,0,
              ProgressBarFrame.LENGTH_OF_PROGRESS_BAR,
              ProgressBarFrame.HEIGHT_OF_PROGRESS_BAR);
    }
  }
```

GiveFile.java

/* This is the server class which should be run on the
   server on which the software package to be installed is
   present. It creates a server socket at port 2000 and
   waits for clients to connect to it.

   First it reads the name of the file that needs to be
   transferred. Then the file is read and its data bytes
   are sent over to the requesting client.
*/

```java
import java.io.*;
import java.net.*;
public class GiveFile
{
  public static void main(String args[])
  {
    ServerSocket serverSocket=null;
    Socket clientSocket;
    try
    {
      serverSocket = new ServerSocket(2000);
    } catch(IOException e)
      {
        System.out.println("Couldn't listen to port
                            2000");
         System.exit(1);
      }
        System.out.println("Waiting for connection at
                            port 2000");
    clientSocket = null;
    try
    {
      clientSocket = serverSocket.accept();
    } catch(IOException e)
      {
        System.out.println("I/O Exception in
                                serverSocket.accept()");
        System.exit(1);
      }
    try
    {

      /* The necessary data streams for communicating
         with the client are created.
      */

      FileInputStream fis;
      InputStream is1 = clientSocket.getInputStream();
      DataInputStream is = new DataInputStream(
      new BufferedInputStream(is1));
      OutputStream os = clientSocket.getOutputStream();
```

```
DataOutputStream dos = new DataOutputStream(os);
String inpu;
String fileToRead;
```

/* **The server reads the name of the file to be
transferred. First the file size is transmitted. Then
the data bytes of the file are written to the stream
through an array of 3000 bytes. Once it receives
confirmation from the client that these bytes have been
consumed, it sends the next set, until the whole file
is transferred. Then it writes an integer to the output
stream to confirm to the client that the whole file
has been sent. After this, the loop starts repeating
until the connection is broken.**
*/

```
while((fileToRead = is.readUTF()) != null)
{
    System.out.println("Sending File " +
                        fileToRead);
    fis = new FileInputStream(new File(fileToRead));
    int fSize = fis.available();
    dos.writeInt(fSize);
    dos.flush();
    is.readByte();
    byte[] buf = new byte[3000];
    while((fis.read(buf)) != -1 )
    {
        os.write(buf);
        os.flush();
        is.readByte();
    }
    dos.writeInt(fSize);
    dos.flush();
    fis.close();
}
os.close();
is.close();
} catch(IOException e){}
}
}
```

12.2 Help Files

dest.hlp

This is the destination directory to which the software should be copied over from the source directory.

insFrm.help

Through this list you can specify whether the software to be installed is present on this machine or on another machine. Make your choice and click the OK button. Depending on your selection, the appropriate text fields will get activated and you'll be prompted for answers.

inst.hlp

Now you're in a stage where you can click Install and the installation will start. You can make any changes to the values that you've specified in the text fields before clicking the Install button.

port.hlp

Specify the port number to which your server is connected. This will be used to establish a connection with the server.

remote.hlp

Specify the name of the remote machine on which the software is residing. You must make sure that the server application that will help in the transfer of files is actually running on that machine.

src.hlp

This is the source directory in which your software is residing. Files need to be moved from this directory to the destination directory.

JDK 1.2

There are several new features and enhancements coming up in JDK 1.2 (which is in the Beta 3 stage at the time of publication). This chapter gives you a brief overview of some of the changes. The purpose of this chapter is to make you familiar with some of the new things you can expect to come up as Java evolves further. Here we mention only those areas that make sense in the context of this book.

For a more detailed look you can refer the Javasoft web site:

http://www.javasoft.com/products/jdk/1.2/docs/relnotes/features.html

2D Enhancements

JDK 1.2 introduces the Java 2D API, which enables the creation of advanced 2D graphics. It enhances the AWT in terms of graphics as well as text. Color definition is greatly improved in the new 2D model. The new API allows you to draw virtually any geometric shapes.

In JDK 1.2, a new Graphics2D object is passed as a Graphics Context to the paint() method of an applet. This allows the applet to use all the new, rich functionality. While doing so, Java has taken care of backward compatibility. To do this, the Graphcis2D class extends the old Graphics class (which was passed as a Graphics Context to JDK 1.1 applets).

The AWT Look and Feel Enhancement

One long overdue enhancement in is a platform-based look and feel. This means the ability to have GUI components that look exactly like the components drawn by native applications on a particular platform. This problem is solved by Swing, which is a part of the Java Foundation Classes (JFC). It implements a new set of GUI components with a pluggable look and feel. Swing is implemented in 100% pure Java. It contains implementations of standard Java components such as checkboxes, buttons, and so on, as well as some higher-level components like trees.

Audio Enhancements

With JDK 1.2, audio is supported in both applications and applets. It supports MID and several other audio formats in addition to the AU format.

A new static method has also been introduced in JDK 1.2, which allows applications to use audio features. The method has been introduced in the Applet class:

```
public static final AudioClip newAudioClip(URL r)
```

Performance Enhancements

In JDK 1.2, an area of major focus has been speed enhancement and memory usage reduction.

Support for Solaris native threads has been provided. The native threads VM pays off a lot with native code because it integrates better than the default threads (green threads) of the 1.1 VM.

Java has also taken steps to use memory more efficiently. For instance:

1. Constant strings are now shared among different classes.

2. JDK 1.2 provides faster memory allocation and garbage collection.

Native libraries that are required by some of the core Java classes (especially for the toolkit) have been rewritten using JNI, which leads to the creation of more efficient code.

Just-in-time compilers are now included. (Speaking very broadly, these are tools that compile the code just before execution, so it doesn't have to bear the overheads of an interpreter during execution.

Java Archive (JAR) Enhancements

The JAR format and associated utilities and APIs have been enhanced in JDK 1.2. The command-line functionality of the JAR tool has been increased. There are new standard APIs for reading and writing JAR files. There's the java.util.jar package, which contains classes such as JarInputStream and JarOutputStream, which can be used for reading or writing the contents of a JAR file. Also, there is a JarEntry object associated with each entry in the Jar file. You may have noticed in JDK 1.1 a package called java.util.zipóthe new jar package is mainly an extension of this, directed more toward Jar files.

JNI Enhancements

In JDK 1.1, native libraries were shared across class loaders, so if one native library was loaded by one class loader, it would be available to all. This caused a namespace problem in which you could potentially end up using a native method you didn't intend to use. This problem has been resolved in JDK 1.2, where each class loader manages its own set of native libraries. Likewise there are enhancements aimed at using arrays, strings, and so forth.

RMI Enhancements

Some additions have been made to RMI. One area of particular interest is Custom Socket Types. This means you can now specify that RMI should use a specific socket type to access a remote object. This expands the use of RMI a great deal, because now you can use RMI over a secure network layer such as SSL.

Another very important new feature is the introduction of the concept of daemons. While in JDK 1.1 you created an instance of UnicastRemoteObject, which was running all the time, in JDK 1.2 your object extends java.rmi.activation.Activatable. There is a daemon, ìrmid,î that takes care of activating the object only when required.

Security Enhancements

As we noted in our chapter on security, this is one area that has been evolving at a rapid pace in Java. This is not a surprise considering the explosion of the Internet. Keeping pace with the general industry trend, Java has made quite a few enhancements in the security model to meet new challenges and provide a more granular and useful security umbrella.

For instance, now you can specify a "security policy," which determines what kind of permissions the code will have when it is loaded. You can provide restricted read/write access to certain files and directories. There is a policy file that determines these constraints. Permission has to be explicitly granted to code, in order to prevent accidental exposure to areas where you wouldn't normally want the code to wander.

Three new tools have been created to support/enhance the security model. They are keytool, for creating keys and to generate/import/export certificates, jarsigner, for signing/verification of jar files, and policytool, for creating/modifying policy configuration files that we discussed above.

INDEX